The Source of
All Things

A MEMOIR

Tracy Ross

Free Press

New York London Toronto Sydney

Note to readers: Names and identifying details of some of
the people portrayed in this book have been changed.

Free Press
A Division of Simon & Schuster, Inc.
1230 Avenue of the Americas
New York, NY 10020

First Free Press hardcover edition March 2011

FREE PRESS and colophon are trademarks of Simon & Schuster, Inc.

For information about special discounts for bulk purchases, please contact Simon
& Schuster Special Sales at 1-866-506-1949 or business@simonandschuster.com.

The Simon & Schuster Speakers Bureau can bring authors to your live event.
For more information or to book an event contact the Simon & Schuster Speakers
Bureau at 1-866-248-3049 or visit our website at www.simonspeakers.com.

Manufactured in the United States of America

1   3   5   7   9   10   8   6   4   2

Library of Congress Cataloging-in-Publication Data
Ross, Tracy.
The source of all things / by Tracy Ross.
p. cm.
Includes bibliographical references and index.
(alk. paper)
1. Ross, Tracy—Childhood and youth. 2. Abused children—United States—
Biography. 3. Adult child abuse victims—United States—Biography. I. Title.
HV6626.52.R674 2011
362.76092—dc22
[B]   2010031245

ISBN 978-1-4391-7297-1
ISBN 978-1-4391-7299-5 (ebook)

Contents

Contents

To Scout, Hatcher, and all children, who must be seen, heard, and believed, no matter what.

Out beyond ideas of wrongdoing and rightdoing,
there is a field. I will meet you there.

—Mowlana Jalaluddin Rumi

The Source of All Things

Prologue

Redfish Lake, Idaho, July 2007

All my dad has to do is answer the questions.

That's it. Just four simple questions. Only they aren't that easy, because questions like these never are. We are almost to The Temple, three days deep in the craggy maw of Idaho's Sawtooth Mountains, and he has no idea the questions are coming. But I have them loaded, hot and explosive, like shells in a .30-30.

It's July and hotter than hell on the sage-covered slopes, where wildfires will char more than 130,000 acres by summer's end. But we're up high, climbing to nine thousand feet, and my dad, who is really my stepdad, says that this heat feels cooler than the heat in Las Vegas, where he lives. Four days ago, he and my mother met me in Twin Falls, a town 140 miles south of here where I grew up. They'd driven north, across Nevada, past other fires, including one on the Idaho border. When I saw my mom, at a friend's house where she'd wait while Dad and I backpacked, she'd seemed even tinier than her four-foot eleven-inch frame. Her sweatpants—

plucked from the sale bin at a Las Vegas Abercrombie and Fitch store—drooped like month-old lettuce over her bum. In the creases of her mouth, a white paste had congealed, proof that she was taking antidepressants again. Officially, she's said that she's glad Dad and I are going back to the place our troubles began twenty-eight years ago, almost to the day. But as I kissed her good-bye, leaving her standing in our friend's driveway, I wondered, *which way is the wind now blowing?*

It was late when we left Twin Falls that night—too late to reach the trailhead to The Temple. So Dad and I slept in a field of sagebrush above the town of Stanley. A gnawing in my stomach kept me from eating our black beans and tortillas, but the smell of the sage helped quiet the fear I felt welling beneath my ribcage. In the morning, Dad parked his red Ford pickup at the Redfish Lake Lodge and we took a boat across the water. On the far shore, we found the trailhead to our destination, which we started hiking toward and have been for the past three days.

At sunrise this morning we slid out of our bags, made breakfast, and caught a few fish. When we finally started hiking, we climbed out of one basin and into another, inching up switchbacks sticky with lichen and loose with scree. At the edge of one overlook, we saw smoke rising on the horizon from a fire that was crowning in the trees. And when we arrived at the lake with the dozen black frogs chirping across the water, we called it Holy Water Lake because it was Sunday and we did feel a bit closer to God.

Now the wilderness seems haunting and dark. The air is thin, the terrain rugged, and my dad's body—sixty-four years old, bow-legged, and fifteen pounds overweight—seems tired and heavy to me. He's been struggling the last half-mile, stopping every few feet to catch his breath, adjust his pack, and tug on the big, wet circles that have formed under the armpits of his T-shirt, which reads *Toot My Horn*. Ignoring his choice of wardrobe, I try to remember the father who first led me into these mountains. That man was lean, with a light brown mustache and hair that fanned out from his cheekbones in beautiful blond wings. In a Woolrich shirt and hunting boots he charged up trails, coaxing me on to ridgelines with views of vast, green valleys. If I whined from heat or wilted with hunger, he'd lift me onto his shoulders so effortlessly it was as if my body were composed entirely of feathers.

I know my dad is hurting because I am hurting too—and not just my legs and lungs or the bottoms of my feet. We have barely spoken since we left the dock at Redfish Lake, left the boat and the worried Texans who said, "You're going where?" I'm sure we seemed an odd pair: an old man and his—what was I? Daughter? Lover? Friend? When we stepped off the boat, I'd wanted to turn back, forget this whole sordid mess. But The Temple—a spot on the map I'd latched onto and couldn't let go of—was out here somewhere. And, besides, I still hadn't decided if I was going to kill him outright or just walk him to death.

We're here for reasons I don't want to think about yet, so I train my mind on the sockeye salmon that used to migrate nine hundred miles from the Pacific Ocean to lay their eggs and die at Redfish Lake. That was before the Army Corps of Engineers put in the dams that obstructed their journey. For decades, no fish have made it back to their ancestral spawning grounds at the base of the Sawtooth Mountains. But when I was young, sockeyes clogged the streams pouring out of the lake, creating waves of bright red color. Mesmerized, I knelt on the banks of Fishhook Creek and stretched my fingers toward their tinfoil-bright fins. My dad told me that the fish were rushing home to ensure the continuance of their species. He said they hadn't eaten in months; were consuming the nutrients in their own bodies. Over the years I have thought of the fish with love and terror. I want to hover, as they did, over the origin of my own sorrow and draw from it a new, immaculate beginning.

Several times as we hike up the trail, I fantasize about finding the perfect, fist-size rock and smashing it against my dad's skull. I picture him stumbling, falling onto the ground. I see myself crouching beside him, refusing to hold him as he bleeds. But even as I imagine it, I know I won't do it, because I can't afford to lose my dad—yet. For twenty-eight years he has held my memories hostage. Without him, I'll never know what he did to me when I was a kid.

We climb for another hour until, a few hundred feet from the pass, we turn off the trail. In front of us is a circle of granite towers, sharp and fluted like the turrets on the Mormon Tabernacle. Loose rocks slide down vertical shafts and clatter to the ground. Quickly but carefully, my dad and I crabwalk across the jumbled blocks, insinuating ourselves into tight slots and willing our bodies to become lighter, so the boulders won't shift beneath us and break our legs.

When we get to the wide, flat rock that looks like an altar, we stop. My dad slumps over, sips water, and chokes down a few bites of food. His eyes, the color of chocolate, begin to melt, and the corners of his mouth tremble, as if he's fighting off a frown.

Hunching next to him on the granite slab, I squint into his red-brown, sixteenth-Cherokee face. I dig in my pack until I locate my handheld tape recorder. Holding it close to my father's lips so the wind won't obscure his answers, I begin the interrogation I've waited most of my life to conduct.

"Okay, Dad," I say. "I'm ready. Tell me. How did it begin?"

I
—

An Untimely Death

How long have I been searching for a father? Nearly as long as I have breathed air.

I was seven months old the day my real dad went backpacking in the Sierra Nevada Mountains and an aneurysm exploded in his brain. He was leading a group of Boy Scouts, teaching them to track a black bear, hook a trout, and build a fire with one match. He collapsed in a scree field, cutting his cheeks on shards of million-year-old rocks. His friends carried him back to the trailhead, because the blood pouring out of his artery impaired his ability to see. They took him home and laid him on the sofa, where my mom found him shivering beneath a wool blanket, though the temperature was eighty degrees.

We lived on the Lemoore, California, Naval Station, where my dad worked as a weapons technician. He rode on the USS *Kitty Hawk*, making sure the bombs on the planes it carried didn't accidentally detonate. When Mom opened the door of our military-issue tract house, she knew instantly that something was wrong. My dad's boots, which he always placed at attention (whether he was standing in them or not) were slumped against the living-room wall. Hearing the story of his fall in the mountains, she dropped my four-year-old brother, Chris, and me off at a neighbor's house, then raced our dad to sick bay, where she was told to come back the following Tuesday because it was Flag Day and all the good doctors were out playing golf.

My dad spent Sunday and Monday in bed. He complained that his head felt like a pressure cooker that couldn't release steam. On Tuesday, he tried putting on his uniform, but he was staggering and sweating, and then he threw up. My mom took this to mean his condition was worsening. Throwing a pillow onto the driver's seat of the family station wagon, she drove back to the tiny naval hospital, sobbing and steering, while holding me on her lap.

The doctors found blood in my dad's spinal fluid and made plans to operate. But the night before his surgery, my parents both knew he was going to die. "I'm afraid," he told her, though he couldn't have wanted her to know such a thing. He was Peter Lewellyn Ross, twenty-nine, youngest chief in the Navy at the time. She was Doris Mary, a twenty-seven-year-old Canadian transplant, who, eight years after coming to America, still said *srimp* instead of *shrimp*. They clutched each other on his hospital bed while my mom kissed his bandages and pressed ice cubes on his lips.

We buried my father a few weeks later in a cemetery in Twin Falls, Idaho. But my mom swears he came back to us after the funeral. She and I were sleeping in his childhood bedroom at my Grandmother Ross's house when he returned. It was cool outside, and the window was open, so my mom said he just climbed in. She remembers exactly what he was wearing: blue-and-black checkered golf pants and a baby blue polo shirt. He had a list in his hand, just like he always had when he'd been living. He gave her the bright, beautiful smile she says I inherited along with his sea-green colored eyes. He stood over my cradle, adjusted my blanket, and laid his hand across the soft spot on my head.

Seeing him, my mom sat up, a little girl in her cotton nightie.

"How did you get here?" she said.

"Can I visit you? I miss you. I need you."

My dad sat down on the edge of her bed. "Go back to sleep, Doris Wakeham," he told her. "I still have work to do. I'm not leaving anytime soon."

Six months later, Mom packed up our belongings, emptied her military pension, and moved us into another split-level ranch house, at 1537 Richmond Drive in Twin Falls.

She says she did it because she wanted Chris and me to be near our grandparents, who, like my dad, loved nothing more than hooking a trout on a caddis nymph they had tied in their own back shop. The Rosses were exotic, comfortably wealthy, and grounded in the outdoors. Both in their early fifties when we moved to Idaho, they made a striking couple. Grandma Liz was five foot six and stately, with a head full of flaming red hair. She'd grown up in Beverly Hills and, as a teenager, swam laps with Johnny Weissmuller—the original Tarzan. My white-haired, crew-cut grandfather was raised in Contact, Nevada, during the Depression. But he was no hobo looking for handouts, like the characters in Wallace Stegner's *The Big Rock Candy Mountain.* He studied his way to an engineering scholarship at the University of California, Los Angeles.

Howard Ross pumped gas to pay his way through college, and it happened that one day my grandma pulled into his station in one of her two convertible Chryslers. When they married, my Grandma Liz gave up a sizable inheritance. But when she and Howard moved to Idaho, she found a new kind of riches. Both learned to fly Cessnas and went on trips to Canada, California, and Mexico. They fished and hunted and camped out in the desert. They also threw the best dinner parties in Twin Falls County. I know, because they're the first and most vivid of all my childhood early memories: imagine lipsticked ladies clinking whiskey glasses while discussing the best way to field dress a sage hen, and you have it. With zero effort I can conjure up my three-year-old self hiding under the dining-room table during one of Grandma Liz's parties. Her German shorthair, Josephine, wags her tail beside me. Dressed in a pair of denim overalls, I feel my way along a half dozen pair of tweed-slacked knees and nylons-encased legs. Occasionally someone looks down to see whose fingers are tickling his or her kneecaps, but for the most part, I am left alone and happy to be surrounded by the sound of so many stories; the sound of so much laughter.

My mom has always said that her decision to plant us close to our grandparents, five thousand miles from her fish-head-eating, whiskey-swilling cousins, was her one true act of heroism. But really she had no reason to return to Canada. Aside from her sister, Marjorie, my grandparents were also the only relatives we had in the States. The rest of Mom's family—a motley but musically gifted bunch of Scotch-Irish Catholics—lived in Newfoundland, where she'd grown up. Her own mother had died of tuberculosis when Mom was two, and her deep-sea-fishing father pawned her off on his cancer-stricken mother to raise. At five, my mom was scrounging the shores of Conception Bay, sent out to look for coal chunks to burn in her stove. At seventeen, she and my Great-Grandmother Wakeham still shared the same bed. When Mom left Petit Forte at the age of twenty, on the day John F. Kennedy died, she swore she would never live there again. But nothing could have prepared her for the desolation she found in Twin Falls, which sits on the edge of the Snake River Canyon, a gash in the earth that, in some places, runs one thousand feet deeper than the Grand Canyon.

Twin Falls. The only reason anyone's ever heard of it is because Evel Knievel tried to jump the Snake River Canyon there in 1974. My mom, grandparents, Chris, and I sat on the roof of our house trying to watch him do it. *Wide World of Sports* even came out from California to film the event. Knievel almost made the quarter-mile-wide leap, but the wind balled up in his parachute and pulled his rocket-powered motorcycle into the canyon. By the time he touched down, unconscious and strapped to his bike by a harness from his stars-and-stripes jumpsuit, he was mere feet from the black coils of the Snake River. A few knots to the west, and he would have fallen in and drowned.

"Twin" sat high above the river on a plateau of sticker bushes and sagebrush. When I was young, it was nothing more than a lonely clutch of brick schools, empty churches, and drab, low-ceilinged businesses. But at the far edge of town, the Snake River dropped abruptly, creating two enormous waterfalls. At 212 feet,

Shoshone Falls is higher than Niagara, though not as wide. The Twin Falls, which drop 125 feet, are shorter but just as beautiful. Together, the misty cascades lent my dull, mostly Mormon hometown its lone drama and distinction. But for as long as I can remember, the streets seemed too empty, the businesses always on the verge of dying. How they didn't is a mystery, what with the mighty Snake dividing us from the lusher, more beautiful parts of Idaho. Only the Perrine Bridge, which stretched across the river 486 feet above the water, provided us access to the ski town of Sun Valley, where, I believed, lived the rest of civilization.

I guess it's no wonder our mom never took to Twin Falls; despite the hardships of her childhood, she still longed for Newfoundland. As a little girl in Petit Forte, she had looked out her window at rolling green hills, dramatic headlands, and fathoms-deep water, where she'd once paddled her own dory across an inlet thick with whales. When she looked out the window of her house in Twin Falls, she saw only sagebrush and piles of lava, remnants of the Yellowstone Caldera's last eruption, 640,000 years earlier. Now, instead of the scent of sea salt and cabbage boiling on her stove, the smell of pesticide-laden cow manure wafted through her house. She never complained, at least not that Chris and I can remember, but she also never forgave whatever forces of destiny that tore her husband away from her and sent her, reeling, onto the cracked-earth Snake River floodplain, surrounded by Mormons and sheepherders, among the largest concentration of dairy farms in the United States.

Not that Chris and I had one problem with living so close to our grandparents, who treated us like their own children. I'd go to their house and shadow my grandpa while he made his patented

Ross Bait Baffler fishing boxes in his backyard shop. At lunchtime, we'd eat potato chips smeared with Adams peanut butter and listen to Paul Harvey on the radio. After lunch, Grandpa would go back to the shop and I'd search for piles of Jo's dog poop, for which he would pay me a penny each. I loved the smell of my grandpa's starched, short-sleeve plaid shirts and the sound of his L.L. Bean work boots clomping across the speckled linoleum of his kitchen floor. I'm sure a part of me extrapolated my real dad from him. When I sat on his lap and wrapped my arms around him, I had to have been channeling my father.

Living near Liz and Howard also meant that Chris and I would be indoctrinated early into the wonders of the outdoors. On dozens and dozens of summer mornings, we'd pile into their white Ford pickup and head to Magic Reservoir, one of their favorite fishing spots. While they sipped bourbon in their float tubes, my redheaded, freckle-faced brother and I drank lake water out of rose-flowered teacups and nibbled on gritty mud cakes. We camped in our grandparents' Airstream trailer and caught tadpoles in Dixie cups. Sometimes we left tiny frogs in their paper prisons until all of the water dried up. We—or at least I—paid for it too. By the time I entered kindergarten, permanently sunburned from the glare off so much water, I'd already had mud-and-lake-water-induced illness twice.

Over time, my outdoor antics became family lore and legend. One day, while camping with my grandparents, we hiked along the bank of a slow-moving river. The water burbled, calling me to peer into the riffles. I looked, lost my footing, and slipped in. Oblivious, Liz and Howard walked ahead of me, scouting for deep pools to cast their lines. But as my grandma used to tell it, at some point they noticed my singing had stopped, and shortly thereafter, that I was missing. Racing back to my last-known location, they once again heard my melody. That's how they found me, hanging onto a root in the bank, my body stretched out and bobbing on the surface of the water.

For us kids, there was nothing better than stargazing with our grandparents or hanging out while my grandma played gin rummy with her girlfriends in the Airstream. But to my mom, the Rosses were a constant reminder of all she was not. They had never liked her, she was sure of it. Not since the day my dad had brought her to Idaho and they insisted on checking the quality of her teeth. Not when they made fun of the way she said *whore-de-oerves*, and told her, after both of our births, that she'd better start dieting or her husband would start looking for a new wife. Even as my dad lay dying, Grandma Liz couldn't stay off my mom's case. When my mom begged to see my father—one last time before they unplugged him from the ventilator—Liz (who was seven inches taller and outweighed her by forty pounds) practically wrestled her into a cradle lock holding her back.

But our roots, however spindly, were planted, so Mom, Chris, and I made the most of our new digs. We played *Chutes and Ladders*, watched *Sesame Street*, and read hundreds of books. My mom loves to tell me how, even as a toddler, I could crack her and my brother up. While she cooked cabbage rolls on our electric four-burner, I'd hook my fingers and toes in the webbing of my playpen and circle around it like a monkey in a cage. Later, when the dishes were stacked and drying, Mom would tuck me into my crib. Since Chris was older, he got to stay up later than me at night. But it was only a matter of minutes before he and my mom would hear the thud that meant I'd hoisted my body over the railing and flopped onto my head. Seconds later, there I'd come, crawling and jabbering in my pajamas, determined to be a part of the action.

"You were the miracle child sent from heaven to quell my loneliness," says my mom. "I know this, because even though God took your daddy, he gave me you."

I wish I could have been the elixir that prevented my mom from bottoming out, but that act of heroism fell to the neighbor ladies, Marlene and Terry. Refusing to let her be single and sad, they went to great lengths to set my mom up on blind dates. When she'd drive off with this rancher or that lawyer, they'd come over and babysit, bringing along their own passels of kids. In most of the pictures from my pre-school years I'm standing next to Terry's daughter, Marcie, looking innocent and sheepish, like we've just finger-painted the wall of my bedroom and then helped ourselves to a handful of Milk Bones (which we probably had).

Marlene and Terry were there when Mom needed to borrow coffee, or cry, or celebrate Chris's first day of school. They invited us to every birthday party, holiday celebration, and parade. And they swooped over to take care of my brother and me on the afternoon our mom decided she could no longer take the loneliness that felt like an anchor around her neck. She was standing at the kitchen window watching Chris and me playing in the backyard when she thought *How can I do this? I have all the responsibility and no help.* She doesn't remember calling 911, but a few minutes later an ambulance screamed up the driveway and two husky paramedics jumped out. After a quick assessment of her mental stability (not so crazy she needed the psychiatric ward but wide-eyed and ranting enough to be monitored), they loaded her onto a gurney and whisked her off to a week of "rest and relaxation" at Magic Valley Hospital.

If there's a moment when Mom's sadness took on a life of its own, it was when she stood at that little window letting the blueprint of her suicide form a picture in her head. She didn't know exactly how she'd do it, but the tools appeared before her in stark relief: a razor blade borrowed from her Schick shaving kit. Scissors sharp enough to cut a perfect line across my bangs. All the leftover Valium from the bottle the doctor prescribed after my dad's funeral to help her sleep. What mattered, of course, was not the method she'd use to snip the cord that connected her to us kids, but that she no longer felt capable of carrying all of our weight.

2

A Knight In Shining Bell-Bottoms

Mom, Chris, and I waited three years for a miracle to sweep us off our lonely, displaced feet. And then one day in June of 1974, it pulled into our driveway behind the wheel of a flesh-toned 1949 Willys jeep.

In my memory from that evening, I am standing under the awning of our black-and-white ranch house at 1537 Richmond Drive. A sprinkler on the front lawn sends cool mist across my toes. Fresh out of the bath and dressed in a pair of summer-weight pj's, I smell like Johnson's baby powder and No More Tears shampoo. My hair, still light enough to be considered strawberry, skims the tops of my shoulder blades.

In the hazy light of early summer, I see my brother come flying down the sidewalk on his red Schwinn Fastback with the sparkly banana seat. He's wearing a pair of tattered cutoffs and a tank top that says *Lifeguard Waikiki Beach*. At seven years old, he is my own personal blue-eyed Dennis the Menace, who likes to wipe Dentyne gum on his buttcrack and give it to me to chew. He pedals his bike as fast as he can, shouting, "That guy you're going dancing with is coming in fast!"

The sight of my brother's skinny legs pumping makes Mom rush into the house for one last peek at her outfit for the night: a tight denim vest over a peasant blouse with pouffy, see-through sleeves. Trailing her cloud of perfume, I follow her into the bathroom, where I find her opening her eye-shadow compact and sweeping a layer of turquoise across her lids. She squints into the mirror at her rosy cheeks, forest-green eyes, and slightly grey, widely spaced teeth, then leans down to tattoo my cheek with a glossy, cherry-red kiss.

We emerge onto the porch just as the jeep pulls into our driveway. A door opens, revealing a lanky, bell-bottomed leg. It's attached to a man wearing tinted eyeglasses, a tan leather jacket, and a silky, wide-collared shirt. I can't place him, but something about the man's warm brown skin and feathered blond hair makes me think I have seen him before. Then he smiles, and a gold cap on his right, top tooth summons a memory into my brain.

I know the man from the boys' section at Van England's Department Store in downtown Twin Falls, where my mom takes me when she needs to buy my brother's plaid polyester pants and matching shirts. Whenever the man sees my mother, he compliments her new hair color, platform espadrilles, or jeans. My mom smiles all the way to the checkout counter and out in the parking lot to her beige Mercury Cougar. When we get into her car, she taps her fingers on the steering wheel and says, "That man sure knows his fashions."

One day, Mom realized she had never introduced me to the man. It was December, and we'd picked out a new coat for me to wear during the holidays. We walked over to where the man was folding a pile of little boys' argyle sweaters. "Donnie, hello!" said my mom. "I'd like to introduce you to my daughter, Tracy." The man looked at me and smiled, reminding me of the way my grandpa smiled when he brought me red roses for my birthday. I liked it when my grandpa did this ritual for me. It told me I was his special girl and deserved to have my own special day. The look in the clothing salesman's eyes suggested something similar. But I wasn't about to sit on his lap and wrap my arms around him like I would my family. I anchored my feet to the warped wooden floor and shoved my hands deep into the pockets of my Kermit the Frog art smock.

The man crouched down, putting us at eye level. "It's a pleasure to meet you, Tracy," he said. "My name's Mr. Lee, but you can call me Donnie. I sure do like that coat you're getting for Christmas. Wear it with a pretty dress, and I can tell by just looking at you that you'll be the slickest thing since Wonder Bread."

It was late afternoon, and sunlight slanted through a giant window facing west. I felt a stirring like a chick cracking through an eggshell in the center of my chest. I was the kind of kid who could live for a week on a compliment. I stood before my future father and fanned him with my eyelashes.

By that summer, Donnie was courting our entire family. Mom and he did the Funky Chicken at his favorite bar, the Cove. They four-wheeled into the South Hills, where they made out to the music of Mormon crickets. But when Donnie picked my mom up, he always brought Chris and me a toy. And when he dropped her off, he snuck into our bedrooms, patting our backs and leaving tender kisses on our sunburned cheeks.

Sometimes he'd pull into our driveway unexpected, gunning the engine of the Willys jeep. Jumping out and leaning against the metal doorframe, he'd yell, "Pile in! We're going out! My treat!" Hearing the siren call of popcorn and drive-in movies, Chris and I would drop whatever game we were playing (me: Barbies; he: cutting the toes off my Barbies) and race outside, forgetting to put on our sneakers. Mom would toss her *Woman's Day* magazine into a macramé basket and chase after us, carrying our shoes and her purse.

As my brother and I clambered up the jeep's metal footstep, we'd kick and shove, each vying for a chance to sit behind our family's date. But as soon as we were buckled into our seat belts, we'd have to pile right back out. Juiced on the knowledge that wherever we were going would invariably lead to ice cream, I'd have forgotten to stop off at the bathroom before loading up. Mom would help focus my mind on the heavy feeling in my bladder by saying, "Okay, who needs a pit stop before we leave?"

Finding me in the rearview mirror, Donnie would tip his hat and throw me an encouraging wink. "You run inside, Trace," he'd say. "Don't worry. We'll wait here for you to come back. But whatever you do, don't fall in."

Looking at his reflection, I would wrinkle my forehead, trying to decode the message he was sending. Chris had told me that alligators and snakes lived in the sewer pipes under our house, but I didn't want to disappoint my new friend. Donnie was the only man I knew who actually picked up speed when he saw me, racing toward me and holding out his arms to wrap me in a fierce, high-impact hug. Once entangled, he'd hang on as long as I did, resting his chin in the crook of my neck and smoothing my strawberry tangles. If I was wearing one of my favorite terrycloth tube tops, our hug would have shoved it up over the top of my belly. An amateur stylist by way of his job at Van England's, Donnie would smooth it back down over the elastic waistband of my polyester cutoffs.

In the jeep, I whined that I could hold it until we got to the Arctic Circle, our favorite ice cream joint. I edged closer and closer toward tears. But before I could stage a full-blown go-to-pieces, Donnie cut the engine and offered to walk me inside the house. He waited in the hallway while I clutched the sides of the toilet, holding my body a few inches off the seat. Who knows how long it took for my bladder to finally relax enough to flush the Kool-Aid or whatever sugary drink I'd been chugging out of my pipes, but when I finally stepped out of the bathroom, Donnie hoisted me onto his shoulders and carried me back to my mom and brother.

I can't say that I ever knew I was missing a biological father, but with Donnie around, a whole new world opened up. It was defined by adventure, excitement, and fun. I also remember feeling encapsulated, I think, by love. Night after night, he drove us away from the depression that still clung to our house like a needy child. I know my mom fought hard to infuse our lives with stability and joy. But by the time Donnie found us, we were all ready for the kind of light only a man in need of a new family can shine.

His favorite thing was taking us on outdoor adventures, a passion ingrained in all of us since birth. On weeknights and official holidays, we'd fish for slow-moving trout at Dirkies Lake, swim at Nat-Soo-Pah hot springs, or four-wheel to obscure ghost towns near Sunbeam Dam or Idaho City. He held off on the big adventures, like weeklong camping trips near the North Fork of the Wood River, because he didn't have a camper-trailer big enough to accommodate all of us yet. But on evenings when the light was just beginning to turn purple, we'd switchback down the narrow road leading into the Snake River Canyon to one of our favorite picnic spots. A supper of cheese, crackers, and Hostess cupcakes would be followed by Chris and me running around like demons, high on sugar and the invigorating feeling of cold grass under our feet. Eventually, the sun would sink below the rim of the canyon, lending an eerie glow to the mist floating around Shoshone Falls. With the birds retreating into the bushes and the heat rising out of the canyon, Donnie would slip off his sneakers and crack his first beer of the evening. Leaning onto his forearms, he'd tell us about himself.

He was born on March 12, 1943, in the mountains above Loveland, Colorado. His mom, Mary Ann, was seventeen, and his dad was a chauvinist a-hole. One day, Mary Ann asked if she could go deer-hunting with her husband. They wouldn't need a sitter, she said, because she'd bring the baby along. When Donnie's daddy responded by saying, "A woman's place is in the home," Mary Ann filed for divorce. A year later, she met a wire-stringer for the Mountain Bell telephone company and baby Donnie got a new pop.

Donnie lived in thirteen different states before he was six years old. Mary Ann and his new dad, Edward, had three more children, including a boy named Larry and two beautiful daughters,

Lori and Debbie. Lucky for Donnie, the family settled in Idaho, the most mountainous state in the U.S. Rivers flowed from snow-capped peaks into wildflower-infested meadows. Pheasants and sage hens soared above the beet fields and Mallard ducks hid in pristine wetlands. As a teenager, Donnie started hunting, a love that would last his entire life. He graduated from high school, joined the National Guard, got married, and got divorced.

All he ever wanted was a son and daughter to call his own, and then his wife cheated on him with her high school sweetheart. When Donnie met my mom, he admired the Stevie Nicks swivel in her size-four hips. More so, he loved the laughing, redheaded children that clung to her slender legs and narrow ankles. Years later, when I was grown with two small sons of my own, he'd tell me that he liked my mom from the second he met her, but that Chris and I were the glue that affixed the seal on their marriage certificate.

"I probably enjoyed seeing you two more than I enjoyed seeing your mother," he said. "I bonded with you. I loved you. There was no chance it wouldn't work out."

I remember the day I first decided that Donnie needed to become our permanent daddy. It was the end of summer and he had brought over his black lab, Jigger, to play. I'd met Jigger a few weeks earlier, on a hiking trip to the sand dunes near Mountain Home. She'd followed me up and down the greasy hills, pushing the top of her head into my outstretched palm.

I was a sucker for any four-legged creature, but there was something about Jigger's eyes that made me want to tell her my heart's deepest desires. Asking Donnie's permission, I slid my hand under her collar and led her gently into the backyard.

We talked for a solid hour—well, I talked and she listened—sitting off to the side of the house under an aspen tree where I thought no one could see us. I whispered, in case Chris was spying.

"I love you, Jigger," I began. "And I love your owner, too. He's the nicest man I've ever met. When you get home, tell him I want him to be my daddy. Then you can come live with us, starting tomorrow."

Jigger listened, breaking her gentle, bird-dog stare every so often to lick my cheek or grass-stained foot. I took each kiss as a form of doggie affirmation, as if she was saying: *I like you. He likes me. Pretty soon we'll all be sharing the same steak.*

She was right. Mom, Chris, Donnie, and I tied the knot nine days shy of my fourth birthday, on November 3, 1974. I say it like that—*we tied the knot*—because that's how it felt: the four of us vowing to love, cherish, and honor each other till death—or some other unforeseeable catastrophe—tore us apart.

3

The Power of Love

Y ou're lucky," my mom told me. "You know what it's like to be loved."

She and I were sitting in the living room of our house on Richmond Drive in February 1976. I wasn't in kindergarten yet because I'd missed the cutoff date at my school, Sawtooth Elementary. My birthday was in November, the same month the valves in my unborn brother's heart filled up with calcium. One day Mom felt him rummaging around near her ribcage, and the next day: nothing. She called the doctor, who told her to lie on the couch and eat Jell-O; that would get the baby moving. A week later, when he still hadn't tickled her kidneys, she knew he was dead inside her.

The doctors scheduled Mom for something she called a D&C, a simple procedure to vacuum the baby out of her body. It happened a few days before my fifth birthday, but, due to complications, the simple procedure turned into a hysterectomy. Marlene and Terry came over to make the ice-cream-cone cupcakes and blindfold the dozen kids at my party for pin-the-tail-on-the-donkey. But sometime between presents and birthday cake, I lured my friends into my bedroom to tell them my mom was in the hospital and that we shouldn't be having so much fun.

Even then, I had a sense for which of my friends would respond best to my dramas and who would give me the wrong response. I'd already been caught—and punished—for showing Marcie and our neighbor Wendy a *Playboy* magazine I'd stolen from my dad's stash in the garage. We were simultaneously horror struck and mesmerized by the models' balloon-size boobs and hairy armpits, and our laughter made Marcie's dad look behind his La-Z-Boy where we were sitting. When he found us, he threatened to call my parents if I didn't tell him where we got the magazine. I could tell from the tone in his voice that magazines with naked ladies were bad, but there was no way anyone could make me rat out my new daddy. When my parents found out I'd stolen the *Playboy,* they scolded me, but only lightly, and later I heard them laughing about it.

At my party, my friends and I grouped up between my white-and-purple bed frame and the wall, buttercup yellow. Marcie stuck her feet in my flowered sleeping bag, while Wendy pulled my Porky Pig nightlight out of the wall socket.

"My mommy is in the hospital trying to get out our baby," I told them. "We can eat cupcakes and I can open my presents. But after that, I think God would want you to go home."

One by one, around the circle, my friends' faces clouded over. Most of them went to church, so they understood the concept of God. If they were Catholic, like I was, they also knew that God the Father could fly down from heaven and light our hair on fire if we didn't put others' needs before ours. Nearly all of my friends prayed "Now I lay me down to sleep" before they went to bed. But when it came time to sacrifice their party favors for a woman they knew vaguely as "Tracy's mommy," they just stared at me, blinking.

"Maybe we could finger-paint your mom a picture," offered Marcie, pitching forward on her corduroys.

"Or save her a piece of cake," said Wendy, picking at the carpet.

"Or maybe all of you can come back to the living room and join the rest of the children who were nice enough to come to your party," said a mother I didn't know, sticking her head through my door and furrowing her eyebrows.

Some people don't know how to recognize a child's strange way of coping with trauma. But when my mom came home six days later, I knew I had been a good daughter. She pulled up her nightgown and showed me the layers of blood-stained gauze wrapped around the center of her abdomen. Her skin looked doughy and waterlogged and blue bruises lined the insides of her arms.

"I'll be good as new in a little while," she said, when she saw me staring at her injuries. But for some reason I knew better than to believe her. We were standing in the bathroom in front of our big oval mirror. Static lifted my hair from its roots and stuck it to my mom's bandages.

A few months after her surgery, though, Mom actually did start feeling better. She came out of her bedroom dressed in a black leotard, matching tights, and glittery, navy blue legwarmers. She turned on the TV, and a man with hair like a space helmet started telling her to do leg kicks. I hopped around behind her, trying to copy her footsteps.

In the mornings before my first year of school, Chris went to Sawtooth Elementary and my new dad drove his jeep to work in the boy's department at Van England's. If Mom was feeling happy, she'd pull my hair into braids and tie my Holly Hobbie pinafore into a bow. We kept ourselves busy, cleaning out the closets and watching *As the World Turns*. But every afternoon, something came over my mother that made her want to go to sleep. Climbing onto the black vinyl sofa in our upstairs living room, she'd mutter, "I wish I knew what it was like to be loved. But no one's ever really loved me." When she said it, she wasn't looking at me, but somewhere beyond me, near the fake oak tree we kept in the living room, flanked by matching statues of Asian kids in kimonos.

I sat Indian style near the base of the couch, studying the bottom of my mom's feet. It'd been more than a year since we'd married Donnie, and I was confused by her confession of loneliness. It made no sense for her to say that no one loved her, because even I could see that my new dad waited on her hand and foot. The stories she told about my old dad made me think he'd loved her too. And what about me? I loved her more than anything.

Besides that, ever since the wedding our life had seemed so much happier than before; even a five-year-old could see it. In my Mother Goose–influenced worldview, everything about our new life shouted love, from the songs we'd sing on our way to go skiing at Soldier Mountain to the TV dinners we got to eat in the basement while watching *Sonny and Cher*. Love is what made my dad jump out of his beanbag during a chase scene in *Starsky and Hutch* to rush down to Safeway for Ruffles, my mom's favorite potato chips, and spend an entire Saturday during the middle of sagehen-hunting season helping Chris build race cars for his Boy Scout troop's pinewood derby.

I was pretty sure love accompanied my parents into their bedroom on the rare occasions when my dad would sneak out of work and surprise us for lunch. After a quick grilled-cheese sandwich and tomato soup, he and my mom would make me go down for a nap, then nudge each other into their bedroom, smooching and holding hands. When I heard the latch on their door lock behind them, I'd sneak out of bed and press my ear into the two-inch space between their door and the carpet. The muffled noises seeping through the gap made me feel weird but happy. They sounded like people licking strawberry ice cream.

So when my mom offhandedly mentioned how alone she felt on that blustery February afternoon, confusion swirled like a cloud of mosquitoes. Even then, a part of me knew that my mom's sadness was more powerful than any love anyone could give her, and that her life before me had been too difficult for her to ever be truly happy. I knew she'd grown up in a place where love was doled out in slaps and insults, and that, more than once, she'd received actual coal in her Christmas stocking. This knowledge made me feel both lucky and guilty. I'd sit with her on the couch looking at pictures of my real dad and hold her hand as sobs wracked her body. But I was young and full of energy. I bounced up and down on the sofa and said, "But I love you, Mommy. *I* do."

"Oh, I know you do, sweetpea," she answered. "That's not what I mean."

The house became melancholy when Mom slept, and the wind sounded like someone scraping against the door. I went to my room and took out my Barbies, then tiptoed back down the hall. On the couch, Mom had covered her face with a blue-and-red afghan someone had crocheted for my unborn baby brother. I sat with my back against our new wallpaper—black velvet trees painted on a white background—and watched her chest rising and falling under the cover.

4

My Pa

O kay," said my new dad, Donnie, "you're sure about this?"
We were in the bathroom of our new house, on November 11, 1977. The previous summer, Mom and Dad had bought
a new place on Parkway Drive. It resembled our old place, with
three bedrooms, a basement, and two baths. But this one had so
much built-in storage that the first time Chris and I went there,
we played hide-and-seek in the walk-in closets for two solid hours.
Now I also went to a new school called Harrison Elementary, and
the next day, I would turn seven, becoming one of the older kids
in my first-grade class. My hair was pulled into two tight ponytails
that were wrapped around pink sponge rollers so they'd be curly
for my birthday party the next day. All afternoon, my mom had
baked, frosted, and decorated nineteen ice-cream-cone cupcakes
with rainbow sprinkles on top. But the success of my birthday
hinged on one thing only: I wanted to lose a tooth.

I'd convinced myself that I couldn't be happy unless a tooth came out before I turned seven, so I begged my dad to extract one for me. A few days earlier, Dad had gotten out his needle-nose pliers and tried to pry a tooth out of my mouth. He yanked and wiggled, scraping off some of my enamel. When I started to cry, he described an easier, more reliable tooth-pulling method. He would tie one end of a piece of floss around the tooth and the other end to a doorknob. When he slammed the door, the floss would yank, tearing my tooth, roots and all, out of my gum.

I sat perfectly still, just like Dad instructed me to, but my insides felt like Jell-O. I held my breath and tried to think happy thoughts. I thought of my grandpa, and how fun it was to steal his Tums, which tasted like minty candies. And of camping at Magic Reservoir, where, during the summer, the water was always warm enough to swim. Dad looked at me while looping the clear floss around the doorknob. When he finished, he squatted down in front of me and put his hands on my kneecaps.

"Your eyes are so big," he said. "We don't have to do this if you're afraid."

I was afraid, but I trusted my new dad. He was the one I turned to when I needed a good adventure or big, strong hands to swoop me out of trouble. Over the summer, he'd taught me to roller-skate, ride my bike, and jump off the high dive at Harmon Park. My mom always watched, but she never urged me to test my bravery. Out in the living room, I could hear her laughing at something Sonny told Cher. I knew she was watching TV because she was too scared to see Dad ripping my bone from my head. I, on the other hand, was exceedingly brave. Even though it was November, I still went outside in my Wonder Woman swimsuit with a towel pinned around my neck. I ran laps around the trailer, flying in my invisible jet. I climbed fences and did cartwheels and chased Jigger around down the sidewalk in my bare feet. So it didn't matter that my mom was hiding out in the basement, because I had my dad, and I had me.

Dad stood with his hand on the door, waiting for my cue to slam it as hard as he could. A jolt of electricity shot through my spine and into my pigtails. Holding on to the backs of my legs, I said, "It's okay, Daddy. Just do it, please?"

A second later, Dad slammed the door, tearing the tooth out of my gum. Hot tears sprang to my eyes and blood-tinged drool trickled down my chin. Dad lunged for the tooth as it shot past him, tiny, square, and Chiclet-white. He scooped me up and sat me on his lap, where he kissed the blood-tinged drool off my lower lip.

"Tomorrow," he said, "You'll be the queen of the first grade."

He was right. The next day, I did feel like birthday royalty. My pigtails bounced like wire springs affixed to the sides of my temples. I carried a small, square mirror in the front pocket of my jumper and took it out often to admire the gap in my teeth. My tongue kept finding reasons to fiddle with the metallic-tasting hole until my teacher, Mrs. Galloway, asked me to stop.

But I didn't need a missing tooth—or anything else—to get me excited about going to Harrison Elementary. I already thought first grade was hitting the jackpot, because it meant I finally got to spend all day at school. In Mrs. Galloway's class, I cruised through my reading lessons in the advanced reading group. Art and spelling were a cinch, and math was a piece of cake too. But after I realized the smart kids didn't get any extra attention, I started intentionally writing down the wrong answers to my addition problems, so Mrs. Galloway would have to "help" me figure them out. (This didn't last long, because it was only after I compulsively answered them correctly that I erased my answers and "recalculated" them. And my erasing skills weren't as good as my math skills.)

At recess Jenny Harr and I played our favorite game, Little House on the Prairie. Like every six- and seven-year-old girl in 1977, we were fanatic about the nineteenth-century capers of our tomboy heroine, Laura Ingalls, and her soon-to-be blind sister, Mary. I always let Jenny play Laura, but only because, deep down, I knew I was the more convincing actress. At home, I was constantly begging my dad to play Pa, and had actually cajoled Grandma Liz (an expert seamstress, among everything else) into sewing me not one but *two* sets of matching gunnysack nightgowns, because I needed one for me and the other for my "sister" Mary (a king-size pillow that I'd stolen from my parents room and slept next to at night).

One day, I was sneaking bites of Milk Bones in the garage when I heard a voice call out, "Hey, half pint. You ready to go to market?" Amazed and confused, I replied, "Pa? Is that you?"

"Sure is, half pint," answered my brother. "I have the wagon ready. Now get your lunch pail and come on board."

Inside the wagon, Chris had placed a pillow, snacks, and my favorite sleeping bag, a gesture of rare, inexplicable kindness that, had I been older, would have raised a million red flags. But I was young and prone to bouts of loneliness, which made me only too eager to pretend. For weeks, I'd been strolling my Baby Alive around the neighborhood, looking for someone to play with. But all my friends were either on vacation or more interested in playing indoors. And besides, in one corner of the wagon, tucked below the lip, sat a plastic cup full of milk and a stack of graham crackers—my favorite.

It was Indian summer, a Saturday, and I couldn't believe what I was seeing. Never before had my brother gone to such lengths to assist me in any game. His role had always been to ignore, tease, and berate me, then tickle me until I peed my pants. But now, the snack-filled wagon was ready, sitting at the top of our driveway. Chris helped me in and encouraged me to zip my sleeping bag up to my neck. I tucked my arms alongside my body while he worked the zipper up. Soon, the only thing sticking out of the bag was my face, shaded beneath the rim of my bonnet.

"You snug as a bug, half pint?" my brother asked. But there was no time to answer. Knocking on the box with a wooden stick, he yelled, "Git up now, horsies!" and pushed the wagon down the steep pitch of our driveway.

For the next twelve seconds, then, I was Laura Ingalls Wilder, rolling down a rutted wagon-train road on my way to Kansas City. I had my lunch pail (a plastic beach bucket) and my baby sister, Carrie (a Madame Alexander doll), next to me, and grand visions for the future. Sitting in front of us and guiding the horses was my one and only favorite and forever father, Pa, on the lookout for Mormons and marauding Indians.

It was the best twelve seconds of my life. And then, on the thirteenth second, I was crashing into the pavement at the end of the driveway, where grey cement met gravelly black tarmac. Rolling out of the wagon but still wrapped in my sleeping bag, I was suddenly awash in a tornado of milk and graham crackers. Toys and dolls flew through the air, whacking me in the face and body. When I landed, I was head down in the gutter and already wailing. Footsteps pounded toward me, interrupted by the sound of my brother's cackling. And then, from the top of the driveway, another voice called out.

"Dammit, Chris, what the hell are you doing?" yelled Dad. "Can't you leave your sister alone for one single goddamn second? Get in the house—or I'll give you a beating."

Dad's footsteps hustled down the driveway and stopped outside the wall of cardboard. He was still cussing, which scared me to death. I'd been at the receiving end of his belt-whippings before and fully expected him to lift up the box, rip off his belt, and whip me, like the time he'd found Chris and me shoving and hitting each other in the downstairs shower and spanked us until we were bawling. He didn't hit us often, but from time to time Chris and I could drive our dad to corporal punishment. I hoped today there would be no spanking.

There wasn't. My dad lifted me out of the gutter and wrapped me in his arms. The harder I cried, the tighter he held me, until it was time to go inside.

Even though we lacked the same genes, it seemed my dad came preprogrammed to protect me. The previous summer, when I could barely swim, the family had gone to Nat-Soo-Pah hot springs. After a few rounds of Jaws and seeing who could hold their breath underwater the longest, Dad got out of the pool to change his clothes, leaving Chris and me under the watchful eye of our mom. Mom had never learned to swim, so I didn't take chances when she watched us. But for some reason, I decided I needed to prove how brave I was to my dad.

While Dad blow-dried his hair in the dressing room, Chris and I clung to the side of the pool, playing Motor Boat and pinching our noses. We probably farted in each other's direction. At some point, I got out of the water and migrated toward the deep end, careful not to slip on the slimy cement. I was perched above the ten-foot-deep mark when Dad stepped out of the change room and back into the pool area.

"Hey Daddy! Watch this!" I shouted and did a half cannonball into the water. Seconds later, when I came up for air and realized that my feet didn't touch the bottom, I started sinking. Fully clothed, in a pair of snug Levi's suspended by a King of Beers belt buckle, Dad dove in after me, outpacing the lifeguard on duty. I couldn't have been more thrilled by my dad's act of heroism, but when we surfaced, Dad was infuriated. "Why would you do that, Trace?" he shouted. "Why leap to your death when no one's looking?"

I'm sure my cheeks burned as I tried to come up with an answer. I hadn't meant to scare my dad, just wanted him to marvel at my bravery. But my leap had unleashed a shock of repressed terror through his veins. I didn't know then that his baby sister, Debbie, had died in the Wood River when she was three. A bank had collapsed beneath her and she slipped in. My then teenage father sprang into action, dropping his fly rod and jumping into the snowmelt-bloated rapids. But it was too late. The last time he saw Debbie alive she was disappearing under a tangle of logs in the river. The last time anyone saw her, she was hanging from a grappling hook that my grandfather had used to comb her water-logged body out of a deep, slow-moving eddy.

At the time, I didn't know the story of Debbie and the grappling hook. All I knew was that my dad always materialized when I was in danger. It felt nice to have someone big, strong, and handsome watching over me. I knew that what I had was as good as—or better than—what any of my friends had, even with their shared-blood daddies.

5

Love Interrupted

On September mornings during my seventh year, Dad, Chris, and I met Gary Mitchell and his daughter, Jeannie, at their farmhouse on the outskirts of Jerome. We drank hot chocolate and ate cinnamon rolls, then slinked along the irrigation canals where the pheasants hid in the sunflowers. Jeannie and I didn't carry guns; we were only little girls. But when our dads dropped a bird out of the bruised autumn sky, we hugged each other with pioneer pride. We strung our bounty on a wire and hoisted it over our shoulders, pulling out the tail feathers and pretending to sword fight.

Dad loved hunting with both of his kids. But given my unending enthusiasm, he especially liked hunting with me. Chris was generally stuck in his own boyhood agenda—playing the piano, building models with his Erector set, and hanging out in the underground fort Dad built in the empty lot next to our new house. Quality family time for Chris included all-day rounds of

Battleship and practicing the various songs he was learning—by Rush, Van Halen, and Led Zeppelin—on the drums and electric guitar. Since his eleventh birthday, it also included chasing me around the living room with a cassette recorder, taping my beleaguered responses to his constant taunting about my being fat.

Dad decided early on that I would be his longtime hunting partner, knowing that if I learned to love hunting, he would get to go more. He wanted us to drink cowboy coffee and eat gritty eggs as the sky turned shades you read about in westerns but never actually see unless you're out there. Sometimes he talked about the day when we would pack our bags with cold meat sandwiches and watch our breath form clouds of exhaust on the windows of the jeep. When I got older, he said, we'd creep through the pine groves looking for deer warming themselves in bright strokes of sunlight. I'd follow my dad, watching his hand signals. At just the right moment, I'd drop onto the crisp, curled leaves that fell from the trees and made the ground look like a giant mosaic, then watch for my dad's signal for me to take a shot. I'd pull the trigger, killing a winter's worth of venison. After cleaning and field-dressing the steaming animal, we'd hike back to camp and share tin plates piled with elk pot roast and campfire-baked potatoes.

"You watch, sis," Dad would say, while we kicked the frost off dead grasses on our chilly late-autumn hikes. "When you're big enough, we'll spend every day of hunting season staked out in Big Piney. Far as I'm concerned, from now on, you're my number one bird dogger in the family."

When Dad talked like this, I knew he was sniffing out the best *me* in me, helping to unearth my hidden talents. At home, I was good at all kinds of things—from ballet and tap lessons to Brownies and gymnastics—but I was also overweight. By third grade, I would tip the scale at eighty pounds, a good twenty more than most of my friends. The girls in my Donna Mauldin's Dance Academy classes were all bones and eyelashes, with beautiful skin and tiny appetites. I had chipmunk cheeks and bumpy arms and could eat an entire six-inch Blimpie by myself. The ladies in my family didn't approve; when I stayed with my grandma, she sent mixed messages, telling me to clean my plate one second and watch what I ate the next, and my mom had already started taking me to her high-end hairdresser, who trimmed, layered, and permed me until I was so ashamed of my appearance sometimes I refused to leave the house.

At home I was just a "big-boned" kid trying to mask my extra pounds with a winning personality. But in the mountains my size was matched only by my desire to fish, hunt, hike, and swim. It helped that there were no mirrors for me to judge myself in. Only my dad's expression, which, when he looked at me, said, *You are strong, and beautiful, and perfect just as you are.*

Dad's pride and joy—after his new family—was the Roadrunner camper-trailer he'd bought in 1976. On Thursdays, and sometimes as early as Wednesday, he'd start loading it with supplies: big bags of chips, Tang mixed with tea, and twelve-packs of minicereals for Chris and me. By the time the other dads on Parkway Drive were cracking their first weekend beers, we'd be chugging across the Perrine Bridge, past the lava flats with their searing heat, and approaching the cool, clean air of the Stanley Basin, where our favorite mountain range, the Sawtooths, top out at twelve thousand feet.

In the long shadows of the Sawtooths, we built castles in the freshwater sand and took turns swimming out to a giant rock a few hundred feet from shore. Sometimes, other families came with us, and all the kids would hike together, searching for bird nests along wooden walkways that stretched over primordial wetlands, or climbing on top of beaver lodges before taking off shoes and pants and jumping into the murky ponds. At the time, the streams pouring out of Redfish Lake teemed with sockeye salmon on their way home from the Pacific Ocean. As a little girl, I stared down at their rotting bodies covered with slime, the bulging eyes, and the long, hooked jawlines dotted with razor-sharp teeth. I was afraid but also fascinated, and though I couldn't have articulated it then, I wondered what demon drove them to travel so far inland—without food or rest, for weeks—to decompose and die while furiously wiggling up the feeder streams that fanned off of my favorite lake.

In my last, best memory of 1979, we're on our way to Redfish Lake. I am eight years old, on the verge of entering third grade. Dad has eased the camper off the side of the road below our favorite hot spring, Russian John. Soaring, soft-edged mountains flank both sides of the road, and the sound of water burbles through brown-tipped grasses. Our clothes—Mom's silk bra next to my size 8 flowered panties, big jeans and little jeans in a heap, a kid's navy blue down vest, and a grown man's camouflage hunting cap—are piled next to a juniper bush near the steaming pool. One by one we slip into water that smells like minerals and sage. My parents slide down the algae-covered rock and laugh—at the urgency, the cold air, and the slight, acceptable indiscretion we're committing, uphill and just out of range of the car beams passing through the night.

We soak until the last rays of sun paint the mountains pink. We all scan the hillsides for deer. Spot one and you earn a dollar: my new dad's rule. A star—my dad points it out—burns itself into view. "Wish on it," he says, and we all do. When our skin begins to prune, we jump out of the water, rushing to pull clothes over sticky goose-pimpled flesh. We run to our yellow Jeep Cherokee, where we blast the heater, screaming the lyrics to "Free Bird," my all-time favorite song. It's dark when I lift Mom's head off my shoulder and move into the front seat. Dad and I call truckers on the CB radio, using our handles, Coyote and Pinky Tuscadero. Outside the window, the Sawtooths rise into the night.

A few days later, autumn light reflected off a burnished Redfish Lake. Decaying aspen leaves smelled good, in a sad, slowed-down way. This was our fifth trip to Redfish that year and the last one until next spring. As we wound down from swimming and sand-castle making, I sat with Dad on the white-sand shore and told him how I wanted to go into the Sawtooth Mountains, next summer maybe, on a real backpacking trip.

Dad stomped out a cigarette and put it in his pocket, then smiled down at me like I was the most interesting thing he'd ever seen. He slung an arm around my shoulders, scrunching the feathers in my blue-and-orange down vest. Dad took my hand and led me back to the trailer, where Mom and Chris were fixing dinner: tacos with hot dogs on the side. We crunched the chalky corn shells and guzzled big cups of milk. Later, at the foldout table, we played cards—Spoons or Go Fish—while Dad sipped beer from his koozie and Chris begged him for a taste. When I went to bed, Mom did too, crawling onto the foldout couch directly below my foldout bunk. She read for a while, then drifted off while I listened to the card game. "Pair of jacks," said my dad. And I fell asleep.

When I woke up next, sandpaper was crawling on my skin. At least that's what I thought it was, until I felt hot breath against my cheek. The bunk bed where I slept was two feet from the camper ceiling, dark as a coffin and covered in dust. I couldn't sit up, so I stayed perfectly still, while my eight-year-old brain tried to grapple with sandpaper and beer breath.

At first, I thought someone had broken into the trailer, that I was alone, or else Mom would jump up, tear at her hair, and start screaming. Dad would grab his rifle and shout, "Identify yourself or I'll shoot." Chris, a gigantic pansy, would run out of the trailer and hide in the trees.

In the dark, the sandpaper kept moving, five round pieces the size of fingertips. I thought I could hear two people whispering, or one person talking to itself. While it mumbled, the sandpaper scraped my stomach, then pulled up my pajama shirt. It touched my belly button, then worked its way to my nipples. When it was through scratching me there, it slid down to the elastic on my pj pants, where it lifted them off my belly and scraped its way south. In the dark I could feel myself sweating, but I was too terrified to move. The sandpaper stopped near the top of my vagina, then found an opening.

I was swimming in tar. I would suffocate. I listened to the wind beat against the trailer until the breath grunted away from my face and the sandpaper pulled up my pajamas, patting the waistband, laying it gently against my skin. In its place two leathery hands pulled up my sleeping bag and tucked it ever so carefully under my chin.

The next morning I waited until I heard Dad go outside to get the fire going for coffee and eggs, then slid out of my bag and climbed down from the bunk. Chris was stretched out on the kitchen table, which folded down and converted into its own bed. Mom was buried in my parents' double-wide Cabela's sleeping bag, cocooned under so much flannel I couldn't find her at first. I burrowed in beside her, the scent of my dad's body still lingering in the air.

For a long time I didn't say anything, just stared at Mom's eyelids, which flitted along the surface of a dream. I rubbed her earlobe with my finger, feeling the superfine hairs. When I couldn't stand it any longer, I leaned over and whispered that something scary had happened while we were sleeping. Someone had snuck into my bunk bed and put their hands on places that had made me feel scared and sick.

"Mmm-hmmm," Mom murmured, "okay honey, you go ahead." Then a switch went off in her muggy brain.

"What did you say?" she said, twisting her ear away from my hand.

"I don't know," I whispered.

"Tracy, what did you just say? Tell me what you just said."

"I don't know. Someone did something to me."

Mom sat up, pushing the covers off of us, which let in a shock of cold air. "What do you mean someone did something to you? I don't understand," she said. "You're right here. How could someone have done something when you're two feet away from me?"

"I don't know . . ." I said again. "But I'm afraid."

"Tracy!" repeated my mom. Now she was yelling, which scared me even more. "What's going on? Where's your dad? Don!"

But Dad had already heard rustling in the trailer, so he came inside to investigate.

"Top of the morning, family," he said. "Who's ready for some pancakes?"

But no one was ready for pancakes. Chris sat up and then quickly exited the trailer. I cowered under the covers trying to become invisible. Mom looked at my dad, relying on him for answers.

"Don?" she said. "Tracy says someone came into the trailer last night. I didn't hear anything. Did you?"

Dad's smile dimmed slightly. He looked from me to my mom and back again, and then he sat down on the bed.

"What's your mother talking about, sis?" he asked me. "What happened last night?"

I'm not exactly sure what happened after our conversation in the camper, at least not the order of events. Dad asked Chris to take me outside, so we rode around the campground on his dirt bike, peeling out and popping the clutch. I was thirsty and hungry, but also sick to my stomach, like I'd been sunburned from the inside out. Chris and I went to the dock, where we skipped rocks and tried to catch minnows in plastic sandwich bags. We dug in the sand for a couple of hours and then went back to the trailer, where I found Mom still in her sleeping bag, reading a book.

Mom said Dad and I needed to talk. They had discussed it at length, and he assured her that no one had come into the camper and that I'd just had a bad dream. To make me feel better, she said, he and I were going for a walk.

It was warm in the sun and cold in the shade. The wind smelled like pinecones and the promise of snow. Dad led us out of the campground to Fishhook Creek, where I liked to watch the spawning salmon, back when they ran so thick it looked like you could Jesus-walk across the river on their wiggling backs.

When we got to the creek, I found a log and inched across it to the center. Dad scooched behind me, lit a Camel, and sat down so that the soles of his boots skimmed the surface, which was metallic and bright. I felt better, because Dad and I were sitting in one of our favorite spots, balanced on a log above our favorite river, with the sun spilling over our skin. Dad puffed on his cigarette, exhaling streams of smoke that hung in the cool fall air. I balanced on the log, hopping from one foot to the other, staring at one spot like I'd learned in ballet. I had to pick a place above my dad's head, because it made me feel even dizzier to look in his face.

"I know what you're thinking," he said after several minutes. "I know what you think that was."

I considered asking him how he knew that I was thinking *Do fish breathe in the murky water that disappears under the grass?* I was imagining, in some abstract and childish way, how, if I wanted to, I could slip into the water with them, swim toward the current, and let it pull me out of sight. I held my breath and waited for my dad to tell me why I'd felt so scared and dirty the night before, in my pj's, in the bunk bed of my trailer, in the safety of my own family. But Dad took one last puff of his cigarette, then threw the butt into the creek.

"I mean it, Tracy," he said. "I was only tucking you in."

6

Agent of Change

As far as I can remember, Mom and Dad never brought up the camper incident again. But on this point my parents' and my memories diverge. Mom says she went to her priest in Jerome and that he told her we all needed to sit down and talk about what had happened. She brought my dad and me into the living room, circling the wagons. She peered into both of our faces, saying, "Okay, you two. Tell me again about that night in the camper." When both Dad and I stared down at the carpet, she sat back and breathed a sigh of relief. Just as she'd suspected: even if something sinister had occurred, it wasn't so important that it needed repeating.

My dad, however, tells a slightly different story, one in which he and my mom both manipulated my memory: "I made up all kinds of excuses that sounded good to your mom. She went along with them. That's how we overran that particular situation."

Deep down, I knew that my dad had done something bad to me. But if my parents were so sure that I'd been mistaken, I must have made myself believe them. Who was I to question the people who fed, clothed, and protected me from things like Bigfoot and monsters under my bed? If there was a God, to me, they were It. I had no business refuting their version of reality.

For weeks following our return from Redfish Lake, though, it felt like static electricity radiated through our house. We resumed our schedule of school, Brownies, Boy Scouts, piano lessons, swim team, track, drive-in movies, and Kick the Can. Mom busied herself with her job as the Bickel Elementary lunch-money lady, and Dad lurked around the basement, loading shotgun shells or tying flies, emerging only when Mom needed his help making dinner. At first, I spent more time than usual in my bedroom, playing with my Lite-Brite or writing in a journal that I could lock with a tiny key. But pretty soon I managed to push from my mind the memory—and all physical sensation—of the fingers scraping across my body.

That was the year Darcie Murray and I ran around the school-yard screaming the lyrics to "Another One Bites the Dust," with our I ♥ Horses shirts over the tops of our heads. Tornadoes of little-girl energy, we did back-flip knee-drops off the high bar and chased boys into the Love Tunnel to pretend make out. One time, a teacher on recess duty heard us yelling "fuck you!" to no one in particular and sent us to the principal's office. When Mrs. Anderson asked where we'd learned such vulgar language, I told her I didn't even know what "fuck you" meant (a lie) but that Chris had taught me to say it (the truth).

My erratic energy bursts earned me sprained wrists from falls off the monkey bars and the occasional catfight with girls on the playground, and Dad was always doctoring me up. He burned ticks out of my hair after they'd burrow into me when Jeannie Mitchell and I played house on fresh deer hides while Dad and Gary Mitchell hunted. When I crashed on my bike, Dad used his best tweezers to pick the gravel out of my knees. If I was throwing up, he'd sit by my bed with an old bucket, ready to catch the green bile that erupted out of my mouth. Later, if I felt better, he'd bring in another bucket and sponge warm, soapy water across my shoulders and neck.

Over time, I'd started trusting Dad again, but things were going downhill between him and my mom. They never hugged in front of Chris and me like they used to, and when they did, it seemed forced—a reenactment of affection put on for our benefit. Somewhere along the line, Mom had started to resent Dad's hunting habit, just as he bemoaned her weekend clothes-shopping sprees. Both of them fought over Chris's now teenaged defiance, which would eventually make him steal our neighbors' Christmas bonus checks and grow pot in an old Studebaker pickup Dad had bought and parked in front of our house. But what really dealt the death blow to my parents' chance for happiness was my mother's deepening despair. Her past seemed to overtake her, plunging her into clinical depressions that required more and more medications, which themselves altered and darkened her moods.

Years later, she would talk to me about how she had never fully recovered from her hysterectomy, which she says ripped out all the parts of her that made her feel like a woman. Not being able to have more babies made her feel ugly and purposeless. Her problems with sex began even before her hysterectomy, when, in 1967, her obstetrician used forceps to deliver Chris, tearing her underside open. As a result, sex had been painful—something to be tolerated while trying to look and sound as if she was enjoying herself. Mom also endured crippling, near-daily headaches, a result of chronic ear infections she had suffered as a child. She had never been properly treated by a doctor, so the infections just sat in her head and festered. The effect was so powerful that despite seemingly weekly visits to ear specialists, chiropractors, and acupuncturists when I was little, she would continue to suffer from severe migraine headaches until the mid-1990s, when a Los Angeles otolaryngologist would cut her ear away from her head and dig out the fifty-year-old bacteria.

I understand, now, that my mom had never really been able to come to terms with her own ragged childhood or my dad's untimely death. But the depressions they evoked were jarring and confusing. One minute she'd be cleaning fish at the kitchen counter, whistling the refrain to "Dancing Queen," and the next minute she would be weepy, lethargic, and unable to sleep. I had no idea that bad chemicals were hijacking the feel-good circuits in her brain, because no one ever bothered to tell me. All I saw was that my mom cried more than the other moms I knew and that she seemed content to collapse into her "comfy chair," a tattered tweed recliner with matching footrest. She did take me shopping more than my friends' moms did, spending her paychecks and a sizable chunk of the child-support checks the U.S. Navy sent us every month on the newest Esprit and Izod fashions. But there's only so much an endless supply of new clothes can do for mother-daughter relations. What I remember more than the weekly shopping sprees was her general discomfort in any and all social situations.

At swim meets and other social functions, she hovered around the edges of large groups, never seeming to know what to say.

"Hey, Doris, come on over. We're rounding up players for a game of pinochle," one of the kids' parents would call out, and I'd see her turn around and walk the other way. When I asked her why she had just ignored an invitation to get to know the other swim team parents, she'd say, "Oh, I'm fine all by myself. I don't know those people. I wouldn't want to ruin their game." So even though I liked the way she cheered for me during butterfly or breast stroke races, her unease and sadness made *me* uneasy and sad, despite my tendency for extreme Pollyanna optimism.

It's also why, less than two years after the Redfish Lake incident, I had so easily gravitated back into the outstretched arms of my dad. Where else would I have gone?

On autumn evenings when I was ten and eleven, Dad took me to the gun club so I could watch him shoot skeet. The atmosphere at home still felt depressed and tense. I spent as much time as possible at my friends' houses, including one in particular, who lived down the street. Her name was Kathie Etter, and I liked going to her house more than anyone else's because her mom was so warmhearted and sweet. But Dad used the gun club, out near Filer, as his escape, and, on occasion, I would go there with him. On the drive he'd nurse a beer, concealed in a koozie that said Bo Derek A Perfect 10. Usually he'd be scanning the landscape, looking for signs of movement in the brush. But occasionally he would mist up and get quiet, and when that happened, he would put his hand on my knee.

"We never talk anymore, sis," he'd say, "You're growing up too fast."

"Dad, I'm only eleven. And you know me. I'm immature for my age."

I did feel immature, even though Dad had recently told me about the birds and the bees. Mom asked him to do it, because she felt too awkward, like she'd leave out an important part of the process or wouldn't be able to say words like "sperm" and "vagina." But lately I had begun to develop, with tiny molehills of breasts rising out of chubby, little-girl flesh. Molehills meant that my period was coming, and Mom didn't want me to be afraid when I saw blood on my underpants.

On the night of the big explanation, Dad and I sat on my bed with our shoulders touching. Chris was at the high school practicing for the 4-by-400 relay, and Mom was in the kitchen making supper. The smell of hamburger and Lawry's seasoning wafted down the hall: beef burritos. I hoped Dad, who was known for being long-winded, wouldn't go on forever, because I wanted to play tag with my neighbor, Charmelle Puka, before dinner.

Dad launched into his presentation, saying that God had made men and women different so they could fit together, like a puzzle. He explained how penises fill with blood in order to make them stiff enough to enter a vagina. When I let out a little whimper followed by an exaggerated eye roll, Dad put a calming arm around my shoulders. This stiffening only sounded scary, he said, because, really, it made men feel extremely good.

"Women feel good, too," he assured me.

I stared at my dad, fighting the urge to recoil. I had never heard the words *penis* and *vagina* in the same sentence, let alone uttered by a grown man. But apparently my reaction wasn't grounds enough for him to stop talking. He went on, describing how men become aroused, and detailing the intricate workings of sex organs. As he talked, his movements became more animated and his breathing quickened. If he could see the horror in my face as he went into greater and greater detail, he didn't show it, nor did he relent. I bounced up and down on my white ruffled bedspread, trying to calm the feeling of ants crawling up my blood vessels.

By the time Dad got up and walked awkwardly and quickly into the bathroom, I knew everything I would ever need to about orgasms, but not one thing about menstruation.

On the road to the gun club, Dad mulled over my thoughts about my maturity level. He reached a hand across the middle console and smoothed a stray hair that was whipping me in the face. "I like you immature," he said. "It means you're bright and beautiful and ready for anything."

I felt nervous when he talked like this so I started to sing. Dad smiled out the front windshield, tapping the steering wheel, eventually joining in. In the Idaho desert the wind always blows. We drifted across the highway with our arms hanging out the windows. We sang the words to "Hotel California," harmonizing during the chorus and banging out the rhythm on the sun-warmed doors of the bright yellow jeep.

7

Bull's Eye

When I was twelve my dad said I needed to start thinking about carrying my own gun. He signed me up for a hunter's safety class at his buddy Al Bolish's house. Every Wednesday evening for six weeks, we made ourselves peanut butter sandwiches and headed to the farm town of Filer, which smelled like the inside of a cow's stomach where milk was curdling into cottage cheese. The class filled up in one afternoon with a dozen kids who'd rather sit inside and watch first-aid videos than shovel hay for their dads. I was one of the few girls in attendance and nervous the first day of instruction. But my dad knew my aptitude for survival; he promised me I'd shoot better than anyone else. All kinds of common sense goes into handling a weapon, and Dad wanted me to know it, mainly so I wouldn't accidentally ping him in the ass.

At Al's we learned how to hold a rifle while crossing under a barbed-wire fence. We turned on the safety and checked the chamber for bullets before aiming. Then we practiced loading and unloading our ammo, making sure to always leave our gun chambers empty when we were finished, "because stupid people stand a fifty percent greater chance of shooting themselves in the foot," Al said.

On the last Saturday of class, we took a paper test, which I aced, finishing a good five minutes before my runner-up. I walked my booklet to the front of Al's living room and accepted a hug from Dad. Al smiled through chew-flecked teeth and threw a fatherly arm around my low back. He and Dad winked at each other when it was time to head outside for our shooting test.

Dad grinned proudly as I slouched past all the farm kids to a line etched in the dirt, dutifully pointing the tip of my .22 single-shot Winchester at the ground. I didn't arch my back and puff my lungs like the other hunters when I hoisted the rifle to my chest. I steadied it on my shoulder, put my finger on the trigger, and pretended to be Annie Oakley as I glared down the sight.

I would have lined that target up all by myself. Probably tore the bull's-eye apart. But then Dad took it upon himself to give me a little help. He walked up, put his hands on my shoulders, and pressed himself into my back. "Look for the target in the center of the V," he said. "Hold your breath. And squeeze."

Leaning into Dad, I felt uneasy. He was solid and strong, but stuck out in places I didn't necessarily like. Since the sex-education talk, something about him had changed, and I didn't think it was for the better. He seemed to spend more time looking at me, letting his eyes pour over my body. He studied me, from my feathered bilevel haircut to my size 6, brown-and-tan Nikes.

Sometimes, when I was in the bathtub singing, he'd barge in, pretending he didn't know I was there. I had no idea how other dads reacted to seeing their daughters naked, but mine seemed to spend too much time apologizing, stammering about how he needed a lightbulb or a bar of Ivory, while his eyes continued to bug out of his face. Little did I know, I was walking the tightrope of ambiguity. Did Dad stumble into the bathroom while I was bathing "accidentally," or was it on purpose? My dad had always gazed at me with affection. But now his gazes made me want to crawl inside my own skin.

Out on the shooting range, I could feel Dad pressing against my back, as he held me to demonstrate how to aim. His breath—a nauseating mixture of maple bars and Folgers—was hot on my ear. When our cheeks touched, I felt the odd texture of his facial skin, which he prided himself on shaving "smooth as a baby's butt." The sensation made my teeth bite the sides of my cheeks. But with Al and the other kids watching, I had to be brave. I couldn't turn around and tell my dad to give me some space. Instead, I steeled myself against him, clenching the back of my body into one big muscle.

Dad either didn't notice or chose not to say anything. He braced himself against me, squeezing his arms against the outside of my biceps. "Atta girl, sis," he whispered. "Keep it up. You're doing great." The next time I shrugged my shoulders, he seemed to get the hint.

Freed from his grasp, I lowered the gun and stamped my boots in the dirt. I resteadied the rifle and stared down the sight. Waiting until I was sure everyone in the class was watching, I pulled the trigger. The bullet tore a hole through the tiny black dot in the center of the target.

The next time my dad asked me to go to the gun club with him, I didn't race outside to the jeep. By my thirteenth birthday, I had begun to feel nervous and worried in his presence. Every time I turned around, it seemed his eyes were glued to my breastbone. He told me jokes—out of earshot of my mom or Chris—that made me hate my own body. I'd come out of the shower and he'd be standing in the hallway, waiting. I'd look for my mom, hoping she was noticing the same thing I did. But Dad chose his opportunities carefully. Mom was usually out of earshot; if she wasn't out shopping, she was cleaning the living room or parked in front of *Knots Landing*.

A few months into my thirteenth year, I stood in Mom's bathroom asking her to shave my armpits. The next day, my swim team, the Magic Valley Dolphins, had a meet, and the last thing I wanted was to show up at the swimming pool with hairy pits. The trouble was, every time I tried to shave I ended up cutting myself.

"Why don't you ask your dad to do it?" Mom said.

"I don't *want* him to do it. Why can't *you* do it?"

Over the past year, my body had continued to quicken, hips spreading and breasts rising out of supple, sun-freckled skin. Now I caught Dad watching me as I pushed out my chest and looked at my reflection in the microwave door. Sometimes I could feel him peering through the hole he'd smashed in the wall of Chris's room during a remodeling project. He would stand as still as a statue on the other side of the three-inch-wide wall. But I could hear him breathing, and that made me want to turn into a caterpillar that had wrapped itself inside a cocoon.

Dad had also liberated himself from merely watching. Now he was coming into my room when I was on the verge of sleeping, asking if I was feeling okay, offering to tickle my back. From the time I was little I had been a bad sleeper, so even though I was thirteen, I still liked it when either of my parents came in to soothe me as I settled in to bed. But lately, I had begun waking up in the morning with cotton in my mouth and a cobweb of bad feelings in my head. I couldn't put my finger on the origin of the feeling, but I sensed that it had something to do with Dad.

"You know I always mess it up," said Mom, lifting her head out from under the bathroom sink. "Have your dad do it. His razors are sharper. You'll get a closer shave."

"But, Mom . . ."

She stuck her head out the door and shouted through her bedroom down the hall.

"Don! Can you help us in here?"

"*Mom.* Don't worry, I'll figure it out."

"What's the matter? You should let him help you. It'll make him feel needed and that'd be good for him right now."

Mom was always dying her hair different colors, from strawberry blond to dark brown to Joan-Jett black. She was studying her roots in the mirror when Dad walked in, so she didn't see the horror on my face as I stood frozen next to the shower door, waiting for my dad to shave me.

"Tracy needs her armpits shaved for the meet tomorrow," said Mom, plugging her blow-comb into a wall socket. "Can you do it? I always mess it up."

Dad looked from me to my mom in a way that made the hairs on my arms stand up like the quills on a porcupine. My whole body tensed, which had the negative effect of making my nipples poke out. I was ashamed, and tried to make myself smaller, folding away again like a piece of origami. But folding only made the towel slip.

"I think I can handle that," said Dad. "Let's have a look-see, Trace."

Dad turned on the faucet, filling the sink with hot water to warm his can of Old Spice. He took a razor from his shaving kit, attached a shiny new blade, and dunked a washcloth in the water. He liked to heat the washcloth up, he said, because it would make the follicles soften. From that point forward, every time I'd hear the word "follicles" my stomach would clench.

With the washcloth steaming, Dad knelt in front of the toilet, taking my arm in his hand and raising it over my head. He laid the cloth in the hollow of my armpit, then sprayed a wad of cream into the center of his palm. The dollop was as big as a popover and pointed at the apex like meringue. Dad was humming as he smeared the cream across my prickly flesh, moving slower than a snail in a heat wave.

"How's that feel?" he asked my left breast.

62

Don't land on me, don't land on me, don't land on me! No!

Ten of my schoolmates and I watched the green bottle spinning on the concrete floor of Maureen Neville's garden shed. One bare lightbulb hung from the ceiling; the ground below it buzzed with flies. The bottle slowed, teetering on the concrete pebbles. When it came to a stop it was pointing at me.

Bart Vies looked up and cracked a smile through beer-can braces. He walked to the door and I followed him, stifling a laugh. The wind kicked up, blowing small pieces of garbage through the azaleas in the yard. A metal trash can clanged onto the patio.

"So," said Bart, once we were outside the shed. "Are we like *obligated* to kiss?"

"You and me? Hell no. No way," I laughed.

"I mean, we probably should, because those are the rules," said Bart. "But I don't know. I'm not feeling it. Not right now. At least not with you."

That last part stung just a little bit, but I let it float away. I wasn't Bart Vies's kind of girl, and he wasn't my kind of guy. He was smart, and popular, but he was also a suck-up and naturally tanned. I could deal with the suck-up-ness; it got you scholarships to college and things. But I couldn't stand the tan part. Outside of Mexicans and Mormon ranchers, tan people signified an elite. They tanned so effortlessly; they were never forced, like I was, to drench themselves in Wesson oil and lie out in the driveway on a sheet of tinfoil while the dog tried to lick their arms. But the main reason I didn't like those who tanned was because they included my dad.

By 1984, he and I were growing apart. An eighth-grade cheerleader of the most self-absorbed order, I was too cool to go hunting, which made him feel hurt and mad. New friends and boyfriends competed for my attention, along with drama class, poetry contests, and track. When Dad heard me say "I love you" on the phone to one of my girlfriends, he flew off the handle, muttering, "Why do you tell people that? You sound like an idiot."

I did have one secret that I'd been able to keep from Dad. Earlier that summer, I met a new boy named Reed at a Christ on Parade concert at the Odd Fellows Hall in Twin Falls. We met through a haze of beer fumes and cigarette smoke—and an introduction from my friend Stacy's brother, Darren. Reed had red-blond hair, yellow-green eyes, and eyeteeth that looked as sharp as a vampire's. He belonged to a nonviolent gang called The Antichrists. The second I saw him, standing in a corner smiling through his fangs, I knew we were doomed to love.

I can't remember who approached whom, but we left the concert and went for a walk. The air outside was warm and fragrant. He asked me about my family, and I lied, telling him my dad was a cop. The impromptu lie sprung up from an unknown inspiration. Was it wishful thinking or the reverse?

In the humid summer, which evolved into the worst season of my life, Reed was a heady, heart-throbbing distraction. We exchanged phone numbers, showed up at the same downtown outdoor dance parties, and clung to our separate groups of friends (mine: girls in thick black eyeliner and black nylons with holes ripped in the knees; his: the chain-smoking, forty-ouncer drinking, skateboard ollie-ing Antichrists). We shared glares and the occasional slam dance.

I think Reed liked me because, even at thirteen, I knew what "the establishment" was and already hated it. Reed was the opposite of normal: he seemed raw in a way no one I had ever met was brave enough to be. From the first time we met, I saw him as both someone I could once-over and someone who deserved to know the darkest, most complicated parts of me. He didn't know it, but he was about to become central to my survival, because he gave me something positive to focus on.

The same couldn't be said for Dad, who had recently begun openly preying on me. Even as he felt me pulling away from him, he pried open the blinds of my bedroom and stood in the backyard barely hiding the fact that he was watching me undress. I tried sleeping in my street clothes, but he insisted that I change out of them at night. Though it had been a year since I'd stopped asking him to tickle my back, he came into my room while I was on the verge of sleeping, and staying until after I had dozed off. Sometimes I would wake up and see him hovering over me, like he was on his way to lying down or had already done so and was just getting up. Seeing the wide, staring whites of my eyes, he'd quickly pull up the covers, saying "You're okay, sis. I'm here. You called out for me in your sleep."

I wanted to tell my mom that something terrible was happening, but I always backed off just short of speaking. Dad's threatening looks would stop me in my tracks. Not only that, no matter how hard I squeezed my brain muscle to remember, I couldn't conjure up a clear picture of exactly what Dad was doing to my body all those nights. It would be years before I discovered how far he was going to molest me without repercussion. But at nearly fourteen, I knew only one thing for certain: now he also wanted to fondle me in broad daylight.

He had started a new job at Intermountain Gas Company, selling natural gas to developers as an alternative to propane, and it allowed him to come home in the middle of the day. During the summer, when I was home from school, he'd slip in the front door, silent, as if he were trying to sneak up on me. With Mom working full-time, Dad had ample opportunity to coax me onto the living room floor and make me tickle his back.

In a sense, this was nothing new, and perhaps I shouldn't have been so surprised by it. As a four- and five-year-old, I had loved grooming Dad. He had always been a willing model, for eye shadow, lipstick, and bright red barrettes. I'd take off his shirt and dress him in my fake feather boas or wrap a sequined cape around his back. I'd brush his hair, then style it with a working blow dryer from my plastic beautician's kit. Sometimes his dark skin charred, despite the teaspoon of Cherokee Indian in his blood, and he'd ask me to sit on his lower back and scratch the peeling skin on his shoulders. I'd responded willingly, happy to be the one who could relieve him of the discomfort even better than Bactine. I'd rake my fingers across the black patches, looking for a scab or loose corner of skin. When I found one strong enough to lift up, I would peel the epidermis back, gently coaxing it from the raw underflesh until I had harvested a transluscent, two-by-two-inch sheet. But I was a baby back then. Now, a few months shy of my fourteenth birthday, I knew I was much too old to be grooming my dad.

"You're so good to me, sis," he said one afternoon. He was lying on the living room carpet with the curtains pulled shut. Dad had always wanted the curtains closed, ever since we moved into our new house. He said it was a way of helping our insulation do its job: keep the sun out during the summer and trap the heat inside when it got cold. But the unnatural dark of our house heightened my sense of some impending danger.

On that searing day in June, the sun outside our windows blazed white-hot and blinding. Walking barefoot on the sidewalk meant risking the bottoms of your feet. Thanks to Dad's advice, lots of people on Parkway Drive kept their curtains closed during the hottest part of the day. But right now I could think of nothing I wanted more than to throw the curtains wide open, so that the world could save me from him.

Dad slid his Ralph Lauren button-down off his ropy brown arms, and then spread out on the carpet, stomach down. I stood next to the piano, in a pale pink summer-weight nightgown. I often spent all day in my pajamas, unless I was going somewhere like softball practice or to my friend, Valkyrie's. I suddenly wished I was going to the North Pole, where I would have to wear three layers of long underwear and a floor-length goose-down parka.

Dad patted his lower back, motioning for me to sit on top of him. I stared at the back of his head, fought the tears I could feel coming. I knew I had no choice but to do what he told me, and without raising a fuss. It was unspoken knowledge that if I told my mom about the abuse, like I'd done in the trailer, I would blow up our entire family. I walked over, sat down, and tickled. But I was ten feet under water in my favorite fishing hole at the bottom of the Snake River Canyon. I held my breath and wished the same thing I had been wishing for more than half my life: that I could bust through the walls of our living room, fly to the edge of the river, and let the rapids drag me under.

"Did I ever tell you how pretty you are?" Dad said, interrupting my wish.

"Yes, Dad."
"You believe me, right?"
"Yes, Dad."
"You know I love you, right?"
No answer.
"Now let me tickle you."

8

—

Run!

Through it all, I wrote poetry. In both 1984 and '85, I won the Idaho Young Poets contest for ten stanzas scratched on notebook paper the night before submissions were due. When my category—Fifteen and Under: Dramatic Poem—came up, I knew before they announced the finalists that I had won the gold medal. I'd guessed that sad or violent poems would beat out happy poems, so that's what I wrote. And besides, sad and violent was how I felt.

I can still remember the look on my mom's face when I handed her a poem I'd written one morning after I'd woken up with Dad shining a flashlight up my legs. I'd bucked away and snarled at him like a wolverine caught in a trap. He spit back, saying, "If you don't want people to do things to you, don't lay on your back with your leg bent up."

The poem was about dark shadows and chanting voices, black widows, and fingers covered in blood. It was heavy on metaphor and light on exposition—a perfect example of how I cloaked my most painful secrets even as I tried to tell them to my mother. I wanted to shield her from the full spectrum of my horror, but at the same time I hoped that she would ask me to explain.

She didn't—not that morning or on any other. Many years later, when she would beg me to forgive her for not knowing what was transpiring just feet from her bedroom, I would tell her that what remains unforgivable is not that she didn't see what was happening in front of her but that she never asked me for the whole excruciating story when the truth finally surfaced. In my mind, her refusal to know the details of my abuse was the equivalent of a refusal to know her own daughter.

On that morning in late May 1985, we bustled around the kitchen, all four of us getting ready for school and work. When I was sure that Dad wasn't watching, I handed Mom the piece of notebook paper, tucked in the palm of my hand. Taking a sip of her favorite Red Rose English breakfast tea, she unfolded the missive. Skimming the lines, she fell quiet. I waited for a change in her expression, a frown, a grimace—something. But my heart sank to the bottom of my ribcage. Instead of screaming, she refolded the paper, sipped her tea, and burned her own message back to me. It said, *Please, please stop telling me this.*

On the same day that I lost my virginity, I ran away from home. It happened—my "deflowering"—on a dirty bed in a small, dilapidated house on the outskirts of Jerome. I was fourteen, and I did it with a Mexican kid named Mondo, whom I didn't even like or desire. I liked Reed, but I wanted to get sex over with.

When it was over, all I wanted to do was go home and hide in the stuffed animals that still sat in a big love pile against my headboard. But Dad had other plans for me. He greeted me at the door, threatening to ground me if I didn't stop running around like a little strumpet. "Freak," I muttered, pushing past him. Dad hated it when I back talked under my breath. But for some reason, on that night, he waited to retaliate.

I slammed into my room, but was in for a shock. Sometime that day, my bed had been broken. When I'd left in the morning, it had been fine, but now it was leaning to one side. It was clear that someone heavy had jumped on it, severely bending the frame. Dad—being the good father—had noticed and leapt into action. While I was out, he set up my sleeping bag on the living-room floor.

I don't know how long I procrastinated before finally forcing myself to walk into the living room and crawl into that bag. At first I zipped it all the way closed, but getting too hot, I unzipped it down to my feet. Dad and Mom watched TV until a commercial came on, and then Mom said goodnight and padded down the hallway. An hour or so later, Dad disappeared, reemerging in a terry-cloth robe. I could smell him before I saw him: Old Spice and cigarettes. I stifled a gag. *Please, God,* I prayed. *Make him leave me alone.*

If I fell asleep at all, it was fitful. I lay on my stomach, with one leg sticking out of the open cover. A faded yellow Tweety Bird nightgown skimmed my abdomen and legs. I was still shaken by my first experience of actual sex—the pressure of a foreign object pushing into a now not-so-sacred space. Though I'd showered, I was sure Dad could smell the sweat on me, along with phero-mones and sperm. I knew he couldn't detect the scent of orgasm, because I hadn't had one.

In a little while, Dad's program ended. He stood up and turned down the TV. He locked the front door and switched off the lights. Tiptoeing across the carpet, he stopped above me, straddled my body like a starfish, and rested his entire body weight on top of me.

I bucked, still feigning sleep, and tried to edge out from under him. And then like always, I gave up and became lifeless. He raised his body for a second, then resettled like a bag of wet cement. Entire centuries passed as the dread of what was happen-ing now became certain; this time, there was no question about what he wanted or what he was doing. He raised up again and was beginning to assert a rhythm. I squeezed my inner thigh muscles together. A voice in my head began chanting: *I won't let you . . . I won't. I won't. I won't.*

As I lay there, a strange feeling overtook me—I felt myself sink down and go limp. I took my mind out of the room, to a refuge I had been to before. It was the Wood River, and I imagined myself floating in the cool, baptizing water. If this was the night my dad was going to have sex with me, that's where I would wait while it happened. Then, instead—a miracle: a dog barked, and Dad almost back-flipped off me.

I was freed, but not out of trouble, so I didn't move or speak a word. Dad stared at me for a long second, shaking his feathered head. His big, brown hands fished around in his robe pockets. Then he turned around, put on his slippers, and went outside.

Run!

I waited, too terrified to move. When he came in, he turned out the lights and headed to bed. I attuned my eardrums to his movements. I could hear him—feet walking down the hall. Teeth brushed. Covers back. A little moan. Asleep. Restraining myself until I was sure I could hear him snoring, I got up, put on my black-and-pink Vans, and slipped out the front door, careful not to let the wind slam it behind me. I sprinted to the end of our driveway with the wind whipping my hair into the corners of my mouth. Without one ounce of deliberation, I turned north, toward the Snake River and the five-hundred-foot-high Perrine Bridge. As I ran past the dark houses where my neighbors lay sleeping, I thought, *This is the night that everyone will remember, but no one will understand.*

I was running to the bridge that people leapt off when they could no longer stitch together the tattered fabric of their lives. I would climb on top of the cold metal railing. And I would jump.

9

Fugitive

The wind howled and thunderclouds built over the desert.
I thought I could hear the sound of roaring water, but it
could have been the blood rushing into my ears. I knew I was five
hundred feet above the Snake River, a few more if I climbed on
top of the railing, where I would balance for a few seconds, and
then—*whoosh*.

I'm surprised I didn't ask God to intervene. But I didn't think
of Him in that moment. Instead, I thought of the people I knew
who had thrown themselves off the Perrine Bridge, including a
friend of Chris's who was so ashamed after learning that he didn't
make the varsity cross-country team he leapt to his death. I was
smart enough to know that I would black out before I hit the
water, or die on impact. But the wind was so strong, I worried it
would push me before I was ready, or worse; blow me back against
the railing.

I didn't want to climb onto the railing and be at the mercy of the gusts. I wanted to leap of my own volition and fall like a sack of potatoes, both heavy and weightless at the same time. I wanted to know that I was in charge of my own destiny, like Wonder Woman, who could ward off evil villains with a one-two shot of her power bracelets. I pressed my collarbones into the steel girders, leaning over water so black and shiny it looked like motor oil. As I was about to climb over, the reality of what that descent and smack onto the water would mean came over me, and even though I knew that death was the only guaranteed way to save me from my father, I also knew I was more terrified of dying than of going home. But going home was out of the question. There had to be another answer. I sat on the bridge until the wind made me shiver. Then I got up and started walking—back in the direction of my house.

It was late, and nobody was outside, just some heifers in a pasture near the irrigation canal where I used to swim. Mist rose off the water, and the smell of cow bums hung in the air. The moon was bright, which helped me decide to keep going once I got back to my street, Parkway Drive. I continued straight, thinking that maybe when I reached the end of the road, I'd slip between the barbed-wire fence and keep walking west, away from the sunrise.

I went maybe a hundred steps before abandoning the plan to walk until my legs buckled beneath me, pitching me onto my face. Instead, I turned up my friend Kathie Etter's street, fixated on a sudden, illuminating vision of her mother. Kathie and I had known each other since kindergarten. Her mom, Laura, was not only big and masculine looking, but she always struck me as fierce and loyal—like, if I needed her to, she could grab a kitchen knife and fillet Dad. I didn't know it yet, but she was also good friends with a cop.

I turned up Kathie's street and continued walking. When I reached her lawn, I sat down and made a pillow out of a pile of dead grass. Lying on my back, I watched silver-rimmed clouds drift past a three-quarters full moon. I knew that if I went home, I would face the worst grounding of my life or, worse, explode my family—or the illusion of a family, anyway. A sprinkler went on in someone's yard, and a dog started to bark. I stood up, walked to Kathie's ground-floor bedroom window, and knocked.

Kathie must have been in a deep sleep because it took her a while to come to the screen. Her giant blue eyes were even wider than I remembered. Feathered blond hair framed a broad, high-cheekboned face. She and I had been friends since we performed "Who Put the Chicken in the Chicken Chow Mein?" as five-year-olds in Donna Mauldin's Dance Academy. It had never occurred to me to tell her about my dad, even when she spent the night.

"Tracy?" she whispered. "What are you doing here?"

I pushed my face into her window, but no words came out.

"What time is it?" said Kathie. "And why are you here and not at home?"

I was about to answer when, inside the house, a light went on. Laura Etter came to the window. She saw me standing in the middle of a juniper bush, a rash already spreading up my shins. My nightgown was smudged from sitting on the bridge, and my hair was matted and tangled. Laura told me to come to the front door, and I did, finding her in a pool of flickering porch light. I must have looked cold, because she wrapped me in both of her arms and hug-walked me into the house.

"My God, Tracy," she said, when we were in her living room, standing on the green shag carpet. She didn't even know what had happened, but she was already starting to choke up. "What's the matter? Why aren't you home with your parents?"

Certain parts of that night are gauzy, but Laura says I began to spin. Literally stood up and turned circles in the middle of her living room. While I twirled, she kept talking, saying, "Tracy, honey. Slow down. I want to help you. But in order for me to do so, you have to help me.

"Please tell me, honey. What happened?" she said.

And then, finally, I did.

"Help is comin', hon," Laura said, after I'd told her as much as I could. It amounted to little more than "My dad. He comes after me. He tries to hurt me." She called the police and told them a little girl needed their help. "I hope you'll be able to tell them what you told me," she said. "But if you can't, I'll help you, alright?"

In the dark of my friend's living room, I hugged my legs and waited for the flashing strobes that would signal the arrival of the police. I didn't even care when Kathie, sprawled out in a tattered green recliner, started to snore. Just as I knew she couldn't feel the adrenaline coursing through my veins, I also knew that I was probably the only girl in Twin Falls awake and on the run at three a.m. I was equally certain that I was the only one about to turn her family in to the authorities.

While we waited, Laura got up and went into the bathroom. I could hear the water rushing into the porcelain basin, the sound of

78

bristles moving across teeth. My eyes burned and my legs twitched from exhaustion. But as soon as I was alone, I felt the overpowering urge to get up and run, as night edged closer to morning and I became more aware of the enormity of my decision.

I don't know why I suddenly felt the need to protect my family, but I wanted to save them from the things I was going to say. If I acted fast, I could rewind the entire evening, go home, and wake up the next morning pretending nothing had changed. When the police came, I would tell them Charmelle Puka must have called, because "Can't you see my sleeping bag? I was right there, on the living-room floor, asleep." They would question me, and I would tell them, No, my life isn't perfect. But whose is? When they left, I would creep down the hall to my bedroom and try to figure out how to fix my broken bed.

I came so close to leaving that I slipped my shoes back on my feet. I pushed my body to the end of Laura's couch. But two things kept me from bolting out of the living room and tearing off into the night. Years of *Magnum P.I.* episodes had made me believe that if I left the scene of a crime, I would become a fugitive. I also knew that if I went home, the next thing on my dad's agenda would be rape. I knew it like I'd never known anything in my life. Deep down, on a level I could barely interpret, I knew there was no stopping my dad.

So I stayed. And told the police as much as I could. Laura held my hand while I picked at an orange thread sprouting out of a couch seam. Shame kept me from revealing the full extent of the abuse—the midday tickle sessions, the visits to my room, and the half-awake fondling that I was only beginning to accept as a reality—to the two officers with handguns and billy clubs who stared at me while tears streamed down my cheeks. Instead of details, I spoke in my usual euphemisms—about my dad "coming after me," about "not feeling safe."

And yet, for the first time ever, my euphemisms were enough. The police asked Laura to watch me until they could alert the Health and Welfare Department, who would take over where they left off. I'd stay put while social services determined if going home was an option. Laura walked the policemen to the door, then came back and bunched up a pile of blankets on the couch.

"Get some rest," she said, putting her hand on my forehead.

I nodded again, but I was too wired for sleeping. I curled up on the sofa and watched the first rays of sunshine pouring across the west. I watched the glittering gold light shine into the windows of the Etters' neighbors, and waited for what would happen.

I must have drifted off, because the next thing I knew a hand was rousing me from sleep. My blankets had bunched up around my legs. I kicked at them, trying to free myself from the bind of piled polyester. The rest of my body lay in a swamp of my own sweat.

The hand kept nudging me, so I made my eyelids unstick themselves from the goop that had congealed around them during my short, post-sunrise nap. My mouth tasted like the top of a battery when you licked it, trying to give yourself a spark. I opened my eyes and saw a man in a blue uniform. A gold badge floated in the empty space above his heart.

It took several more minutes for me to orient myself to my surroundings. My head felt like someone had vacuumed my brain and refilled the empty cavity with mud. I picked at my eyes, continuing to urge the sleep scabs off them. Then a voice I recognized brought my full attention into the room.

It was Laura, sitting at the far end of the couch. She touched the top of my exposed foot gently, as you would a newborn puppy or baby rabbit.

"Hi, Tracy," she said, shooting me a warm smile. "I'm glad to see you fell asleep."

I blinked hard, tilting my head toward her, putting flesh to the outline of her presence. But even though I wanted to respond to her, I couldn't form the words that I was thinking. They swam recklessly as I tried to knit the events of the previous night together. Nobody asked me to get up, so I stayed where I was sitting.

Around that time, I heard the police officer sigh. His footsteps swooshed across the carpet, headed toward the front door. For a second I thought he was going to slip through it, leaving Laura and me alone to figure out my future. But he stopped halfway across the living room, at which time Laura continued talking.

"Tracy," she said, "sit up now. I want you to see who came back for you. This is Officer Miller. He wants to take you to the Health and Welfare Department so they can ask you some questions."

The policeman came over and stood before me, asking if he could settle in beside me on the couch. I scooched to the corner, worried that he'd put his hand in my pool of body sweat. He towered over me, smelling of aftershave and dry-cleaning starch. But the air that hovered around him as he sat down next to me evoked a certain kindness.

Shivering from fear and sleep-deprivation, I slumped against him, sinking into the strength of his body, feeling the gun in the holster near his hip. For a few short seconds I let myself relax into his powerful, law-enforcing presence. I could have fallen asleep and dreamt a whole different ending for the night that had just passed behind me. But I got up, changed into one of Kathie's sundresses, and followed my civil servant into the blue-and-white squad car marked Twin Falls County Police.

Many years later, in emails from both of my parents, I would learn what happened at my house on the morning of August 7, 1985. Walking into the living room, my dad found my empty sleeping bag and the front door propped open. It being August and generally sweltering, Mom figured I'd gone out early on a run. But when Dad saw my empty sleeping bag on the living room couch, he knew he was in serious trouble. By the time his Folgers crystals had dissolved into coffee, his ears were already burning.

At ten that morning, social services called my mom, telling her I'd accused my dad of abuse. She dialed his office and demanded he meet her at home. He said, "Now? Can't it wait? I'm at work," to which she answered, "Get to our house this second." When she asked him why I would have told the police that I was being molested, he answered that he had no idea, but that he'd found marijuana and cocaine in my dresser.

At ten thirty, Chris rolled out of bed, just as two cops and a social worker were walking up the driveway. They'd come to get my clothes and toothbrush because, they said, I'd be staying at a safe house until they decided if I could come home. Instead of choosing the softest pajamas and packing a note, my mom flew into hysterics. "Why are you doing this to our family!" she screamed, while Chris tried to push the social worker off the porch.

Later that day, my dad went to the police station, where he was questioned in a room with a two-way mirror. Again, he played his "no idea" card. He agreed to take a lie-detector test but only because he believed he could outsmart any machine that plugged into a wall. But when he got home, Mom told him to get a lawyer, who advised him not to take the test, because, no matter what the results ended up showing, they wouldn't hold up in court.

The questioning continued. At the police station, social workers cross-examined Mom and Dad in two separate rooms. Dad maintained his innocence, while Mom cried into stiff, government-issue toilet paper, saying, "What kind of people do you think we are? My husband would never do anything to hurt my daughter."

And yet, on three separate occasions, she had caught him, in the middle of the night, walking quickly and awkwardly out of my room. And what about the incident at Redfish Lake?

While Dad lied—boldly and blatantly—and Mom commiserated by omission and self-imposed blindness, I was led to a room at the Health and Welfare Department where a woman in denim overalls asked me to trade euphemisms for straight talk, generalities for specifics. I tried, but clammed up when she asked where Dad put his hands when he wanted to show me he loved me in the middle of the night. Unrelenting, she gave me an anatomically correct doll and told me to point out the places instead.

This time, I explained better. So well that the social workers decided it wasn't safe to "place me back in the home." They made me a ward of the State of Idaho under the Child Protection Act.

The court put a restraining order on my dad that prevented him from coming within five hundred feet of me. Still on the fence about his innocence, Mom refused to kick him out, which meant I would be going to a shelter for abused girls. Run by Mormons, it would smell like rotting floorboards, scented tampons, and bulk cheese.

In the days before the district attorney finalized the paperwork that would take me out of my parents' custody, I stayed with Kathie and Laura. If my mom knew I was there, she didn't bother calling.

I was terrified, but I refused to let myself feel it. I knew that what I'd set in motion couldn't be reversed. I was also a kid, and kids don't dwell in their emotions. I put on my strongest, happiest face and tried to act like everything was normal.

During the hottest hours, Kathie and I stayed in the house watching Nickelodeon and eating huge bowls of Honeycomb cereal. But in the evening, when the temperature dropped into the low eighties, we drifted out onto the lawn.

That's where Chris saw me parading around like a Solid Gold dancer in my Tweety Bird nightie one week after my escape. Kathie had put her boom box in her windowsill and we were making up routines to Duran Duran's "Rio." Kathie had just executed a perfect roundoff-to-moonwalk dismount when my brother swung around the corner in his cherry-red Sirocco.

He didn't stop, but I could see him squinting as he checked out the two girls dancing on the lawn. At first he and the kid in the passenger seat were laughing, probably because girls made them nervous. But then I saw it dawn on my brother just who was dancing. The way he stopped, in the middle of the road, without checking to see if anyone was behind him, made me think he was going to jump out of the car and run up to hug me. But as I watched, I saw him form the words "What the . . . ?" and jam the gas pedal.

"What was that all about?" Kathie asked, after Chris sped off, burning rubber. Her eyes were wide as saucers. "Wait. Holy shit, Tracy! That was your *brother!*"

"Yeah? I know. So what?"

"I don't know. You'd just think he'd stop if he saw you and didn't know where you'd been for half of eternity."

I stared at my friend, unable to answer. Under the cushion of grass, I felt the heat rising off the desert and climbing into my feet. "Rio" had ended and a tune I don't remember rocked Kathie's boom box. For a few seconds when he'd stalled the car in front of me, I thought I'd found an ally in my brother. But the look on his face was indisputable. It told me I had betrayed my family.

At the shelter where I stayed while the State of Idaho found me a foster home, I ate the cheese, and used the tampons, and walked across the creaky wooden floors. I slept in a row of bunk beds next to a dozen other girls. The girls reminded me of the ones who'd picked fights with me in the bowling alley across the street from the cemetery where my real dad was buried: Mexicans, headbangers, lesbians. I didn't talk to anyone but spent a lot of time inspecting the floorboards.

I stayed just five or six days. In the afternoons, we gathered in a dusty living room with big, square windows that looked out over the thirsty wheat fields. Crows scoured the roadsides, flying over them and then landing to pick at piles of carrion. Our shelter parents told us about the power of faith and the importance of surrendering ourselves to God. But every night, when the lights were out and I could hear the other girls snoring, I stared up at the mattress of the bunk bed above me and thought about my dad.

I can't explain the guilt that came over me then, or the depth of self-doubt that threatened to crush me. My abuse had been hidden, always cloaked in darkness. My dad played tricks to make me think I'd played a part in the molestation. During our midday tickle sessions, he had finessed the boundary between acceptable and unacceptable touching so that I couldn't be entirely sure that, at least in those circumstances, what he had done was wrong. Nor could I be certain that I hadn't somehow enticed him. Looking back, I chided myself for spending so much time in my nightgowns. Why did I insist on doing Jane Fonda in the living room? The other instances—the nights when my dad came to my room and fondled me after I was sleeping—were his fault and his fault only. But a lie he'd once told me, after I'd woken up and asked him what he was doing, had always stayed with me. "How dare you accuse me of anything," he'd said. "If you don't want people to touch you, don't sleep on your back."

While the rest of the lost and molested girls slept, I tortured myself with stories. I told myself my abuse couldn't have been as bad as I remembered. My mind began mixing good memories of my dad with bad ones, until the good ones usurped the bad. I know a part of me just wanted it all to be over. The uncertainty about what would happen next seemed even worse than my dad's abuse. Life at the shelter was the opposite of fun. All the girls shared one bathroom, and we weren't allowed to do anything without asking. Phone use was strictly off limits, meaning I couldn't call my friends, grandparents, or parents. Because our foster parents were Mormon, on the Sunday I was there, I had to attend church at the local temple. My mom packed me no dresses when the social workers demanded my things. With nothing acceptable of my own to wear to church, I had to borrow an outdated Gunne Sax dress that was two sizes too big. Dozens of kids from my junior high were Mormon, and when I walked down the aisle of the church with my "shelter family," I could see them staring at me quizzically. A kid named Ted Smack watched me the entire service. I knew that when school started a few weeks later, he'd go back with a story. It went like this: Tracy Ross was in a whole heap of trouble.

But at night, I worried about my dad and, believing him in jail, fretted about how he was being treated. I imagined him cooped up with real criminals who committed real crimes: killers, serial rapists, thieves. It didn't matter how terrible he'd been to me, my heart cracked open at the thought of his suffering. I don't know if this says I was empathetic beyond belief or just a kid who would suffer anything to be in the relative comfort of her family. No matter. I couldn't wipe my dad's image from my brain.

I thought about the days we swam to our favorite rock at Redfish Lake. It sat in the middle of the water at what seemed like a few hundred feet from shore. Dad and I were the only swimmers in our family brave enough to make it all the way to the distant boulder. The trout and tiny silver minnows we swam among flickered in our peripheral vision, and the sun over both of our bodies made us seem beautiful and fast. I felt warm, even though the water was freezing. When I got to the rock, Dad was already there, floating on his back.

"Only you could make me swim this far to a rock we can't even climb onto," he teased, when I came within earshot.

"Come on, Dad! Get over it," I answered back.

"No, I'm serious," he said. "Just listen for a second."

"Okay. I'm all ears. Watch me wiggle them."

"I'm serious, Trace. You're special. People don't say things like that enough. I know sometimes I don't show it. But I love you. Got it?"

I knew I was loved—by him, my mom, and my grandparents. But my dad and I also had a secret, something we'd shared ever since I met him and immediately started hiking and fishing. While other people knew about feeding and clothing children, Dad taught me the beauty of taking risks in the mountains.

He never stopped me from swimming too far out into freezing mountain lakes, or skiing down steep, icy slopes at Soldier Mountain. Most of the time he came with me, for the sheer thrill of the experience. When we camped, it sometimes seemed that all Mom and Chris wanted to do was sit around and read or play cards in the trailer. But my dad gave me the tools of excitement—like the Honda 80 dirt bike I rode, and crashed, into an aspen grove when I was eight—and cut me loose. I jammed the throttle when I meant to squeeze the break and went flying over the handlebars, landing hard on my back. At first I thought I was dead, and then I howled in fear and pain. But for those few, frozen seconds that I was zinging through a grove of bright yellow aspens? All glory; all wild girl in the wilderness.

At the shelter, I sang myself selections from *Paint Your Wagon.* *"I was bo-orn, under a wandrin' star . . ."* But Dad's image continued to haunt me, even through my quiet humming. When I couldn't stand the torture of my imagination any longer, I slipped out of bed and snuck down the hallway, to the top of a creaky, double-landing staircase.

The stairs were so old and whiny they broadcast my every step. But I crept down them even though I knew that phone use was off-limits. On that night, I would have taken solitary confinement in return for hearing one of my parents' voices. I found the phone and dialed their number. On the third ring, my dad picked up.

"Hello? Who is this?" he said, just as I was pulling the earpiece away from my head.

I waited until I was sure no one upstairs was following me, and then said, "Dad? It's me, Tracy. I'm scared. I hate it here. I want to come home."

It was a miracle.

Dad had heard the pain in my voice and experienced a change of heart. On the phone, he sounded worried, apologetic. He told me how much he missed me and how bad he felt that I was living in a shelter, like a refugee or Little Orphan Annie. He said he and Mom wanted to come to my rescue, but they couldn't, because they didn't know where to find me.

I wanted to tell them where I was staying so they could spring me. But a tiny voice in the back of my head said, *You'll get everyone in big trouble.* After Dad and I talked, he put Mom on, who said *I love you I love you I love you.* Neither of my parents said *I believe you* or *I'm sorry.*

Still, talking to them only made me want to go home more. I obsessed about it for days after our phone call. I was going over our conversation for the hundredth time when my social worker, Claudia Vincent, pulled into the shelter driveway. A jolt of relief shot through me. Claudia had brought me to the shelter after I left Kathie Etter's house. She must have come back because Dad confessed everything. The court must have decided to reunite us.

But Claudia ignored me as she stepped inside the slanted, sun-peeling safe house. She smiled, but she said nothing. When I heard her tell my foster parents that she'd been court-ordered to remove me, I shot up the stairs and started packing my belongings. Bounding out the front door, I threw my small, black duffel into the backseat of Claudia's Impala; then we took off across Twin Falls. For a while we went in the general direction of my house, but as we neared the Snake River Canyon we veered left, stopping in a small cul de sac. In front of a one-story, off-white ranch house, Claudia killed the ignition.

I looked around at a neighborhood of identical houses.

"Where are we?" I asked.

"Reach around and grab your bag," she answered. "Social Services found you a more permanent placement. Let's go inside and meet your new foster parent. She's been waiting for you. Her name is Joy."

I fought the tears that came, quick and sizzling. Claudia's words didn't compute. On the drive across town, I'd fantasized that she was taking me to *my* house, and that my parents—or at least my mom—would be waiting in the driveway to greet me. I was so sure of it, I didn't bother asking.

In my head I told myself that going home would be just like the time I'd had my tonsils out, or broken my foot after landing on a sprinkler head while doing an aerial cartwheel: the freezer would be full of popsicles; MTV hours unregulated.

Instead, I stared out the car window, looking at my third "temporary dwelling" in two weeks. The longer I stared, the more I wanted to punch someone—Claudia, to be specific—in the face. When I finally composed myself to speak, I said, "But I want to go *home*. To *my* house. I'm sick of living in places where you have to ask to use the bathroom. Those foster people might pretend they like girls like me, but really they think we're all fuck-ups. I wasn't going to tell you this, Claudia. But I talked to my dad. He sounded sorry. I know he is. I know he wants me back."

Claudia sighed. "I know this isn't easy, Tracy. We all know it isn't. But I have to be honest with you. Your dad is still insisting that he's innocent. And your mom still believes him. That's why we're keeping you out *here*, away from your house, where we can watch you and make sure you're safe. As long as your dad stays in the home, by law, we can't let you go back."

"But what about my mom?" I asked. "Can't *she* protect me?"

"I'm sorry, Tracy," said Claudia. "But she's not ready. She hasn't asked your father to move out."

I moved in with Joy, the next stop on the homeless-teenager house tour. Joy served as a temporary foster mother to girls in trouble or at risk—I seemed to be both.

All I remember now about Joy is her name and a smoky image of her physical appearance. She was tall and quiet, and her hair rose up in a metallic black corona that reminded me of Brillo.

In many ways, Joy was the perfect foster parent. She kept to herself and rarely asked questions. The court made sure my mom gave me money, which they filtered through Claudia and Joy. If I needed deodorant, or a new jar of Noxzema, Joy would take me to the local Albertsons and wait in the car while I raced through the aisles hoping no one would see me.

By some stroke of luck, Joy had also forgotten to put a screen on her guest room window, where I slept. At night, when I was feeling lonely, I'd climb through the open window and sit in the gravel watching thunderstorms build over the desert. Sometimes I'd sneak a phone call to Reed, who would drive over in his teal blue pickup and take me to the rim of the Snake River Canyon.

We'd sit on the hood, and he'd ask me how I was doing. I don't know when I told him about the abuse, or how much detail I went into. But I remember the surprising strength of his bony arm around my shoulders and the feel of his cheek, also a surprise, so soft and warm against my cheek. We sat in silence, except for the sound of the river, faint and far below us.

On nights when Reed didn't appear, I stood in the dirt outside my bedroom, wondering if I would ever go home. Even though I raged at my parents, I missed my yellow Labs, Dusty and Brandy. I wanted my clothes and my room, my freedom and independence. I know how crazy that sounds. But there are times when familiarity trumps even safety. The strangeness of living as a transient unnerved me. All I wanted was to crawl back into my own, familiar cage.

But the court system didn't agree with my definition of "normal," even though it (the court; not my definition) would ultimately fail me in all matters regarding my abuse. I stayed with Joy while school started, and I went back, hoping no one had heard about my summer. I knew my classmates suspected something, but few, if any, ever stepped up and asked me what had happened. Years later, someone would describe my situation like this. "If you're a kid and you get hit by a car in a crosswalk, people visit you with balloons and well wishes. But if you're a kid who gets hit in the crosswalk of life by sexual molestation, nobody will even talk about it. They expect you to brush it under the carpet."

If my classmates wondered why a strange lady was dropping me off at school, or why I'd stopped wanting to sleep over, they never asked me about it. Scared of soiling my image—or losing my spot on the freshman cheerleading squad—I don't remember telling anyone I'd been molested: not friends, school counselors, or teachers.

Three weeks after I moved to Joy's house, Claudia came over, telling me to pack up my things. This time, she said, she was taking me home.

"But why?" I'd asked. "Why all of a sudden?"

"Because your parents finally decided to do the right thing," she answered. "They're going to work within the system."

Claudia was right, at least in theory. In late August, Dad went to the Health and Welfare Department, asking what he needed to do to "get our family back together." After so many weeks of not knowing my whereabouts, he and Mom said they were worried sick.

Within weeks, the Health and Welfare Department struck a deal with my dad. In exchange for his signed admission of guilt, eight weeks of court-appointed group therapy, and ten months of abstinence from me, they would forego prosecution and return me to my mom. If, by the following June, Dad could prove that he'd been "cured" of his obsessive need to molest me, he could join Mom and me at home.

In September, Dad moved out. He went to live with his brother across town. He didn't take much with him: just some work clothes, his shaving kit, and a few copies of *Field and Stream*. His job, he told my mom, wasn't to enjoy himself, but to do anything and everything to get himself home.

It felt to me like a bit of redemption. I finally thought my family believed what I'd been saying. Years afterward I'd learn that Dad's admission had been anything but honest; he told my mom he was only *telling* the Health and Welfare Department he was guilty because she was so frantic to bring me home. Mom was inadvertantly in on the lie too. She believed my dad when he said he was only paying lip service. She didn't actually commiserate, because she didn't have to. He never told her the full extent of my abuse, and she never bothered to ask him.

Early September, 1985. Five weeks after I bolted out of the living room, Claudia and I pulled into my parents' driveway. Dusk was spreading across the desert, laying a blanket of purple over the scratchy, yellow earth. The grass on our front lawn looked like somebody had doused it in gasoline and then lit the whole thing on fire. I hoped Dusty and Brandy were in the backyard waiting for me, but if they weren't, I also hoped wherever they were, the grass was greener than at our place.

Imaginary piranhas gutted my intestines. I kept my seat belt buckled, even when Claudia turned off the car. Neither of us was in any rush to get moving. We sat in the driveway while the light deepened from periwinkle to purple. Claudia said my mom would probably act nervous for the first few weeks I was home, that most families struggle to resume normalcy after a family member has been accused of abuse. At any rate, she said, I shouldn't expect miracles my first week back.

I heard her, but I wasn't really listening. I was watching the windows of my house. At one point a curtain shifted, and I saw the outline of my mom's face peering into the night. I figured she didn't see us, because she didn't wave or come to the door or turn on the porch light. Reluctant to make the first move, I stayed glued to the car seat until Claudia told me to get moving.

"Only if you come with me," I said.

"Of course I will. But you have to lead, and I'll follow."

Silently cursing her, I opened the car door, grabbed my duffel, and slowly began walking up the concrete.

And for those first few steps I felt a small rush of happiness. After five weeks in foster care, I was finally going home. I took refuge in the clean, cool air of evening and the thought of my dogs, restless from a summer of sitting around and desperate for a game of fetch. I even smiled at the Roadrunner trailer sitting on the pavement with the snot-colored swoosh my dad never bothered to repaint yellow. But the closer I got to the front door, the more I questioned the Health and Welfare Department's decision.

I wanted my mom to be waiting for me, putting the final

touches on my homecoming celebration. There'd be cans of Tab, a new bedspread, a card that looked like a giant doily. The card would say something about how much she loved me, how sorry she was for the suffering she had caused. But I knew from years of experience how her actions could detour from her words.

The front door opened just as Claudia and I mounted the first step of my family's AstroTurf-covered porch steps. Mom stood before us in a pair of tattered blue sweatpants and matching hoodless sweatshirt. She was thinner than I'd expected, and deep dark bags hung beneath her forest-green eyes.

We surveyed each other, halting. Then she took a small, shaky step toward me. She was smiling, and at first I thought she was laughing. But the laugh I thought I heard was really the sound of her crying.

"Oh, Tracy," she choked, pulling me to her collarbone. "I'm so glad you came back to me. You have no idea what those people did to us. I told myself I wouldn't cry when I saw you. But I needed you, and now you're home."

10

Girl, Interrogated

Mom kept hugging, squeezing me tighter than a Vise-Grip. I haloed my arms around her, patting her on the back. I'd sworn off hugs from adults when Dad started using them as an excuse to suction me into his body. But Mom was so weepy and emaciated, I let her hang on as long as she wanted.

When we were finished, Claudia said good-bye. She told us to take care of ourselves, watch out for each other, and that she'd be back to check on us in a week. She had to check in even if she didn't want to, because although the court had returned me to my mom, I'd stay in the custody of the state for another ten months. It was Claudia's job, for the duration, to make sure Mom and I got along. She wished us good luck, gave me a reassuring arm squeeze, and turned around.

Mom went inside before Claudia reached the bottom step. I kept watching as my temporary guardian's curly, salt-and-pepper head, atop her tiny, round body, ducked into the Impala, where she sat for several minutes, then threw the car into reverse.

I stared after her until even the tracers off her headlights disappeared around the corner, then took a deep breath and picked up my bag. Mom had left it, along with my running shoes and a milk crate of textbooks, sitting a few inches from my feet. At first I thought it was weird that she didn't wait to go inside with me, but I quickly dismissed her actions. Slinging my bag across both shoulders, I picked up my belongings and stepped into the house.

I was curious to see if anything about our house had changed in my absence. Mom prided herself on her near-constant interior decorating, so I stepped into the living room and looked to see which vase had been replaced or which picture moved to a different hallway.

To my disappointment, everything looked exactly the same. The bright orange sectional where I'd recovered from various bone breaks sat in front of the glass coffee table, which sat in front of the wood burning fireplace. Chris's Steinway piano hugged the entryway wall. Dad's leather recliner hovered a few feet from the front window. And Mom's comfy chair, where I'd spent so many nights lying across her lap and forcing her to tickle my back, still slumped in front of the TV.

And yet, it wasn't really rearranged furniture I was looking for. What I wanted was some sign that I'd been missed. I'd had weeks to construct the ultimate fantasy homecoming and now I wanted results. Kicking off my Birkenstocks, I put down my duffel, and walked into the kitchen, where I expected to see a welcome home sign, balloons, and a mason jar full of flowers.

Instead, I saw my mom, sitting on a beige swivel barstool at the far end of the counter. Her nose was red and swollen from crying. She kneaded a soggy Kleenex, which she stretched in my direction.

"Come over here, stranger," she said, patting the barstool next to her.

I smiled, but didn't walk over.

"Sit down," she prodded again. "I want to look at my beautiful daughter."

"I'm not beautiful, Mom. And I'm good. I feel like standing."

"But you must have been standing all day."

"No . . . Actually, I was sitting. Waiting. You know, for Claudia to pick me up."

"Well, come over here anyway and give your mom a hug."

Slowly, dragging my bare feet across the carpet, I went to her barstool. She stood up and wrapped her arms around me. She smelled like Clinique face wash and Redken shampoo. I noticed her breasts, and how they hung heavy against her chest. My mom's bosom was warm, but the feel of it against my own chest made me want to worm away from her as quickly as possible.

"What's wrong?" she said. "You don't want to hug your mother?" Then stepping back and sighing, she added, "I know how strange this must be for you, Tracy. But this is where you live. Dad's gone, so you can feel safe here. It's just you and me for a while."

Standing before her, I tried to come up with the appropriate response. Something that would make her feel good but also show her that I hadn't come back to play games with her. I knew I was the one who would have to prove that our lives had returned to normal, just as I knew that I couldn't because they never would.

But Mom was too quick on the draw. She continued talking before I could answer. "You feel good being back here, right? I mean, if you don't, we can call Claudia and tell her to come get you. You don't have to stay here if you don't want to, Tracy. I know what you must think of me, but I'm still your mother."

"No, Mom. That's not it. I just got here. Give me a second and I'll feel better."

"Okay, then," she said, turning back to the counter. This time she chose a different barstool, in the middle. "Take your time. I'm perfectly happy to sit here and wait forever."

Mom and I sat at the kitchen counter, reacqauinting ourselves with each other. When we ran out of things to talk about, we turned on *60 Minutes*. After a while, though, my stomach started growling. Still believing my mom had planned a special homecoming, I hadn't eaten for hours.

"So, Mom," I said. "What's for dinner?"

"Oh, gosh, is it that time already?"

"I think so; at least that's what my stomach is telling me. Make anything special? You know, for my first night back?"

Her face fell. She seemed to know instantly that she'd forgotten to do something important. It wasn't like her, either. She'd always made sure I had birthday parties, Christmas trees adorned with presents, and obscenely full Easter baskets. But now she searched for an answer to why she hadn't recognized me with anything special.

"I didn't make anything," she said. "Because I didn't know *what* to make you. It's been so long since you've been home, and Dad and I barely ate all summer. We were too sad to eat. We stopped cooking."

"But it should have been easy, Mom," I said. "You know how much I like lasanga."

"I know, honey," she said. "But you know how your tastes change. What if you'd found some diet in *Seventeen* that I didn't know about." Then her face brightened. "You know what though," she said, "check the cupboards. I got you all kinds of goodies."

I got up and rifled through the cereal cupboard, finding boxes of Trix, Cap'n Crunch, and Golden Grahams. Mom had definitely been to Albertsons. In the Lazy Susan I found potato chips, Oreos, and Triscuits, and when I looked in the fridge, I saw milk, eggs, cottage cheese, and mini yogurts. I pulled my head from the frosty compartment and managed a weak smile at my mother. At least I'd get to eat junk food.

"Check the freezer too," said my mom. "The Schwan's man stocked us up on fried shrimp, frozen hamburgers, and bean burritos. You know I hate that stuff, but Dad likes it. Pick something, and I'll pop it in the microwave."

I peered back into the freezer at the bright blue boxes of fish sticks and egg-and-cheese biscuits. The remnants of Dad's last gallon of ice cream sat on the bottom shelf. When I was sure there were no homemade lasagnas hiding behind it, I said. "Bean burrito, I guess."

"Perfect," said Mom. "Then that's what I'm having."

For a few weeks that autumn, Mom and I lived together like roommates. It was great. She'd go to work at Community Action, and I'd go to school, cheerleading, and cross-country practice. If I didn't have extracurriculars, Reed would come over for a visit. We'd fall on my bed and make out; then he'd tell me that he wanted to build a pipe bomb and put it in the gas tank of my dad's Jeep. I loved this show of strength and solidarity, but it also scared me, because Reed seemed crazy enough to kill my father. We'd kiss and grope until we heard my mom's car pulling into the driveway; then he'd glide out the sliding glass door and hop in his truck, which he'd hidden around the corner.

But then one day the beautiful lawlessness at my mom's house ended. It was a Saturday, and we were sitting at the kitchen counter, eating breakfast.

"Can I ask you a question?" Mom said.

"Sure, Mom," I answered. "Shoot."

She paused, lowering a Red Rose tea bag into a cup of boiling water. She dunked it up and down, pinching the white paper pull-tab. When she was sure enough tannins had seeped into the water, she removed the bag, squeezed it, and set it on the counter.

"But I'm not going to ask it if it's going to make you angry," she said.

Now it was my turn to pause. I stalled because I heard something dangerous in Mom's voice. For weeks she'd been summoning me to the table and asking me questions about the abuse. "Yes, Mom," I'd answer. "I still believe everything I said in family court," or "No, Mom. I don't think I'll hate Dad forever." But either I was a masochist or too stupid to know better, because every time she summoned me, I went back for another round of interrogation.

But this time sounded different. Mom had never predicted my anger before. I used my spoon to push my apples-and-cinnamon goop into a circle, constructing a static oatmeal whirlpool. Into the center I poured a splash of milk. When I was finished pouring, I dipped my spoon into the eye of the maelstrom: *voilà*, apples-and-cinnamon-flavored milk.

"Well," I said, licking the sugary slurry off my lips, "if you think it's going to make me angry, don't ask it."

"But I have to," said Mom. "It's something I've been thinking about for a long time. Father Lafey and I talked about it. I met with him at the priory."

Mom put her faith in Father Lafey, the Jesuit priest at the Jerome Catholic Church. I liked the priest because he had acoustic guitar at mass. I figured he'd be fair to the whole family when it came to our situation, especially as a man of the cloak. But I'd also seen Mom trap people in conversations; I knew how she'd pretend she didn't know what she was saying, so she could say anything she wanted.

"Okay, then," I said, digging my spoon into my oatmeal. "Whatever you want, Mom. Go for it."

The words blasted from her mouth like machine-gun fire:

"What if it was the devil?"

"*What?*"

"I said . . . What if it was the devil and not Dad who hurt you?"

"*Mom!* How can you think that? How can you even say that?"

"Say what? You're taking it too literally. I'm talking about how the devil can get *inside* people. Make them do things they don't want to do. I'm not saying Dad *became* the devil. But the devil can make people do things they don't want to. Father Lafey and I talked about this. He agrees: whatever's ailing Dad can be healed with your forgiveness."

I chose my words carefully.

"Well, if you put it that way," I answered, "I guess it could have been the devil."

Mom questioned me again, a few weeks later.

This time her friend Nan was with us. We were sitting at the kitchen counter, eating boiled eggs and English muffins.

Mom and Nan complimented me on my new haircut, the short/long Eurythmics style I'd given myself over the summer. They *ooohed* and *aaahed* over my new clothes style, a preppie/punk rock fusion that consisted mainly of super-short mini skirts and Hanes men's size large T-shirts. My new favorite band was the Sex Pistols, so I'd permanent-markered NeVeR MinD tHe BoL-LocKS HeREs THe sEx PiStOLs across the front of several shirts.

But after a while, the conversation shifted to an episode Mom had seen on the *Phil Donahue Show*. She'd been at home, nursing a migraine, when she turned the channel to a row of women sobbing on a stage. Instantly captivated, she watched until the last commercial.

"It was horrible," said my mom, glaring into her teacup. "These women were raped by their husbands. They had to sit there and take it. Some of them were hurt so badly they had to be hospitalized. And nobody helped them. They had to take themselves to the doctor."

I sat on my barstool, listening to the conversation. I liked it when Mom talked about important things. We never discussed concepts like social justice or women's rights when my dad was around. This sounded like a new beginning.

I was just about to tell Mom and Nan about Laura Etter, and how brave I thought she was for being the only female brakeman on the Twin Falls branch of the Union Pacific Railroad, when Mom changed the subject again. Or maybe she didn't change it, but shifted it ever so slightly. It's obvious she didn't think about what she was going to say because the next thing out of her mouth hit me like a sledgehammer to the tonsils.

"You know, though," she said, "sometimes I wonder if incest has been blown out of proportion in this country. I mean, Americans can be so *Puritan*. In Newfoundland we put up with old men grabbing us all the time. But we never *did* anything about it."

I'm trying to remember what came first: the constriction behind my ears that felt like someone was pinning them together or the hot tears that jumped to my eyes, blurring my vision. Mom's comment had come out of nowhere. I caught the tears before she and Nan could see them, but I couldn't stop the words that tumbled from my mouth like a rockslide down a muddy, rain-soaked mountain.

"*Mom!* Do you have *any* idea what you're saying?" I shouted.

"What? What's the matter?" stammered my mom.

"Do you really think Americans are *too sensitive* about abuse? I'm sitting *right here*, Mom. Does that mean *anything* to you?"

I stood up, accidentally slamming the barstool against the refrigerator. Mom and Nan looked at me in horror. But instead of apologizing like I'd normally do, I turned around and took off down the hallway.

"Tracy, stop!" Mom yelled from behind me. "I didn't *mean* anything by it. I was just *saying* . . ."

But I didn't want to hear what my mom was *saying*. I'd spent fourteen years listening to what she said. She'd told me—about the poverty in Newfoundland, the neglect in her childhood, and her uncles, all raging alcoholics, who did things like shove their wives' heads in oven broilers while their children stood watching—so often I'd never forget it. What she'd always failed to realize was that a *person* with her own thoughts and feelings sat at the other end of her conversation. I wanted to scream that it *mattered* how and when she said things, and more important, *who* she said them in front of.

I got to my bedroom just as Mom was rounding the staircase, and jammed a Soft Cell cassette into my tape recorder. Mom banged on the door of my bedroom, yelling that she was sorry. She carried on so long that eventually I started thinking of Nan out there listening. I liked Nan, so I turned down the music on my stereo.

Mom was leaning into the door, pushing her sentences through it. "Tracy. I'm so sorry," she said. "I did it again, didn't I? Said something stupid and made you angry. I *know*. I'm an *idiot*. A *poop*. But I promise I didn't mean anything by it. Whatever you heard, Tracy, you took it the wrong way."

You've heard about the camel, and that tiny straw that crushed its back? That last sentence was my straw. I stood up and pressed my body against the door, waiting for my mom to finish talking.

"I'm so sorry, Tracy," she pleaded. "I promise, I'll never say anything like that again. You know I love you and would never do anything to hurt you. I just got overexcited. Now open the door, please, and let me in."

When it seemed like she was through begging my forgiveness, I unfastened the deadbolt I'd installed after my dad left and opened the door of my bedroom. Mom stood in the hallway, in front of the linen closet. She opened her arms, offering a make-up hug. I lifted my arms too, but when I got close enough to wrap them around her, I shoved her into the linen closet.

Looking up at me with wild, injured eyes, she said, "So is this it? Is this what I can expect now that I'm the evil mother?"

"Yes, Mom," I answered. "It's *exactly* what you can expect."

Mom got me. I got her back. But it was the shock of what happened to Dad that threatened us all. Among the stipulations of my homecoming was that Dad couldn't come within five hundred feet of me. If Claudia—or one of the cops assigned to keep an eye on us—drove by and saw his Jeep parked in the driveway, he'd be in serious trouble.

Apparently it didn't matter.

One Saturday morning in late November, the Jeep pulled into the driveway. Mom was dusting the furniture, and I was perched in my dad's leather swivel chair watching *American Bandstand*. Dad walked through the front door as if he still lived with us; he went straight to the kitchen and hoisted himself onto the counter. Mom hurried to him. I hung back, nervous.

Dad and I hadn't talked since the time I'd called him from the abused girls' shelter. Not really talk, like we used to before the abuse. He'd called us nightly over the past month, and when he did, Mom made me say things to him. She'd raise her eyebrows and point into the receiver. I'd concede but keep it brief—"Hi, Dad. How ya doin'? See ya later"—because the pain in Dad's voice scared me. I knew he hated living with his brother, and my mom had told me that the sex-offender meetings the court required him to attend were filled with thugs who did things like rape babies. I could see why she was proud of him for going, but I wasn't about to be the one to congratulate him.

Mom saw the Colt .357 handgun the second Dad pulled it out of his waistband. And the second she saw it, she started screaming. Then I saw the gun, too, and froze where I was standing. I started to shake, and my chest wall cramped over my heart. My heart hammered: *Would he fire? At us? Himself?* Across my mind flashed a common headline: "Man shoots family, then self."

My mom started walking in circles, pulling on her earlobe. "Don?" she said. "What is that? Is that a gun? You have a gun, Don. Why do you have a gun?"

But Dad just sat there with his legs dangling over the counter. The glance he threw me made me want to throw up. I'd known a girl whose parents tried to kill her in a fit of insanity. They'd been drunk and had hacked at each other with kitchen knives during a fight. The girl ran to our house, and my dad let her sit on the couch under an electric blanket while he called the police. Now my dad could be her dad, but unlike her, I had nowhere to run for help. I watched my dad and wondered if he was going to kill me. I figured he must have been contemplating it, because in hell, like in Newfoundland, incest was probably considered normal. Behind me, a small moan started in my mom's throat. It grew until she was screaming.

Her hollering made Dad stand up. He put the gun in his back pocket and started for the front door. Mom sprinted after him, reaching for his shirt. She couldn't swim, ride a bike, or ski except for cross-country, but she clung to his light blue Izod like one of the Wicked Witch of the West's flying monkeys.

I still don't understand how my dad reached his arm around his body and grabbed her, casting her off of him like a tick that hadn't yet burrowed into his skin. It didn't seem like an arm should have been able to bend that far backward. But she hit the floor and crumpled. I watched the commotion from the spot I'd wedged myself into between the piano bench and the wall.

My dad took one last look at us before he continued walking. He was still smiling . . . and still crying. He was about to step through the door, when he turned around and spoke in a voice that sounded like his vocal chords were coated in butter. "What other choice do I have?" he said. "People are going to find out what happened. Then what? What's left?" My mom must have been in shock, because when I looked at her, she was poking her tongue between her cracked red lips. She pulled at the collar of her sweatshirt, as if she couldn't get enough air.

Years later my mom would tell me that, after my dad drove off "to kill himself," she almost copied him. She thought she could no longer live with such a pitch-black feeling. While I sat in the living room waiting for someone to save me, she went to her walk-in closet, dug under a shirt rack, and located a different gun. This one was a Smith & Wesson Chief 38 Special that my dad had given her for protection. She cocked the gun and bit the barrel. But just as she was about to pull the trigger, a voice inside her spoke up. *Doris. Think of Chris and Tracy,* it said. *What will they do if you take the easy way out?*

Bandstand was still playing when she emerged swollen-eyed, rumply-clothed, and tearstained from her bedroom. I pushed myself around in my dad's swivel chair while she picked up the phone and dialed a number. I figured she was calling the police, to alert them that my dad was on a suicide mission. But she wasn't. She phoned my uncle, who told her, Doris, you're overreacting. Donnie took the jeep into the South Hills this morning. But he's back now, and he's in his room napping.

Where There's Love, There's a BMW with Heated Seats

C an I smoke another cigarette? It's almost time to board."

"Don't smoke, Trace. You know it's bad for your health."

"Don't you think it's a little late to start preaching, Dad? Children learn by example."

Mom, Dad, Chris, and I sat in blue plastic bucket chairs in the dingy one-runway terminal at the Twin Falls County Airport. Outside, even the air seemed brittle. February in Twin Falls is grey and cold or cold and grey, with no other combination. That must be why the official Groundhog Day groundhog doesn't live there: the sun is too weak to create a shadow.

In a little while an American Airlines twin prop would skid onto the tarmac, belching a trim, pinch-mouthed stewardess from the belly of the plane. Smiling and waving like a prettier version of our own Miss Idaho, she'd summon me and the half-dozen other passengers lounging around the candy dispenser onboard. Fingering the lighter I stole from Chris's glovebox, I'd hurry across the tarmac, trying not to look back at my family.

"It doesn't have to be this way," said my dad. "We're not asking you to leave."

Except that they were—Dad, Mom, Claudia, and the Health and Welfare Department, everyone who claimed to have my best interest in mind. In early January—after our big fight, the suicide threat, and several other minor infractions that led my extended family to believe I was within inches of running off and joining the circus—Mom went to Claudia and told her I'd become too difficult for her to control. This was partly true: after the suicide stint, I stopped listening to either of my parents, believing that neither was sane enough to give me orders. The less I listened, the more terrified Mom became, until we were having colossal, blow-out fights on a near-nightly basis. We bickered about everything from whether or not I could go to the Dairy Queen after a football game to why I borrowed my mom's favorite sweater without asking. I'd end up screaming that I'd rather live in hell than have her for a mother. Afraid of the twitching in my arms that made me want to grab her and throw her out a window, I'd tear outside and sprint down Parkway Drive. All I wanted was space, and a few puffs of a cigarette to stop my blood from searing my arteries, but instead of letting me kick the curbs until my toes broke, Mom would chase after me, shouting, "TRACY! COME BACK! DON'T LEAVE ME, PLEASE!"

Seeing her like that—keening and wild-eyed, like a character out of a Greek tragedy—had the opposite effect on me from the one I believed she was going for. Her hysteria drained my compassion and filled me with disgust, making me vow to become emotionless.

Claudia did a cursory search for foster homes in the greater Twin Falls area. And apparently no one wanted me. Even Joy refused to take me back to her beige ranch house, like all the other ranch houses, on Indian Trail. Her name, along with my mom's, my mom's attorney's, Claudia's, and the Twin Falls county prosecutor's, all appear on the document filed by the Twin Falls county magistrate on January 27, 1986. It's four pages long and states that the "present residential placement, as well as the placement options presently available to the Health and Welfare Department, do not appear to be consistent with the best interests and emotional well-being of the child. An alternate placement, with the child's relative in Oregon, has come to the Guardian Ad Litem's attention, and the Guardian Ad Litem is of the belief that it should be presented to the court."

Nobody asked what I wanted. If they had, I would have told them that Reed and I were going to California. We'd find a beach where we could sleep under the stars. We'd surf and swim and eat scallops cooked like marshmallows over an open fire. If things worked out between us, maybe one day we'd have babies. The whole family would take up skateboarding, which we would do on the boardwalk where they filmed *Three's Company*.

But nobody wanted my opinion. The court decided I should move to Tigard, Oregon, a suburb of Portland, to live with my dad's sister, Lori, and her accountant husband, Nick. In exchange for helping Lori care for my infant cousins, I could camp out in the family's guest room, go to a school where nobody knew me, and give up my spot on the Robert Stuart cheerleading squad. *Bitchin'.*

Out on the runway, the plane skidded to a stop and a ladder ejected from within. It was time to go. Dad put his hands on my shoulders and looked at me like he used to when I'd beat myself bloody riding my bike as a kid. I'd come home with gravel in my kneecaps, bawling about not being able to pop a wheelie over the curb, and he'd tilt his head and puff out his lip, reflecting my expression back to me. Sad face got me again. I let him hug me, but jutted my butt out so our vital organs wouldn't touch.

Then it was Chris's turn to say good-bye. He stood before me in a pair of dark-blue shrink-to-fit Levi's and a navy blue Ralph Lauren shirt. He didn't smile or wink at me like he had before that summer. We'd talked only once since I'd run away, and that was during Christmas vacation when he got drunk at a party and drove me to the very airport we stood in now, watching crop dusters dive like swallows over the wheat fields. Parked in the gravel at one end of the runway, he'd blazed Bacardi-fueled anger at me, saying, "I don't know what happened and I don't want to. I love you and Dad the same. Can't we just make this go away?"

And now it was going away because I was going away. Dad would move back in with Mom, and Chris would return to the University of Idaho. Four months from now, my parents would drive to Oregon, pick me up, and take me home. We'd all resume the lives we had before Dad started fantasizing about wrestling me in the shower. I said good-bye, leaving a chapped-lip kiss on my mom's tear-streaked face, then followed the other passengers across the tarmac and onto the plane.

Less than forty-eight hours later, I stood at the bus stop in front of my aunt and uncle's house, awaiting my inaugural ride to Whitford Middle School. Dark clouds clotted the sky. Half a dozen kids milled around me, joking and trying to shove one another into gutters swollen with rainwater. I froze my face into an expression of friendliness and tried my best to avoid eye contact.

That morning I'd sugar-watered my hair into a great wave that crested one eye and swooshed down across the other, and I had smeared my lids with metallic gold and green shadows. From my dad's army duffel I pulled an oversize purple silk shirt and an enormous yellow sweater, layering them over black, ribbed leggings. On my feet: a pair of soft-soled jazz shoes that I'd spray painted metallic gold.

Lori's eyebrows shot up to her hairline when I showed up at the breakfast table dressed like Annie Lennox. "That's what you're wearing on your first day at a new school?" she asked when I sat down next to her at the table. Her blue eyes clicked. She was getting ready to do volunteer work and was dressed in a grey sweater and pleated khaki trousers. Nick had already vanished, on his long commute to Portland, ten miles away, where he worked.

"I think so," I answered. "Why? Does it look stupid?"

"No, not stupid," she said, smoothing the edge of her place mat. "It's just a little . . . noisy, don't you think?"

I didn't, and wore the outfit in spite of her poor opinion.

I went outside and stood in front of the house with the other kids at the bus stop. The longer I stood there, the more I wished I hadn't worn the gold jazz shoes. The kids around me splashed through rain puddles in K-Swiss sneakers, Guess jeans, and Polo oxfords. Next to them I looked like a thrift-store version of Punky Brewster.

I stepped onto the bus anyway and made my way to the back. I found an empty seat and scootched across it to the middle. I dug into my pack for the dog-eared copy of *Romeo and Juliet* Lori had lent me for freshman Shakespeare. But my hand landed on a hard, plastic bubble.

I pulled it out, and saw that Nick or Lori had slipped me a Valentine's Day present without my noticing: a heart-shaped container filled with red-and-white heart-shaped candies. Below them I found another heart-shaped box, this one full of miniature chocolates. Putting both of these on the seat beside me, I kept digging and found a pair of pink-and-white ankle socks with more hearts embroidered around the cuffs. Beneath all of this was a card that had the words, "Dear Tracy, Love exists if you believe it" scrawled across it in Nick's high-powered ink.

My heart lurched. I stared out the window at the rain pelting the greenest earth I'd ever seen. I hadn't felt love—for love's sake, with nothing attached to it or weighing it down—for many, many months. I pulled my valentines onto my lap before the bus could hit a pothole and knock them onto the floor.

If I'd have thought someone was watching me, I would have shoved them deep into the bowels of my backpack and kept them there until I could look at them again, in the privacy of my own bedroom. But because I was the new kid, and sad, with pain etched into the creases of my forehead, I lined them on top of my backpack and gave them—and myself—an awkward, secret hug.

I made friends at Whitford Middle School the way the Nazis made enemies: by wearing a swastika over my heart. I was standing on the basketball court, trying not to sweat through my running shorts, when a voice a few feet away from me said, "Hey, bitch, what's up with that shirt?"

I looked up from the spot on the free-throw line I'd been examining to a girl with hair so red it was purple. She was glaring a hole though my Sex Pistols shirt. I noticed with a sizzle of self-vindication that her hair was also long on one side and short on the other, just like mine. She stood apart from the other girls, who were lined up against a cinder-block wall waiting to be picked for volleyball.

I honestly had no idea what she was talking about. Beads of sweat, generated by hormones and anxiety, popped onto my forehead. I checked my posture and slouched over.

"I made it. It's punk rock. Don't you like it?"

"No I don't *like* it," said the girl, stepping closer. I wondered if she was going to shove me. "And if you keep it on, you're gonna get your ass kicked. There's a lot of Jewish kids in this school. Some of their grandparents even went to Auschwitz. They're not gonna like it if they see some Nazi lover walking around. What are you? A member of the Aryan Nations or something?"

Aryan Nations. Aryan Nations. I wracked my brain, trying to remember where I'd heard that term before. *Oh no.* Chris had told me about them when he came home for Christmas from college. His school was in Moscow: Idaho headquarters for the neo-Nazi skinhead organization, which was responsible for murdering anyone who wasn't white and which, I'd heard, cavorted with the Idaho chapter of the Ku Klux Klan. Now that the real meaning of my swastika was being revealed to me, I wanted to sprint out of the gym and burn it. But with the purple-haired girl breathing stale smoke breath into my face, I decided it was smarter to feign ignorance.

"Aryan Nations?" I said. "No way. Never heard of them."

"Well . . ." said the purple-haired girl. "You're lucky, cuz I'm gonna take pity on you. But only because you seem so innocent and stupid. My name's Mary. Go tell Mrs. What's-Her-Face that you got your period and you need me to take you to the locker room. I keep an extra T-shirt stashed there. It probably reeks, but whatever. Anything's better than that thing."

And that's how God, or the Holy Spirit, or some other benevolent deity took pity on me for the first time in teenage memory. Because from that day forward Mary treated me as a friend. She and her parents lived in a big, beautiful house with lots of windows that let in the sun. Mary's mom believed that kids should make their own decisions about things like smoking, so she let Mary torch up whenever she wanted. When we met for lunch, Mary would feed me cigarettes and let me listen to New Wave bands on her Walkman. That's how I became addicted to nicotine and first heard Flesh for Lulu, the Smiths, and the Jesus and Mary Chain.

I doubt Nick and Lori would have liked Mary, who, for reasons I still don't understand, was allowed to hang out in seedy bars in Portland's Burnside district. My aunt and uncle, on the other hand, kept their conservative chains shackled tightly around my ankles. My territory when I lived with them consisted of school, track practice, home, and church. I joined them for service at their Methodist church on Sundays, but while theirs was the god of affluence and corporate conservatism, my god reigned over the world of music and imagination. Its disciples were my friends at Whitford, who turned me on to David Bowie, the Romantics, and Yaz. After my Shakespeare class read *Romeo and Juliet,* we went on a field trip to the Ashland Shakespeare Festival, where I saw people who'd committed themselves to the arts. For the first time in months, I got out my journals and started writing poetry and short stories again.

From there, things got better. In late April, after weeks of training with the school track team, I broke the school record in the mile with a time of 6:05. I also finished second place in the Portland Trail Blazers creative writing contest. These accomplishments kept Nick and Lori, my parents, and Claudia Vincent happy. But in my room, I dreamed of the day I would go back to Twin Falls.

Mostly I wanted to be with Reed, and on a more permanent basis. When I left for Oregon, he'd promised me he'd write. I dreamed about his red hair and yellow-green eyes—everything that made him different from the world to which I was exiled. I wrote him letters, some inspired by Mary's experiences, which exaggerated the "badness" of my new life. In one letter, I hung out with skate punks in downtown Portland, and in the next I went to see INXS at the Rose Garden. Determined to return to Twin Falls looking hungry and strong, I stopped eating junk food, ran every day, and spent most of my nights in my bedroom doing leg lifts, stomach crunches, and push-ups.

And I became thinner, stronger, and more focused on what I wanted, which was to leave Oregon and return to Idaho a different kid. I missed my parents and the freedom they gave me. In the short time that I'd been reunited with my mom, I'd gotten used to doing whatever I wanted, wherever and whenever. I knew that when I went home, both parents would feel too guilty to try too hard to control me. Even if they did, some part of me knew how easy it would be to manipulate them. I was the victim, and that carried certain privileges.

It's sad that none of my therapists, or the Health and Welfare Department, or Claudia Vincent ever taught me the language I needed to both express my love for my parents and establish post-abuse boundaries. I can see my own mixed messages in a letter I wrote to my parents on March 24, 1986. I was fifteen years old.

Dear Mom & Pop!
    So how's life going Sonny & Cher? Er, I mean Romeo & Juliet? No. I mean, um, oh ya, Mom & Dad! There! I got it! Yay! Life here is groovey, but I'm still kind of lonely. I mean, I'm close to Lori but not like you guys. She and Nick don't hug me or play around like a "real" family does. And I want, so badly, to be tucked in. Oh, well. Only 3 more months to go, and besides, what's life w/o sacrifices. And who wants to be a spoiled brat anyway. At least I know that when I come home every hug will be 100% better, longer, sweeter than if we'd not been separated. Now we have a 4 way hug too . . . I can't wait!

The letter's main body is filled with reports about going to Portland and seeing my friend, Erin, all scrolled in loopy g's and j's with curly tails. But by the third page, after complaining because Lori wouldn't let me go to a Romantics concert at the Starry

Night, I reverted to treating them like the parents I so desperately needed.

> That's cool that you're doing all that stuff (going to Bible study at the Catholic Church; attending individual counseling) Mom. I'm proud of you. You really need this and I'm glad you're finally getting the chance to do it. Keep it up! And what about you dad? Any special activities? . . . If you even *mention* "the group" (referring to the sex-offenders meetings he had to go to) I'll kill you! I feel so bad that they put you through that shit. But keep going. Let my hugs be an inspiration. [smiley face] Remember your infamous Pee-wee Herman laugh? I can't wait to hear it. You're so good at it. Three cheers for Dad. Yay! Yay! Yay! and Mom, Yay! Yay! Yay!

Judging from the closing paragraph of my letter, by the time I'd spent two months at Nick and Lori's house, my feelings for my mom had softened, and I had chosen a deliberate amnesia regarding Dad. When I read this now, I see—it was my invitation to my own downfall.

> Don't feel fat, Mom. You needed to gain a few. I'll bet you look so vibrant and healthy! You better eat too, Dad. When I get home you better have a B-E-L-L-Y! I love you both and think you're the best parents alive! Seriously!
> Slugs and quiches. Yours truly.
> Your *only* daughter,
> Tracy

Three months after I wrote the letter, Dad called, saying he wanted to talk to Lori. She went into her study and closed the door. I lay low in the guest room, doodling on a pad of construction paper. A little while later, Lori came to the guest room and got me.

"Your dad's on the phone," she said. "He wants to talk to you. Go into my study. You'll want some privacy."

Fear stabbed my gut. I looked at my aunt, who smiled. Her face appeared softer than normal and more encouraging. I went into her office, where I sat down in her leather armchair.

My dad was taking long, rattly breaths, which he exhaled into the receiver.

"Hello?" I said.

"Tracy? It's Dad. How're ya doin', sis?"

"Good, Dad. I guess."

I wondered what this was going to be about. I'd been caught smoking at the freshman prom a week earlier, when Lori came to pick me up. She'd hated my date, a kid I now remember as slightly albino, in a baby blue tuxedo with ruffles down the front. She'd called my parents the next morning, saying I didn't appreciate what people did for me.

"Well, I wanted to talk to you," said my dad. "You know, before your mother and I come to Oregon."

Silence.

"Trace? You there?"

"Yeah, Dad. I'm here."

"Okay," he said. "No crying, okay?" He was crying. I would not cry.

Another long silence, as long as a minute. I stared at the arrangement of family pictures—Lori and Nick at the beach, Lori and Nick at their wedding, Lori holding the babies—on my aunt's desk, saying nothing. If my dad had something important to tell me, I wanted to give him all the time he needed. When, after several more seconds, he said nothing, I said, "I'm here, Dad. I'm still listening," even though he didn't ask me.

"Oh, Tracy . . . Okay. I want you to know, before I . . . before we, your mother and I, come out there and get you . . . before we all three come home and live under the same roof . . . that I did something to you. I did. And I'm sorry for that. So sorry you can't imagine it. I did something and you caught me and you ran away. How could I do something so bad to someone I love so much? How could I have done that?"

When he finished talking, another long silence followed. I sat with it because I wasn't sure what to say. It appeared he was asking me a question, looking to me for answers I couldn't give. I held the phone away from my ear, muffling the sobs that were coming out of the receiver. But something inside me said *Don't hang up. Here is something important.* So I stayed on the line and waited.

But Dad was done talking. He went on snorting and gagging, trying to catch his breath. I sat with my feet tucked under me, like a bird perched on a branch.

"Trace? You there?" Dad asked.

"I am, Dad. I guess I'll see you in a week."

I wish I could say that the phone call was the end of my troubles. But family traditions die hard. The first place Mom and Dad took me, even before the trip home, was to the mall. Mom wanted to show me how sorry she was by buying me a few things that would make me feel pretty. Desperate to go home looking as hip as possible, I was happy to concede—and use her charge card. We went to the closest Lerners, and I picked out a few shirts, a white cotton prairie dress, and a pair of white boots with fringe on the back. Mom said I looked so cute now, on account of my running, that I should pick out a new swimsuit. I chose a white nylon one-piece with a deep, V-shaped neckline and a seductive, to-the-belly-button black zipper.

"I don't know, Mom," I shouted from the dressing room.

"Come on out!" she shouted back.

I peeked through the slats and saw both of my parents standing together. It seemed strangely okay. I hadn't known how I'd feel when we finally reunited, but at least for now, on a shopping spree, their togetherness made me happy.

But not so happy I'd come out of the dressing room in a bathing suit in front of my dad. I cracked the door just wide enough to poke my face out.

"Mom? Come here! I need you!" I shouted.

When she got to me, I lowered my voice so my dad wouldn't hear me. "Are you sure I should come out like this, in my swimsuit, in front of Dad?"

"Of course I'm sure," she said. "What's he going to do? You look so cute. Let him see you. He's proud of all the hard work you've done too."

12

New Roles, New Rules

A ge fifteen, wide-eyed and cardiovascularly inflated from so much long-distance running, I returned to Twin Falls ready to prove that no one could break the girl with the dirty-minded father.

On the trip across Oregon, skirting first the Columbia and then the Snake rivers, I sat in the backseat of my parents' Toyota Camry planning my reintroduction. Once I was home and settled, I'd cruise the mall wearing my belts draped low around my hips. I'd seek out only the most alternative kids, ones I'd heard about through letters from Erin Cecil and Angie Nichols. If my old friends wanted to hang out with the slimmer and more sophisticated me, they'd have to get in line behind Reed, the Antichrists, and the foreign-exchange students.

These things occupied my thoughts as my parents and I pulled into our driveway on June 17, 1986. Already the heat was rising off the sidewalks. My dad had been home through the first yawning of spring and had mowed the grass into a perfect chlorophyll crewcut. Through obsessive pruning and watering, he'd even coaxed a few leggy tulips out of the sun-cooked earth.

But behind the flowers loomed the windows Dad had kept covered so he could unhook my bra strap. I saw them and felt my heart drop to my flip-flops. Though he'd apologized on the phone at my Aunt Lori's, it had sounded halfhearted. As much as I dreamed of the day when my family would be packing the camper for our next trip into the Sawtooths, I also knew our troubles were far from over.

Now I was climbing the steps to the home ground of my sorrow. It wasn't the birthplace of my abuse—that had been Redfish Lake. Had I known the rules set forth for my father by the Health and Welfare Department, I might have felt a little calmer going home. But no one had taken the time to explain how my dad would keep himself from molesting me now that we'd be living together under the same roof. No one thought to show me the court document that made it illegal for my dad to even talk with me about the abuse while unsupervised.

ORDER

Good cause existing, IT IS HEREBY ORDERED that the Order dated August 27, 1985, be amended in the following ways:

1. That the no contact order between Donnie Lee and Tracy Ross will be changed to no unsupervised contact. That the order be further amended to allow Mr. Lee to live in the same home as Tracy Ross and her mother, Doris Lee.

2. That Tracy Ross return to the state of Idaho and live with her mother and stepfather, and not leave the state of Idaho without further order of the Court.

3. That until authorized by Mr. Lee's therapist and the Department of Health and Welfare, Mr. and Mrs. Lee will assure that the below listed restrictions are followed:

    a. Both Mr. Lee and Tracy will be clothed whenever moving about the house.

    b. Mr. Lee and Tracy will not spend any time together without another family member or adult present.

    c. Mr. Lee will not discuss the molest [sic] with Tracy other than in the company of the therapist.

    d. Mr. and Mrs. Lee shall continue in counseling and follow the recommendation of their counselor to insure the safety and well being of Tracy. Tracy Ross will participate in counseling as recommended by the therapist.

    e. That all other previous orders remain in effect until changed.

Looking back on the court order, which I found in a pile of papers at my parents' house twenty-five years later, it's hard to find any protective measures in it. Even then, I doubted that my dad had been "cured." It didn't make sense; even I knew how hard it was to give up on a crush who didn't return my advances. My dad had gotten a lot of physical satisfaction out of me. Why would he stop if no one was right there, every second, preventing him from abusing me?

Dad and I unloaded my belongings and carried them into the house. We hauled my clothes, books, and a dozen shopping bags from the back of the Camry and up the front steps. I paused at the door, thinking of Dad's suicide threat, my attempt to run away, and my mom's interrogation sessions. Dad must have seen the fear in my face, because he shot me a look so warm and reassuring I followed him inside.

Stepping into the dark, air-conditioned living room, I smelled recently shampooed carpets and surfaces polished with Endust. My parents had gone all out to welcome me home. Trying not to get my hopes up, I hurried down the hallway and into my room.

Mom stood at the doorway, holding her arms like Vanna White. "Like it?" she said. "We worked on it for a week."

My eyes popped. The whole room had been redecorated. A fluffy blue comforter replaced my white, ruffled bedspread. Dad showed me the illustration of the "Bearly Ballet" (with dancing teddy bears) that he'd hung on the wall over my dresser. And Mom pointed out a new stereo, cued up for my listening pleasure.

I took it in, smiling like a little kid on her birthday. But my heart didn't stop pounding until I'd scanned the frame around my bedroom door and saw that the lock I'd installed when Dad moved out was still in place and ready to be bolted.

It took no time at all for Dad and me to realize that our relationship was forever altered. That meant the good parts too, like the moments we'd shared fishing for trout or hiking through the South Hills under the showering aspens. In the weeks following my homecoming, we tried to reestablish a new order, but with no one to show us how to deal with our emotions, our tempers—

heightened by the tension we still felt in each other's presence—flared into bonfires. The vibes he sent me when we were alone made me feel like my safety with him was merely temporary. I could feel it when it was just the two of us together. I'd stand in the light streaming through the sliding-glass window, and his eyes would affix themselves to a certain part of my body. The gaze lasering through my nightgown made my muscles tense.

Maybe I'd say I wanted to go to the Potholes, a favorite natural swimming spot above Shoshone Falls, with Reed, or to a party in the desert. My dad's "No," or any criticism of me, would set me off in a rage that was disproportionate to the immediate circumstances.

"What makes you think you can order me around?" I'd shout. "You're the reason our whole family hates each other. I didn't do anything to cause this. And I don't have to do anything you tell me!" Both of my parents cowered at the thought of what I could do now that the Health and Welfare Department had identified them as high risk. They knew that one phone call from me could send my dad to prison. Maybe that's what kept Dad from breaking my jaw when I used my fingernails to claw at his cheeks.

His temper blazed, too, when he couldn't stand my shrieking any longer. He'd grab my wrists and shove me against the wall. We'd stand chest to chest, and I'd see something in his eyes: the self-hatred he felt over what he was capable of doing, and the despair for what could not be undone. When he realized he was actually physically shaking me, he'd let go. Then, with indescribable tenderness, he'd wipe the sweat from my forehead.

The July days that summer were too hot to venture outside except to go swimming. But by the time I came home from Oregon, I was addicted to running. When my drive to run became too strong, I started sprinting into the night. Mom and Dad would be sitting in front of the television, watching the ten o'clock news and spitting watermelon seeds into a Tupperware bowl, when I'd shout, "See ya later!" and slip out the door in my silk running shorts. But the routes I chose could take up to two hours, and Dad didn't like my running alone. Breaking the first rule of the Health and Welfare Department—no unsupervised contact—he started jumping on his Honda 750 motorcycle and riding alongside me in the dark.

Dad looked more peaceful during those runs than at any other time of the day. I never felt obligated to talk to him, and I doubted he could put words to the way he felt about me. We passed the miles in silence, except for the few times he'd call out my split time, or shout, "Good job, sis! Keep it up."

We ran while the rest of the world lay sleeping, and we found some comfort in it. I like to think of him sitting on that bike with the wind blowing through his sideburns. I knew he was suffering, even though he never said so. As badly as he'd abused me, we shared something no one could take away. I'd hated the way he harmed me, and never wanted to go through it again, but still I knew instinctively how badly my dad was struggling. I hoped one day he'd ask about my struggle too.

Junior varsity cross-country. Sophomore class vice president. As hard as I tried to be Twin Falls' version of Nancy Spungen, I was a fresh-faced kid with too much ambition. By October of 1986 I'd been elected to the student council, run hard and steadily on the cross-country team, and been chosen to represent Twin Falls High School at the Hugh O'Brien Youth Ambassador Conference in Boise. I joined the declamation team, which traveled around the state with the debate team but specialized in public speaking, so I could get out of the house and party with my friends. We rode in big, luxury buses with deep, plush seats and air conditioning. My specialty was Dramatic Interpretation, for which I wrote intense, tear-jerking monologues about girls who'd been abused by their fathers. During my first year, I won nearly every competition I entered.

As good as I looked on the outside, though, on the inside I was hurting. My home life was still tense and confusing. The worst part was that I couldn't say anything about the way I was feeling. Since we'd come home, we were officially over the past. Mom made it clear that we wouldn't talk, think, or cry about the events that had "turned all of us into monsters."

"It's a new year," she'd said over our first home-together dinner. "Everything's going to be better."

But it wasn't better; not for me. I worried about my dad when I went to bed. I closed the curtains and locked the deadbolt before I changed out of my street clothes. But if I became lost in a day-dream and walked in my underwear from my bedroom to the bathroom, I'd get a guilty feeling, like I was intentionally trying to lead Dad on.

I wanted to tell somebody—anybody—about the scary vibes that kept me awake, listening for footsteps at my door. But I didn't have anything concrete to tell. Dad didn't grope me, walk in on me while I was in the bathtub, or ask me to tickle his back, but I was experienced in sexual tension. I could feel it when I sat in the living room with my dad.

Maybe I was expecting things my parents couldn't demonstrate. Like the instinct to not make such a big deal about my appearance. I thought they should have known better than to talk about my face or my body. But my mom couldn't get over how cute I looked since I'd dropped my baby weight while in Oregon, and she still asked my dad to do things like hook the eyelets of my prom dresses or squeeze a pimple that was bugging me in the middle of my back.

As a sophomore in the mid-1980s, I had no way to express this to anyone, not even to Reed. It didn't seem like he wanted to talk about it anymore, anyway. In fact, I wasn't even sure he still wanted to be my boyfriend. He flirted with other girls and sometimes said things that made me feel fat or stupid. I was hurt by his comment that when we had sex, my stomach rolled like a water bed, but I couldn't accept being called stupid—especially since, after watching him struggle in his English composition class, I started writing his essays for him. His stunned teacher never understood how he went from Ds to A minuses in the course of two papers.

For a little while, I went to a therapist, but I quit after a short time because he picked his nails while I talked to him and acted blasé and judgmental. Dad and I never attended joint therapy, so we never got to talk about our feelings for each other. I went to school and tried to feel normal, but I was reeling with self-hatred. With no outlet for my anger, I started drinking, smoking pot, and snorting cocaine.

The beer and pot I got from Reed, but the cocaine I got from older kids during our declamation meets. Because I won so often, my declamation teacher let me party with the juniors and seniors. I drank with them, did cocaine with them, and sometimes even had sex with them. At meets, we'd out-orate other kids from other schools and then celebrate with beers in a senior's hotel room. When we grew bored of playing quarters, though, we'd snort the fine white powder that always made me feel instantly lighter, more beautiful, and *capable*.

The first time I tried LSD was at a party with Reed at Darren Bolster's house. I was doing shots with my girlfriends, when he sat down beside me and showed me the small, white, perforated tab on the tip of his index finger.

"What's that?" I asked.

"The body and blood of acid."

He took my hand and led me into the bathroom, where I placed the piece of paper in the hollow spot under my tongue. I let it dissolve, swallowed hard, and waited for something to happen.

Reed noticed the white paint bubbling on the bathroom walls first. I looked at my hand and saw a million pores, staring at me like eyeballs. We ignored the people pounding on the door, laughing, "Hurry up, or we're going to piss on the floor!"

"Go in the bushes!" Reed shouted back. It wasn't even that funny, but we laughed until we were crying.

A little while later, we went outside. The rain on the streets looked sequiny and bright. A half-dozen kids wandered with us, all staring out of unblinking, liquid-bottom pupils. I don't know why it took me so long to notice the stars, probably because I spent half the night with my nose stuck in a tulip. They lined the yards like teacups full of weird inverted spiders. I sniffed them so hard and powerfully, I suctioned several seeds into my nostrils.

After a while, we all started to come down. Reed took a bong hit to ease his reentry, while I sat in an armchair watching him smoke. I might have drifted into a jittery, uncomfortable sleep, but Reed grabbed my hand and led me into Darren's mom's bedroom.

I didn't want to, but I trailed behind him, reaching for but failing to grab on to his shirttail. Reed had told me a million times that if I didn't start giving him more "sexual attention," he'd find it from some other girl who liked to "do it" 24/7.

On the other hand, Reed had stuck with me from "this close to prom queen" to girl with no respect for anyone or herself. Even though he could be rude and judgmental, it was important to me that he cared, that I could trust him.

We lay on the bed, and he began rooting around for the damp spot on my panties. He whispered that acid made his body more—and less—sensitive at the same time, which also made it impossible for him to have an orgasm. I lay beneath him, watching his starchy black T-shirt gyrating above me. But courtesy of the acid, a memory was forming on my eyelids. It was an old family slide-show, filmed in Super 8. Chris and I were eight and four, and we were running around in circles on my Grandma Liz's lawn. My dad stood in the driveway, watching us while sipping a Budweiser. Chris raced across the grass, and I chased after him, shouting.

For a little while, I liked what I was seeing. It reminded me that we had once been happy, crazy little kids. But the longer I watched, the more the movie on my eyelids deviated from the actual movie my mom had stored in a cardboard box in our basement. I saw my dad put down his beer can and walk into the grass. I ran past him, screaming for him to chase me. Shiny, curly ponytails sprung from the sides of my head. They bounced as I ran, as my dad raced after me. He was on me almost instantly, but instead of snatching me up and hugging me, he stuck out a foot and tripped me. When I landed hard on the grass, he fell down on top of me.

When I opened my eyes again, I saw Reed and felt him sanding off the edges of my hipbones. "Yeah, baby," he murmured. "I can feel your body tensing. Now let me feel you come."

But I was not about to come. I was about to spin off into the darkest place I'd ever been. I tried to tell Reed that he was hurting me and that he needed to stop so I could think about the meaning of the movie. But before I could explain anything, the door to the bedroom swung open, and five Antichrists stormed in.

They rushed past the bed and started yelling.

"It's in here!" someone screamed. "Right here! I found it!"

"Nasty cat shit!" another one shouted.

They gathered at the foot of the bed, where Darren's cat had left its smelly package, apparently while Reed and I were having sex. The smell was so pungent that it wafted out into the hall. The Antichrists all kneeled down and inspected it. Someone gagged, and someone else shouted, "Don't puke! That'd be even grosser!" Then another one realized that Reed and I were lying under the covers in the middle of Darren's mom's bed.

They walked over, surrounding us. "Dude," said a kid named Justin. "Are you seriously boning her right now? That's so rank! I'm about to hurl just looking at you."

Reed sat up, pulling the covers off my body. The boys' eyes

lasered over me, making me feel like a cow that was about to be branded. I rolled onto my side, smashing my face into Darren's mom's pillow. It was white, with a powder blue, scalloped edge.

Fortunately, my movement made the boys stop gawking. They resumed their show of disgust. "Nasty!" someone yelled again, and they shoved each other out of the room, shooting final glances in my direction. The last person to exit was Darren, the leader of the Antichrists. He looked behind him, saying, "Come on, Reed. Important meeting in the basement. Antichrists only."

As Reed got out of bed, he threw me a loving wink. He pulled on his shirt and Levi's before following his friends. I lay where I'd been left, curled away from the overhead light. I tried as hard as I could to vanish from sight.

Five minutes—or three hours—later (I couldn't tell) I got up and dug around the bedposts looking for my clothes. They were all there, minus my bra and undies. Darren's mom would find those later, reprimanding Darren, who'd reprimand me. I slid into my jeans, wishing they were softer and less scratchy, before shoving my arms into a faded green army fatigue coat my dad gave me as an early Christmas present the previous December.

Night was morphing into morning when I finally left Darren's house and started walking across Twin Falls. I hurried, hoping to sneak into my bedroom before my parents were up and drinking their tea and coffee. The sun broke across the horizon just as I turned onto Pole Line Road. This was the street I ran down when I left home, hoping to save myself from my father. I stared down the sidestreets at the rows of newly built houses and wondered how it happened that I was back in the place I'd started from.

Did I have to descend further? For what? The following year, I got caught sneaking away from a journalism conference in Sun Valley to party with my friends. All we did was sit around and share a fifth of Bacardi. But when I returned to my hotel room, my teacher, Mrs. Barry, was waiting.

"Well, Miss Out-and-About," she said. "Where have you been?" And then, quickly, "Wait, don't answer that. I can smell alcohol on you from here."

"What are you *talking* about?" I slurred. "I'm not drunk, but you're crazy."

I was drunk, of course, and also incredulous. Mrs. Barry was the one teacher I hadn't been able to win over since coming back from Oregon. Even though I was a three-time gold-medal-winning Young Poet and runner up in the Portland Trail Blazers Creative Writing Contest, I was one of the worst students in her class. Jessica Tingey could crank out three column inches of newspaper copy at lunchtime, while I couldn't figure out how to string together the who-what-why-where-when of a simple story. Ironically, since I already considered myself a writer, journalism class was destroying my faith in writing.

"Watch your mouth, young lady," I recall Mrs. Barry saying. "You're lucky tomorrow is the start of the weekend. But come Monday, I think we both know where you're going. The principal's office. With me."

I started to argue that Mrs. Barry couldn't punish me because I'd already been punished in ways she couldn't imagine. I started to say that neither she nor the principal nor any of the Twin Falls High

School establishment had any right to hurt me any more than I'd already been hurt. But as soon as I opened my mouth, the words burned like bile on my lips. The only people I'd used my abuse against had been my parents. My MO since coming home from Oregon had been to let everyone believe that my life was perfect. It's fine that I didn't speak, because Mrs. Barry was in no mood to argue. She stood up and walked out, leaving me in my stupor. When the room didn't stop spinning, I lurched into the bathroom, where I heaved Bacardi-scented vomit all over the linoleum.

The following morning, I boarded the bus back to Twin Falls. A raging hangover manifested itself as a jackhammer drilling into my cranium. Mrs. Barry poured salt on my wounds by making me sit directly behind her. I did as I was told but used the opportunity to shoot lasers of hatred into the back of her permed, black-haired head.

I wanted to reach out and tear those curls, yanking her head until she was looking at me upside down. I wanted to ask her if it took a brain surgeon to see that I needed someone to save me from myself. It wasn't just the drinking and drug-taking. I still have a pale pink scar on my forearm from when I used a piece of wood to dig the letter *R* into my skin. I put cross tops, a pill form of speed, on my desk and popped them with sips of Diet Coke. How was it that none of my teachers ever noticed when I got so high my hair felt like it was standing straight out of its roots?

Two hours later, the journalism bus pulled into the Twin Falls High School parking lot. I got out, found my car, and drove slowly to my parents' house.

When I arrived, I opened the door. I took two, maybe three, steps, and collapsed onto the carpet.

"You okay?" my mom asked. She was sitting in her comfy chair, reading the Saturday paper. When I didn't answer, she came over.

"Trace? What's the matter? Are you drunk?"

Instead of getting up, I started moaning.

"*Tracy?* What's the *matter?* Talk to me. You're acting crazy."

But I couldn't talk to her, because I knew the second I opened my mouth I'd have to take on her feelings too. And I'd spent too many years making sure that she was okay at the expense of myself. Had I been stronger, I would have gotten up and walked into my bedroom before the feeling of drowning came over me again. But my legs and arms were full of lead. I wasn't strong enough to lift them.

The next thing I knew, Mom lay down on top of me, pushing her fleshy breasts against my neck. I tried to squirm away, but she held on tighter. When I realized she wasn't going to let go, I went limp and gave in to her embrace.

She cooed, rocking me against her. When she'd had enough of that, she sat me up and pulled me onto her lap.

"I didn't do it," I whined. And then: "I did it, but it's not my fault."

Mom must have sensed that I didn't want to tell her more, because she stood me up and led me to her bedroom. We sat on her bed until the last, huge sob had shuddered through my body. As dusk fell, she walked me to my room, where, without asking, she helped me under the covers. She crawled in beside me, and slept with me all night.

13

Escape to Art School

Angels lived in Twin Falls. I was looking at one in the face. Her name was Mayz Leonard and she was tan, although not so tan that I didn't trust her. A halo of golden hair surrounded angelic features—high cheekbones, pink cheeks, red lips. Her eyes were the color of hazelnuts, not unlike my old black lab, Jigger's.

"I'm just going to pray over your knee," she said.

It was the middle of summer, 1987, and Mayz and I were sitting in City Park across from St. Edward's Church. I was performing in the JUMP Company's performance of *Seven Brides for Seven Brothers*. JUMP—Junior Musical Production Company—was the closest thing Twin Falls had to a professional children's theater. My first show with them had been the summer of 1986, with a chorus part in *Bye Bye Birdie*. A year later, I'd moved up in the world. I was going to play Dorcas.

But several weeks into rehearsals, I attempted an aerial cartwheel in rehearsal and landed the wrong way, partially tearing a ligament in my knee. My whole body buckled, causing me to cry out in pain. Our director, Robyn McCracken, yelled at me to get up and keep dancing. I tried, but my knee dislocated again, sending me back to the floor, writhing and moaning. I guess Robyn hadn't realized I was truly broken.

Mayz did, though, and she rushed over to sit with me until my Dad came to take me to the emergency room. I'd never met her, but she'd been watching me. She was thirty-five and married, the mother of five beautiful white-blond kids under the age of nine. Our families both went to St. Edward's Church, and she'd seen me when I slumped down the aisle to take communion. I pretended to sing *Holy, Holy, Holy* with everybody else, but really I was thinking *Anarchy in the UK.* It's not like I was hard to miss. No other kid in the congregation dyed her hair purple or wore Doc Martens with white cotton prairie dresses.

Mayz laid her hands on my bright purple, grossly inflated knee. It sat between us, pulsating in the heat. It was so swollen it reminded me of a jelly roll, all gushy and gelatinous. Looking at it also brought to mind how disgusting I'd let my body become.

In the year since I'd returned from Oregon, I'd quit cross-country, dropped all of my extracurricular activities (except Declamation, which I continued because it allowed me to party), and ruined almost every friendship I'd had. When I started doing acid, every one of my "good" girlfriends dropped me like a hunk of moldy cheese. Then Reed joined the Army. With no motivation to be the coolest kid in Twin Falls anymore, I'd stopped exercising, dieting, and respecting my body.

But for some reason Mayz didn't notice the girl rotting before her. She cupped her hands around my kneecap like it was a baby turtle, like she didn't want to hurt me. I wanted to tell her that she couldn't hurt me even if she wanted to because I was already damaged beyond feeling. But she lowered her head, inhaled deeply, and started praying.

I froze, doing my best to summon a picture of Jesus.

"Sweet Lord," said Mayz. "I don't know why you've drawn me to this beautiful girl. But she is sweet, too. I pray that you'll bring your light into her knee, and wherever else she has wounds. Look upon us, Lord, on this beautiful day with the sun glinting through the elm trees. Show us your mercy and cradle us in the mystery of your wound so that we may be healed in the image of your own suffering."

When Mayz finished praying she took another long breath. She tranced out for a good four minutes. I tried to decide if she was a spy hired by my parents to find out how bad I'd become or truly one of God's messengers when she opened her eyes and looked at me like she wanted *me* to start praying.

Oh, no, you don't, I thought, the words coming to me all of a sudden. They rose up from the hot place in my stomach. I'd seen that look before, the kind that says something better than words can say it. But Mayz could go straight to hell if she thought I was going to pray to an invisible deity who obviously couldn't care less about me.

I gave up praying on the night that I ran to the Perrine Bridge. The wind had been howling like the breath of God, but I knew God had already forsaken me. At sixteen, shame ate at my insides like a fast-growing cancer. But there was no way I could voice my feelings of fear and loneliness to Mayz. I closed my eyes and hoped that she wouldn't actually ask me to start praying.

By some miracle, she didn't. *She* kept praying, closing her eyes again and tilting her face toward the sun. The calm on her lips made me close my eyes too, and I saw an image of God performing surgery on my knee. He stood over the operating table with a couple of lady angels in white feather bikinis. His long, grey hair brushed the top of a shiny, metallic jacket with the words HELLO, I'M GOD. written on the back. When he was ready to start cutting, he sliced into my knee with a scalpel made of light. The whole vision was so funny, I accidentally started laughing.

Oh crap, I thought. *Mayz is gonna kill me. Here she is trying to help and I'm making fun of the whole thing.* I shut my trap as fast as I'd opened it. But then Mayz started giggling. When I opened my eyes, she was two inches from my face and smiling. "I don't know what just happened," she said, "but the color in your cheeks just became a hundred shades brighter."

And then we were really cracking up, the two of us at once. The harder she laughed the harder I did until both of us were clutching our stomachs. A part of me felt self-conscious about losing control like that. But we howled until tears were streaming down both of our faces, and then we stopped, and then we started up again.

I doubt either of us had any idea why we carried on until we were exhausted, sitting under an elm tree on that sweltering summer day. But it was fun, and I felt connected to something bigger than Mayz. I liked how she seemed to appreciate me for no other reason than who I was. And our laughter seemed to seal our friendship in a way that even praying couldn't.

Later that year, I met another Twin Falls angel. His name was Andrew Durham, and we performed school plays and in the JUMP Company together. Andrew had neck-length hair, burnt-butter skin, and bones that stuck out above his waistband. We liked to dance in fields of dried wheat blossoms. I'd pick him up in my Volkswagen Rabbit, and we'd drive ten miles outside of Twin Falls.

"Watch this!" Andrew would shout, pulling at my attention. He'd place his viola behind his neck and try to play it, while hopping on one foot. I'd clap my hands and tell him what he wanted to hear: that one day he'd be first violin in the New York Philharmonic. Then we'd lie in the weeds, feeling cockleburs bite our skin.

I didn't love Andy, who insisted I call him Andrew because it sounded more serious and lyrical. He was too weird and skinny, and he believed in things like chakra cleansing and breathetarians (they're like vegetarians, but live on air instead of broccoli and tomatoes). But he knew of a place called Interlochen Arts Academy, a school in northern Michigan where kids like us—actors and writers, musicians and weavers—spent five hours a day practicing their art forms. Andrew's brother, Paul, said Interlochen was like *Fame*, only older and more respected. The four hundred kids accepted there lived in dorms in the woods surrounding a lake. It was expensive—$10,000 a year—but the cost didn't deter me. I had more than that sitting in a bank account my real dad left me when he died.

There was no conceivable reason why I should have gotten accepted. But I went for it, flying to northern Michigan with my JUMP Company director, Robyn McCracken. On the day of our arrival, we took a tour of the campus. It sat on 1,200 acres under a canopy of pine, oak, and maple trees. The air was cool, and small birds flitted through the branches. Dirt paths linked small buildings like the textiles shop, where, through a giant glass window, I saw a boy with long hair weaving a tapestry on a wooden loom. Wispy girls in leg warmers wove past kids with their noses stuck in

Stanislavski's *An Actor Prepares*. By lunchtime, I knew I would do anything to get in.

But to get in, I had to audition. So the following day, I found my way to a small, brown building called Grunow Theater. I knew the theater directors, Jude Levinson and David Montee, were seated inside. Jude was the big, bodacious director of the theater department, who caked her lids in bright blue eye shadow and always, always wore black. Slight and cerebral looking, with feathered brown hair and big, blocky glasses, David had joined Interlochen the previous spring and specialized in something called the Lee Strasberg technique.

I waited backstage until David called my name; then I went on and recited Blanche's monologue from *A Streetcar Named Desire*. I sang "I Met a Boy Named Frank Mills" from the musical *Hair*. When I finished, I stood in the light, waiting for Jude and David to say something, anything, that would indicate whether or not they liked me. But all David said was "Thank you, Tracy," at which point I walked, trembling like a grocery bag in a windstorm, out of the darkened auditorium.

My acceptance letter came on a day in May when the wind whipped my hair into a million different directions. I ran to the mailbox, crossing all of my fingers. The shining white envelope seemed to warm the cold, steel container. I held my breath and peeled open the back flap, which was sticky, I was sure, with the spit of a creative genius.

By the time I saw the word "Congratulations," I was already screaming.

My parents drove Andrew and me to Interlochen. They used up all of their vacation time to do it. I remember singing as we pulled up to the bucolic campus. Sun-dappled cabins peeked through columns of giant pines. The entire school was tucked in the woods between two shimmering lakes. Loons called through the mist, accompanied by the sounds of violin, flute, and bass.

My classmates poured out of cars with license plates from New York, California, and Rhode Island. Most of them, I'd later find out, started at Interlochen when they were freshmen but had practiced their disciplines since before they could write their own names. I had done approximately two community theater shows when I arrived there in late August of 1988. But despite my lack of professional experience, Jude and David made me a part of the theater company. During the first week of school, I auditioned for and was cast as the understudy for Ruth Hunsdorfer in *The Effect of Gamma Rays on Man-in-the-Moon Marigolds*. Ruth was the perfect first role for me; she, too, was the product of abuse.

Overnight, my life not merely changed but vaulted upward at Interlochen. The place seemed designed specifically to crack me out of my shell of shame. I knew that I had escaped something dangerous, potentially lethal, in Twin Falls. I sensed how close my reckless behavior had brought me to killing myself, which made me all the more thankful that I'd found Interlochen's artistic Eden.

On the musty stage of Grunow Theater, Jude led us through improvisation and visualization exercises meant to free us of our inhibitions. We lay on the floor and imagined ourselves as another person, in another life. I had been doing this for most of my existence, so transporting myself was effortless. Over the course of the year, I scored the roles of Tiresias, the blind seer in *Antigone* who is punished by the gods when he reveals their secrets; and Hattie, a scrappy, single mother of four who shuns the abusive men in her life in James McClure's *Laundry and Bourbon*. Over and over, Jude and David praised me for my ability to "inhabit" a character, while also pushing me to do it better. And each time they pushed, I felt myself expand into a braver version of myself, a person who had talent and worth. For the first time, I was good at something that was all my own; for the first time, I felt connected to the girl I might have been if the abuse had never happened. As we rehearsed our scenes from various plays, Jude would yell from the back of the theater, "That sucked! Do it again!" But while the other students cringed at her crassness, I reveled in it. I became free to reconstruct the girl I knew myself to be, and Jude gave me the tools to expedite the process.

It helped that the campus was surrounded by thick, dark woods. Most kids went there to do illicit things like drink and smoke pot, but I remember retreating to them to fill up. Not since I'd been to the Sawtooths had I seen such thick, dark forests. With my friend Jessica, I'd slip out the door of Thor Johnson Hall and ride my bike into the state park, adjacent to the campus.

We'd pedal across the leaf-strewn earth until we found a spot where we knew we were hidden. Smelling the rich, musky scent of rain mixed with rotting oak leaves, we'd drop our bikes and start pretending. Jessica liked to perform scenes from *The Lost Boys*, which had come out the previous summer.

But more than the characters we chose, I remember the smell of those crisp, cold, fall evenings. Jess and I both liked cigarettes, so my memories are tinged with the scent of smoke. I see the sun, dropping behind the lake, and birds—chickadees, pileated wood-peckers—darting through the mixed-wood forest. At Interlochen I found a world that was clean, and unblemished, and filled with people who were dedicated to a higher power. The power was art. And in its reflection, I saw myself.

That Christmas, I rode the train back to Twin Falls. I wore my navy blue corduroys and light blue oxford, the Interlochen school uniform. I didn't have to wear it—I should have been dying to change into anything else after donning it daily for four months—but I held on to Interlochen as tightly as possible in the hopes that it would protect me as I made my reentry home.

I arrived three days after leaving northern Michigan, and immediately realized that my parents had established a new order: abuse would be in the past, something we didn't bring up. Chris took me partying, bragging about how his little sister went to the same school as the mom in *Family Ties*. "Don't forget about the guy who played Mozart in *Amadeus*," I added, laying it on even thicker. Mom made us all go to Christmas Eve mass, which we did, buzzing on beers and eggnog and belting out *We Three Kings* without caring that we were off-key. Mom had found her comfort or at least her compromise; she clung to her prayer book and kneeled.

As for Dad, he was distant, but I kind of liked it that way. Now that I went to a fancy boarding school, I didn't feel like listening to his simplistic philosophies or stupid jokes. When he talked I listened, nodding my head and squinting to show him I was interested. But Dad had never been book smart; his spelling was sixth-grade level at best. Finally presented with an opportunity to show him how far I'd overreached him, I used words I knew he'd have to ask me to define. He never did, and maybe my attempts at belittling him flew past him. But I knew that I'd superseded his intelligence, and it made me feel better than amazing.

One night toward the end of my stay, Dad asked me to join him outside. It had been snowing, and we kicked our feet at the dirty piles of snow. Dad reached in his pocket and produced a bottle opener and a cold Bud, which I guzzled while he told me about a job he was applying for in Las Vegas at a natural gas company. When it was my turn to catch him up, I recited a few lines from *Arsenic and Old Lace*.

Nothing about my old life in Twin Falls appealed to me anymore—not the football games, the school dances, or the Antichrists. How could I return to *that* after delving into Dostoevsky? With his hands jammed in his pockets, Dad reminded me of the pre-Interlochen times. He shook his head and looked up at the streetlamp we were standing under, where great lacy snowflakes appeared out of the darkness and spiraled into the light.

A part of me wanted to ditch him, as I'd ditched the rest of the boys in Twin Falls. But because I loved him, and it was Christmas, I stayed, even when I got cold.

"I'm proud of you, Tracy," he said, taking a swig of his beer and clearing the clog out of his throat that had been there since the night I ran away from here. "Not only because you're the biggest thing that's ever come out of this place, but for getting yourself out of this mess."

After Christmas, Interlochen lay buried in snow. For weeks on end, the wind howled, and the temperature hovered around zero. Most of my classmates stayed in their dorm rooms, drinking chamomile tea and listening to James Taylor. But an old passion rekindled inside me. The hint of sun drew me out of my cramped room and onto the flat, white sheets of snow that covered the campus. I donned sweatpants, a Patagonia fleece, and a pair of L.L.Bean cross-country skis Reed had bought me for my eighteenth birthday and headed across the highway into the trees. I found my way back to trees and rocks and snow, the absolutes of the world, which I had once relied on and cherished. As I skied, a sadness crept over me, and I welcomed it, because I couldn't let it creep in on campus.

My sorrow was an old puddle, flecked by pieces of treebark and soft white fuzz. I could look in it and see the girl I once was. I knew her—then, still—because she hadn't left me. Despite all my successes at Interlochen, my old, wounded self still roamed along the edges of my psyche.

She wanted things: retribution, an apology, a nonsexual hug. She wanted them from her father, not her mother. She felt alone, even though her mom sent her cards on her birthday, Valentine's Day, even Feast of the Ascension Day. She wanted one person who could know her and understand her and still love her even when she failed, or felt robbed or broken.

I skied loops and loops through the forest, burning through the pain in my chest. It was for a lost father, followed by a bad father, followed by all the people who refused to help. But the trees never wavered.

When I graduated from Interlochen in late June of 1989, I'd been accepted at Los Angeles's American Academy of Dramatic Arts and Seattle's Cornish College of the Arts and was wait-listed at Hampshire College. My new best friend, Amy Burtaine, got into Brown, Harvard, Hampshire, and Sarah Lawrence. Unsure of what we would do over the summer, I scored jobs for both of us in a place called the Escalante Desert in southern Utah. With zero experience in either desert travel or peer counseling, a company called The Challenger Foundation hired us to lead troubled teenagers on 130-mile treks across the desert. We would work with the most rebellious teens: kids who'd robbed places, become addicted to drugs, run away, or been overly promiscuous. Their parents paid our new employer $15,000 to "kidnap" them in the middle of the night. Blindfolded and still in their pajamas, they boarded planes from wherever they originated and flew, guarded by college wrestler thugs, to a remote airstrip. From there, they were blindfolded again and driven deep into the Escalante, where our future bosses, Horsehair and Wallwalker, would meet them. Horsehair and Wallwalker sounded like the names of people who belonged in the Anasazi Pueblo. As it turned out, they were actually fat, white ex-military guys who'd had some success using forced marches and applied starvation to beat the rebellion out of children. At least their reputation was such that desperate parents turned their kids over to them as a last resort.

The program was infamous for its last challenge—called "Handcarts"—during which the teenagers would have to push thousand-pound wooden handcarts (similar to the ones the early Mormons used to transport all of their belongings to Utah in the 1800s) for three weeks through the searing heat. The kids took turns sliding under a metal crossbar and rolling the contraption across the desert. They'd end their three-week hell walk by running down a two-track road into the arms of their hopeful, expectant parents.

Amy's and my job, for which we were paid $1,000 a month, was to force the delinquents to survive in the worst desert conditions—in 120-degree heat, amidst scorpions, rattlesnakes, and a host of other dangerous critters. Challenger's founders believed that this regimen would awaken the kids to what was important in life and correct their hostile, destructive behavior. Privately, I wondered who I was to pretend to be a role model for these kids. I wasn't sure if I should be jealous—or relieved—that my parents were too oblivious—and poor—to have sent me someplace like Challenger. But the lure of the wilderness won me over—I bought a new pair of hiking boots, tank tops, and shorts, and borrowed one of my dad's old military-issue backpacks.

I felt an instant camaraderie with the "campers" the first time I met them, during their transition from Primitive Camp to Handcarts. A kid in a filthy, soiled red headband whispered, "My parents don't give a shit about us, but they think my sister and I should be angels." He was smart and articulate, the kind of boy I liked to hang out with. Then he pointed to a skin-and-bones girl who was sucking on a handful of juniper berries, rolling his eyes and shaking his head. I looked around to make sure Horsehair wasn't watching, and then nodded. Most of the kids looked like they could use a giant steak dinner—or ten—just to put some flesh on their skeletons. I knew that part of our job was to cleanse our charges of the drugs and alcohol coursing through their bodies, but I also knew how hungry I felt after just days in the desert. All we ate during our three-week walk was water and half a cup of oatmeal for breakfast, a dry package of ramen noodles for lunch, and a cup of rice with canned corn or peas for dinner, so it was important that someone knew how to forage the rest. Wallwalker warned us that the kids we'd be counseling were prone to run away, starve themselves, fake all kinds of illnesses. But it was obvious from the second I met them that they were truly suffering for their indiscretions.

My first night on the job, a scorpion headed for my bedding—with me in it. When I say "bedding" I mean a single wool blanket. None of the kids or low-level instructors were allowed to bring sleeping bags and inflatable air mattresses. We slept on the cold, red earth, shivering beneath our one layer. The most incorrigible of the kids, a boy named Xavier, who allegedly broke into someone's house and stole a stereo, came to my rescue—sort of.

"I'll stab that motherfu. . . . if he gets too close to you, but if he stings you, I ain't going to be the one to suck out the poison," he said. I countered his hostility with understanding. My abuse, and the pitiful way I tried to deal with it (by freeing myself and then recovering, but giving in, again and again), made me a conduit for Xavier and the rest of the delinquents.

I felt our similarities poignantly when a little girl named Chicken asked me to walk with her to the top of a rocky outcropping. It was days into our expedition, and Chicken had been trouble all along, cussing and refusing to share group chores like cooking and cleaning the dishes. Standard Challenger procedure was to punish kids who cussed by making them hike alongside the handcart while carrying an eight-pound rock. Not only did the rock detail compound the exhaustion of the person carrying it, but it made the other kids mad, because it meant one fewer person to push the handcarts.

By the time Chicken came to me, whispering that she needed someone to talk to, she was skin on bones with bruises and sores mottling her arms and legs. Her lips were cracked, and her eyes overlarge and overly bright. I knew I couldn't tell Horsehair that I thought Chicken needed more daily rations, but I got permission to hike her to the top of the outcropping, and we picked our way to the apex of a sandy red boulder. It looked out over a sea of saline washes and wind-scoured badlands.

"Neat, isn't it?" I said, picking a spot with a view that extended for what seems now like a million miles. Chicken sat so close that our sun-warmed arms were touching.

"What's neat?" Chicken asked.

"The desert. All that earth with nobody in it."

Chicken looked at me like I'd just piloted a unicorn out of a cloud of cotton candy and landed it on the boulder where we were sitting. She picked a scab at the center of her forearm and looked at me forlornly.

"You're serious?" she said.

"Yeah, I am serious. I like being out here, even if we're not on a vacation. The desert makes me feel small and invisible, like a mosquito or a piece of dandruff."

"Dandruff?" Again, Chicken looked at me like I was crazy. "Come on. Dandruff's gross. Why would you say that?"

I thought about it and silently chided myself for saying something so stupid. I was joking around when I wanted Chicken to see what I saw. The desert in front of us was different from the one in Twin Falls. It was softer-looking and rounded, with no trace of skin-tearing lava.

What I meant was that I loved the simplicity of walking all day only to lay my head on the sandy earth at sunset. I liked the stars buzzing over my head. The desert killed people who didn't know how to find shade or water. But it didn't hate them or prey upon them, the way dads sometimes preyed on their daughters.

We sat and watched the shadows change directions. The sun crept a couple of inches across the horizon, and the wind kicked up the scent of fossils. Every now and then, Chicken looked up from a beetle she was poking and acted like she wanted to say something. I waited until she was ready.

Ten, maybe fifteen minutes passed. She was ready.

"What I want to know is how you managed to get through high school without getting sent here," she said. "And why I couldn't grow up like you did, because maybe then I wouldn't be here."

I felt like a liar, wishing I could tell Chicken the truth about myself and my circumstances. I wanted her to know that I'd been through *everything*. Well, everything short of being raped and getting pregnant by my own father, like the *worse-worst* cases of girls who are abused. But I wished she could see that even a fuckup like me, who'd been seriously jilted and tried to fill her emptiness with her so-called sinful behavior, had found a crack and seen the light shining on the other side of her life. I knew if Chicken could know this, it might be the best thing she learned during Challenger. But the "rules" of my job kept me from telling her the one thing that might have helped her. I knew, as counselors, we were supposed to show only our glossiest sheens.

Sitting on my perch above the desert, I leaned over and knocked forearms with Chicken. "You're not all those bad things people say you are," I said. "And trust me. The only reason you think I'm better than you is because you don't know me."

At the end of Handcarts, the kids ran eight miles into the arms of their parents. Amy and I didn't have to, but we joined them. We ran until we saw the faint outline of Challenger's institution-green Chevys, surrounded by adults: Wallwalker and Horsehair, plus most of the kids' parents.

As we approached the yellow tape that marked the end of the kids' worst nine weeks in history, many rushed into their parents' arms. They collapsed, overwhelmed, exhausted, and enlightened. It was the first time many had seen the people responsible for having them ripped from their beds and shoved onto a plane bound for Utah. I could sense their anger, as well as their relief.

Amy and I sprinted behind them. We loitered in the emotions around us, wondering if we had something to do with it. Amy had already decided that she'd come back to Challenger for two more hitches, while I'd decided to spend the rest of the summer in Twin Falls. We hugged and congratulated each other, reflecting on our accomplishments. In the desert, we'd learned to be patient, open, and fearless. Challenger had taught us leadership, kindness, and perseverance. Though I still thought I would become an actress, I now added "youth counselor, wilderness guide, and social worker" to my list of possible professions. I knew that my successes were even greater than Amy's: in the course of one year, I'd pulled myself up from the dregs of teenage society to become one of the top students in my class. I also knew that instead of tarnishing me, my past had given me the gifts of empathy and understanding. I felt pride and gratitude for the chances Jude, David, Wallwalker, and Horsehair had given me, which allowed me to prove that I was far greater than my circumstances.

Amy and I were just about to get too self-congratulatory, when we heard footsteps shuffling up the dusty road behind us.

Xavier lumbered toward the finish, his shirt soaked through with sweat. His fists were clenched, and he pumped them along the sides of his waist. At first I thought he was pumping with joy, or maybe pride. But then I saw that he was frowning. "There he is. The boy we've been waiting for," I heard a female voice behind me say. Another, gruffer voice, responded, "First time in God knows how long I've seen him running without being chased."

Xavier didn't hear what they were saying. He trotted up to the crowd, looking for his parents. I caught his eye and smiled but was overshadowed as his dad extended a giant, Rolex-draped arm for what struck me as an overly formal handshake. But instead of taking it, Xavier recoiled. Spitting into his father's face, he shouted, "FUCK YOU! FUCK YOU FOR DOING THIS TO ME!"

Before Amy, or I, or anyone could move, Wallwalker grabbed Xavier by the neck. Xavier struggled, contorting his body like he wanted to slam it into Wallwalker. But our leader was too strong for even a big, rage-filled boy to overpower. He wrestled Xavier into one of Challenger's Chevys and got in, firing up the engine. As they headed back to Sheep Camp, where Xavier would start his second, nine-week round of wilderness rehabilitation, I stood on my tiptoes and peered over the dust cloud billowing up behind them.

Whispering, but hoping the sound of my voice would travel, I said, "It's okay, Xavier. Hang in there. I know how wrong it is for them to ask you to forgive your parents."

14

The Hospital Blues

The explosion occurred during an improvisation class the third week of my second semester at Cornish College. I jumped, my knee buckled, and I crashed, screaming like I was being murdered. A doctor at the University of Washington said the operation would be serious; I'd be in a cast from my ankle to my hip for twelve full weeks. I practically fainted when he told me, but I was in for a much bigger surprise.

I needed someone to help me through the operation, so I called my mom, who passed me to my dad. Mom couldn't help: she was too busy, or afraid of flying, or couldn't get the time off from her job at Parole and Probation in Las Vegas. I knew better than to complain about her lack of guts when it came to coming to my rescue. Mom couldn't make it, period. But my dad could. He said he was free on the days leading up to my surgery, the surgery, and the days after the surgery too.

I was nervous when Dad said he was coming, but also glad to

have a parent who would drive so far to sit beside me and hold my hand in the hospital. At nineteen, I still struggled to navigate my way through the world. I had thrived at Interlochen and Challenger partially because they both consisted of controlled environments with clearly defined leaders. In the city, I was overwhelmed. Maybe it was the constant rain or the fact that I'd once again started dabbling in hallucinogens, but in Seattle, I'd also fallen back into depression. Knowing my dad was coming filled me with comfort but also fear. This would be the first time we'd spent a moment alone together since he'd last abused me, five years earlier. But as the day of his arrival approached and my mind started burrowing into the past, I told myself to buck up; there was no way the same dad was coming to Seattle.

I lived in a one-bedroom apartment on Capitol Hill. When Dad arrived, he insisted on sleeping outside. He said it was because he wanted to protect his new Toyota Celica from possible break-ins, but the decision only planted further suspicion in my mind. I couldn't help but think that his refusal to stay in the condo, with both me and my roommate, came out of a fear of what he'd still want to do to me. Now that he was there, a part of me wanted to tell him *Thanks for coming, but I changed my mind. Go home and I'll see you at Christmas.*

Clearly, I was still embroiled in playing my role as loving, forgiving daughter. And Dad, for his part, was nothing if not a doting father. On the morning of my surgery, he knocked on the door of my apartment at four thirty. I remember thinking two things when his hammering rattled me out of a sleep I'd only recently fallen into: gratitude, for all the times he'd let me snore until the last possible minute, and fear, for what I was about to encounter.

At the hospital, Dad filled out my paperwork, while I sat whimpering near his shoulder. He waited outside my room while I changed into my surgery gown. When a nurse came in—wielding a six-inch-long needle that he stuck into my spinal cord to deaden my entire lower body—Dad hovered nervously nearby. The last thing I remember before going into surgery was crying as Dad walked alongside my stretcher. "Don't worry, sis," he said. "It'll be over before you know it."

The surgery lasted three hours. Not only had I torn my ligament, but I'd ripped a silver-dollar-size chunk of cartilage off the end of my femur. Both of my doctors told my dad that any other person with such an injury would have spent the past eight weeks hobbling around on crutches. "Well, that makes sense," said my dad. "She's always been good at tolerating her own suffering."

If only my dad could have been someone else's dad when the nurse rolled me back into my hospital room on a massive dose of morphine. I barely recognized him, sitting in a recliner watching TV. I was shivering so badly from the anesthesia that my teeth actually chattered. Dad flagged down a nurse and asked her to bring me more blankets, which he wrapped around me like a paper towel around a microwave burrito. When I woke up later, gagging and coughing, he shoved a pink, kidney-shaped container under my mouth.

The night went from dark to darker. As it did, I stared at my dad's hands in his lap and thought that the temptation to touch me must be killing him. I tried to stay awake, fearing for my own protection, but every time I whimpered—for the pain emanating from my leg seared through my entire body—Dad pushed the mechanical button in my IV drip, sending another shot of morphine into my veins. The relief was so powerful that it prevented me from telling him to stop. I needed every ounce of that morphine to get me through the night.

I fell in and out of sleep. Sometimes I awoke and felt glad to have my dad sitting beside me. He'd smile and dab my head with a cool, wet washcloth. Other times he'd reach out and tickle my arm. I knew he loved me and hated to see me hurting. But I was terrified of the monster that lived inside of him.

Soon, the knowing overwhelmed me, and in the fog of my painkiller-induced paralysis, I became convinced that I was about to be molested by my dad. I tried moving away from him, but the cast stretching from my ankle to my hip made all movement impossible. I strained my neck, searching for my dad's hands to assure myself that they were still in his lap. My mouth wanted to scream out at him, "Get away from me! I know why you're here!" But before my brain could communicate with my lips, a shadow moved in the hallway. A nurse stuck her head into my room and said, "We okay in here? How's Tracy? She need anything?"

Once again, like I had for so many years, I wanted to say that I needed more than anyone could ever give me, but my dad jumped out of his chair and spoke for me.

"She's been sleeping like a baby," he said. "Whenever it seems like she's hurting, I just give her another shot of morphine."

"Well, she's lucky, then, isn't she?" said the nurse. "Not every girl has a daddy who will sit beside her and keep her comfortable in a hospital room all night."

The next time Dad looked down, tears were pouring across my

temples. He leaned in close and used his thumb to stop them from rivering into my hairline. I wanted to tell him to bring the nurse back, that I was scared to spend the night with him sitting beside me. But I did what I seemed doomed to do forever. I looked at him and convinced myself that he really was there to help me.

Too scared to ask my dad what had happened in the hospital—and too terrified to face the possibility that something unsavory had—I started running again. Only this time, instead of jogging, I drove as fast as possible away from the Pacific Northwest. I needed to be far away as possible from any thoughts of my parents, because I was confused about what they meant to me. The fear I had felt in the hospital erased years of "healing" that I thought I'd already accomplished. I thought I had come to a place where I could move on from the past. But the memories rose like a tidal wave. I still didn't trust my dad.

Three semesters after enrolling at Cornish I dropped out in January of 1991. A friend, Ladan, and I left Seattle on a long vacation. We drove south to the sequoia-studded mountains of central California, and later, to the white sand beaches of Baja, Mexico. Ladan had grown up in Iran but left when the Ayatollah Khomeini overthrew the government in 1979. In the Sierra Nevada Mountains, we camped under trees so big you could drive a car through them, and in Baja, we swam in the bright turquoise waters of the Sea of Cortez with stingrays and glowing phosphorescent plankton.

At the end of June, Ladan and I crossed the border back into the U.S. We were out of money and in need of summer jobs. Ladan wanted to go to Northern California, where she'd heard we could work as laborers on an organic farm. But ever since I was little, I'd been fixated on the Teton Mountains in Wyoming. I convinced Ladan that we should go to Jackson Hole, where we could camp for free on public lands and find jobs in one of the most amazing natural settings in the West.

We landed there a week after leaving the Baja. Almost immediately, Ladan found work waiting tables. Since I had zero job experience—save for my month-long hitch with the Challenger Foundation and a short-lived stint at a bakery in Seattle—I found nothing. I didn't try that hard, though. At the time I still received my war-orphan checks the navy sent to remind me that my real dad had died while in the service. My mom had bought me a pair of Hi-Tec hiking boots and a Patagonia fleece jacket when I went away to Interlochen, and before we left for Baja, Ladan and I splurged on one, faded blue extrernal-frame backpack. I bought a roll of Glad garbage sacks, a couple of water bottles, a box of gallon-size ziptop bags, and a summertime's supply of Fig Newtons. Ladan and I set up our tent in a small valley outside of Jackson where other transient kids were spending the summer. While she waited tables at a cafe called V-Jays, I explored the Tetons.

What I found was a beauty so harsh and ephemeral I could barely stand it. The Tetons shot straight out of the ground in ragged hunks of sepia-toned granite. They stabbed the clouds at elevations of 12- and 13,000 feet. Black bears, grizzlies, and moose wandered up narrow canyons filled with yarrow, Indian Paintbrush, and bright periwinkle fireweed. I hiked with a pocket guide to flowers and learned to identify dozens of different blooms. Where crisp, metallic creeks tumbled over slick, black boulders, I took off my boots and soaked my feet until they were freezing. The sun's rays always found me, turning my arms and legs a toasted brown color and dusting my cheeks with freckles. Though I was terrified of rounding a switchback and surprising a grizzly sow with her cubs, I kept hiking deeper and deeper into the mountains. Leaving the Jenny Lake parking lot at dawn, I followed climbers headed toward basecamp on the Grand Teton, never letting them hear or see me. Once a black bear stepped onto the trail between us, and I followed her for at least a quarter mile. She ambled along, stopping occasionally to browse the blueberries lining the trail. She even glanced at me a couple of times, then kept walking, disinterested. I felt no compulsion to run from her, or hide behind the giant moss-covered boulders that lined the lower path. Maybe I was naive, but, for some reason, I knew she wouldn't hurt me.

It went like that all summer. I'd leave Ladan at V-Jays, telling her I'd be back by the time her shift had ended. Driving into the Gros Ventre Wilderness, I'd look for the mountain shaped like a sleeping Indian. Below it, I would find my favorite swimming hole and hide in the reeds along its banks for hours. Whitewater kayakers would congregate to practice self-rescue in their boats, and I thought about how the mountains themselves were rescuing me, because they let me be exactly who I wanted. I liked the simplicity of walking just to get to the top of something, and then, if I was lucky, finding a snowfield that I could glissade, skiing on the backs of my hiking boots, back down. When I came to a river and knew no one was near me, I stripped to my underwear and waded, just like I had as a child. Rainbow trout hid in the deep, shadowed pools and peregrine falcons sat on treetops waiting to swoop down and catch them. When I climbed out again, I'd lay on the hot river rocks until the last drops of water evaporated off my skin.

I look back on those days and wish I was still living in them, when the mountains and rivers washed my brain as much as my body. After so many years of insomnia, ironically, camping in a land of moose and grizzlies allowed me to access a calm so deep I could finally sleep through the night. Under the scattershot stars my sleeplessness abated, and I drifted off—for the first time with any consistency—free of the worry that someone would invade my body during the night.

15

Search and Rescue

When the last pink petals of the fireweed plants dried up and fell onto the frost heaves, I knew it was time to leave Wyoming. Ladan went back to Seattle, and I was going to a small liberal arts school called St. John's College in Santa Fe, New Mexico. The entire curriculum was based on the great books of Western civilization; every student started as a freshman, no matter how many credits they had from other colleges. To learn geometry, they studied Euclid. They translated the Bible from Ancient Greek into English.

On paper, as I filled out my application, I loved St. John's. In reality, it took less than a month to realize choosing to go there had been a mistake. The academics were too rigorous, and I felt small and stupid. It seemed to me that every other student had been genetically endowed with a pre-existing understanding of Plato's cave allegory and Copernicus's retrograde motion. I sweated through three layers of cotton trying to explain the parts of a point in Euclidean geometry. (Hint: A point is that which has no part.) When the pressure to perform became too great, I reverted to my partying ways.

But the kids I partied with at St. John's didn't just party. They partied their brains out. A girl overdosed on heroin on my bed. (I was away, spending the night with a boyfriend.) Another friend got drunk on the top of a cliff, fell fifty feet, and broke his back. I escaped real injury but had my own near misses. My first year, a friend and I became stranded in a snowstorm on the way to San Francisco. We took two hits of acid and spent the night splitting a case of beer in a cheap hotel room. Jumping between the double beds like kids on trampolines, I convinced myself—without falling or tweaking my body in any way—that I dislocated my thumb and needed to go to the emergency room. My friend fishtailed through the snow-clogged streets until she found a clerk at a 7-Eleven who directed us to the Indian hospital on the Zuni reservation. When it was my turn to be treated, an annoyed physician's assistant took one look at my quarter-size pupils and said, "You're not hurt, you're high. Now get out of here and let me go back to helping people who really need me. You don't need a doctor; you need to get your act together."

I continued my descent in San Francisco, where I took a hit of ecstasy, went to a rave, and met a man who took me home to his apartment-cum-motorcycle-repair-shop in the Mission District. At the height of the AIDS epidemic, we had unprotected sex. When I returned to St. John's, the dread in my stomach manifested in painful sores all over my body. Too afraid to ask for help, I avoided going to the school nurse for a week and instead wandered the aisles of the new health food store with new-age music pumped through ceiling speakers. I had no money, so I couldn't buy the soothing salves and magical tinctures that promised to heal my body. I hovered around the bottles of Arnica, Rescue Remedy, and Weleda rose misting spray, hoping that the love I believed went into creating them would seep out of their containers and help me.

It didn't, and eventually I went to the nurse. She looked at my sores and told me they weren't even herpes. The lesions turned out to be relatively benign: impetigo—horrifically painful but curable.

Was a part of me disappointed to find out I wasn't dying? I have to believe so, for I kept trying to kill myself by other indirect methods. But as I put myself through treatment over the coming months, three things happened that taught me critical lessons about life and death. As I lay in my bed, I knew in my heart that no one could help me before I was able to help myself. Psychiatrists and antidepressants were out of the question, along with any kind of talk therapy. Prozac, Klonopin, and Zoloft—those "uppers" reminded me too much of my mother. Besides, I knew the one thing that could lift me out of my depression. It took a week for the life to return to my body. When it did, I got up, dabbed the pus off my cheeks, and went back into the mountains. Only this time I went with a mission. St. John's had a search-and-rescue team, and I was eager to sign up. Induction required baptism by fire. If a student went to more than one meeting, that meant he or she immediately became a searcher. I went to meeting after meeting, acquiring an entirely new skill set within weeks: everything from map-and-compass navigation to basic first aid, CPR, and simple hiker psychology. On Wednesday nights my teammates and I practiced base-camp and radio operations. I could barely complete a Euclid assignment on time, but on St. John's SAR, I was learning how to coordinate a search with the Civil Air Patrol and state police. At night, I placed my backpack, along with my hiking boots and clothes, next to the door of my dorm room so that I would always be ready.

The year I joined the SAR team, 1991, was a bad year for hikers in New Mexico. During my first two months, we responded to what seemed like a half dozen searches. Not once did we make a "live find." Most of the time, we arrived on the scene after a hiker had been pronounced dead, or we were stopped midsearch when another team found a missing person's body. This didn't mean that we were bad searchers; it just meant we were lucky to be in the wrong place at the right time.

But our good luck ended one day in the early winter of 1992. A call came in for a family that had crashed their airplane in a meadow near Taos ski resort. Riding in the bed of the rescue truck, I saw the contents of the Cessna scattered over the ground: cassette tapes and books, winter hats and warm coats. Those things were fine. That debris said "adults." But as we drove closer I saw stuffed animals and picture books, at which point I realized I was coming to rescue little girls and little boys.

Someone told me to help a nurse who was treating a burning five-year-old boy. I ran to her but was stopped short by the smell of charred flesh and baby lotion. Flakes of skin floated above the child. I would dream I held his ashes in my hands, in an ornate ashtray, for weeks afterward. "Don't just stand there," a triage nurse scolded. "Get me some gauze." I jumped-to, collecting rolls of white tape, a CPR mask, and water for the little boy to sip. But there would be no sipping. He was too broken, too burned. I stared as the nurse tried to keep his heart pumping. I watched her realize it was too late.

That year I not only saw the burning family but searched several times for people who turned up dead. It was always eerie—and thrilling—leaving school in the middle of the night and hiking into the rugged lower Sangre de Cristo Mountains looking for lost souls. On one of my most memorable searches, we departed a trailhead in the middle of the night and hunted for a pair of young Italian brothers who'd rented a plane and crashed it in the mountains. The emergency locator on their aircraft gave us a good idea of their location. The moon was full and mist rose off the meadows.

As we began to hike, everyone talked and joked—something we always did to lighten such heavy situations. And as we always did, everyone eventually fell into a quiet rhythm. We all knew that if we found the missing plane, it could tax us in ways we'd never experienced. I think we were always preparing ourselves for the worst.

The moon was blazing, so I didn't need to wear a headlamp. On the horizon I saw something that looked like a woman dressed in a nineteenth-century nightgown. Her long, silver hair flew behind her in the moonlight. I couldn't hear her, but I could tell by the way her hands were raised to her white, skeletal face that she was screaming.

I stopped in my tracks asking, "Did anyone see that?" But no one else had. I kept hiking, but then I saw her again. This time I stopped the group and asked them to wait for the third return of the apparition.

I must have drawn too much attention, because she didn't show herself again. "Just wait! She's coming," I said. But someone told me to be quiet so we could hear if one of our victims was calling for help. I shut up and continued hiking.

We continued our search for the missing pilots, who had crashed their plane in a dense part of the forest. Another team found them, but we heard about what their bodies looked like after the fact. They weren't dismembered or even all that bloody. But the way the plane had crashed left one of them smashed up against a tree, in a position that made it look like he was hugging it.

I never forgot about the ghost. The experience had been so intense that when I returned to the St. John's campus, I couldn't talk for days. Over time, I stopped fixating on her and went back to studying Euclid, Ptolemy, and Plato. But the following summer, while working on a trail crew in Bridger-Teton National Forest, I told the story to a native New Mexican kid who knew exactly what I had seen.

Or rather, who. He said it was the ghost of La Llorona, who has haunted the arroyos of New Mexico since as early as the late 1500s. He said several versions of the legend existed, but that in the New Mexico version she mourns the death of her two sons, who drowned in the Rio Grande River.

The ancient Celts believed that "thin places" exist in the wilderness, where it's easier to hear God, or where the dead can more easily visit the living. When I heard about La Llorona, I thought of my own biological father and all the times I'd felt his presence while I was out hiking or skiing or sitting perfectly still and watching rain collect in the indentation of a leaf. For the first time, I knew that the few occasions when I thought I had felt him were real, and that his presence was as true as if he had still been living.

By the end of my freshman year at St. John's, I had become a certified mountain junkie. So in June, I signed up for a program called the Student Conservation Association, which places young, strapping kids with land agencies to do things like restore wetlands and clean up forests after wildfires. Pay was minimal, but I scored a coveted spot on a three-person work crew, rebuilding trails damaged by the 1988 fire on the outskirts of Yellowstone National Park.

Traveling with two horses, my crew hiked for ten days at a time, camping in dewy meadows and using two-person handsaws to cut through pine trees that obstructed the trails. It was backbreaking work—and just the thing I needed to continue exorcising the demons of my past. I loved that summer because of its simplicity. Life was pared down to its most basic elements: rise at dawn, feed the horses, eat, work, eat, hobble the horses, sleep. Whether hiking or digging trenches with my pulaski, my mind wandered forward and back. Sometimes, when I was sun-cooked and dehydrated from heavy lifting, I'd pretend I was digging a grave, into which I fantasized I was burying every bad memory, terrified shudder, confusion, and emotion surrounding Dad. Other times, on a particularly cool evening, say, or when the sun shone through the woods at a certain slant, I would feel only tenderness for the man I had once deemed king of my world.

The summer flew by, and at the end, when I looked in the mirror, I barely recognized myself. A few months shy of my twenty-second birthday, I was tan and freckled, with sun-bleached hair and lucid, bright green eyes. For the first time ever, I saw beauty in my own reflection: strong shoulders, lean biceps, lightly browned legs. I still preferred not looking, but I'd leapt a huge hurdle over that summer and was now closer by half to self-acceptance.

By late August, I had completed my last backcountry hitch, and, basking in overblown confidence, I decided to hike out from my trail crew and back to civilization alone. The Thorofare Region, where we worked, consists of a confusing network of Forest Service, horse packer, and hiker's trails, and at some point I became lost, wandering up a faint game path where I was nearly trampled by a deer. It occurred to me that the deer must have been more scared of something *above* it than me to come so close to a human, but I continued hiking, oblivious to a 300-pound grizzly working itself into a lather a few hundred yards up the path.

I knew a creature was lurking—and he wasn't far—and I began to sweat in anticipation of a run-in. I imagined a cougar; the buff-colored mountain lions were known to live there, though they were shy. The lions were fast, efficient predators and, I would be the first to point out, humans were invading *their* land.

Thinking, "Man, I hope bear spray works on mountain lions," I took the safety off my pepper spray, which was still attached to my backpack, and continued walking.

I knew I was lost, and could hear branches crunching ahead of me. Sensing an animal's presence, but unclear if it was a mountain lion or bear, I continued moving toward it. In a vain effort to protect myself, I started yelling: "Hey motherf...! Watch out! It's not just me, Tracy Ross, but whole *group* of me! Whatever you do, don't f... with us! Cuz we're big, and rowdy, and we like to cuss!" Then I'd rattle off the longest, most vile string of swear words I could think of.

Apparently grizzlies are immune to profanities, because I climbed to the top a little knoll, looked down, and saw a medium size, dark brown grizzly walking out of a tree stand. It looked up to where I was now waving my arms and shouting. It stopped and turned to face me.

I'd learned a few things about bear encounters, both from my Forest Service supervisor and from a book I was reading called *Bear Attacks* by Stephen Herrero. So when the bear turned to face me, I turned my profile to it. I couldn't remember if I'd read or just thought that my backpack would make me look bigger—and more menacing. I started to wave my arms and continued cussing.

But the bear wasn't in any rush to get going. I was the visitor in its home, a potential threat to its food source. It stood still for a few seconds; then began pounding the ground. The pounding turned into jumping, and then the jumping turned into charging—straight at me. The grizzly lunged three times, stopping short—but not that short—of my quivering body. I knew too well all the tales of hikers who had ended up being ripped apart and devoured, to be retrieved only as "stomach contents." Standing before the bear, it was too easy to envision my own death.

The grizzly stopped some thirty yards away, then proceeded to bluff charge me again. Only this time I was too petrified to continue standing my ground. Going against everything I'd learned about bear safety, I dropped to my knees, buried my head in my arms, and started singing *Yellow Submarine*.

I kept my head down, waiting. If I was going to die, I didn't want to see my killer approaching. I wanted it to lunge, chomp, and kill me quickly, so that when the pain came it was a shock to my system. I thought of my parents, probably sitting in front of the TV in Las Vegas; my brother, somewhere in Georgia; and my real dad, who I hoped was still hanging around, watching over me.

He must have been, because the bear came within feet of my body, circled around me, and left without so much as taking a lick of my sunscreen. I kept singing until I could no longer hear claws crunching across the ground cover. Then I stood up and started running. I lapped a ridge above me several times before finding the trail I'd come in on and linking it back to my trail crew. When my trail crew supervisor saw me sprinting beneath weight of a full backpack, he knew exactly what had happened.

Laughing, and pointing to my sweat-soaked shirt, he said, "Welcome to Wyoming. Where even little hippie girls get charged by grizzlies."

That fall I went back for one more year at St. John's. But I knew before my first Monday night seminar was over that I was finished hanging out with "society." I knew that, for me, wilderness could provide the perfect meditation, analgesic, escape. I knew any relationship with my parents would plunge me back into the darkness, so the following spring, after two years at St. John's, I packed my car, and headed to a place where, during the summer at least, the light shines all day and all night.

16

Disappearing Act

A laska. I went there after a friend told me that people in the forty-ninth state partied till dawn in the endless gloaming of the Arctic summer. My plan was to hike up glaciers and hang out on the banks of rivers loaded with salmon as big as small dogs. I might work; I might not. The town I was headed to, McCarthy, didn't have phone service and was accessible during the winter only by plane.

In May, I dropped a load of boxes in storage, picked up a friend named Dan, and drove out of New Mexico, kicking up dust. Dan and I had dated at St. John's, but we both knew that we'd go our separate ways when we reached McCarthy. An entire continent passed beneath our wheels as we drove across the United States and then Canada. As gas stations became roadhouses, milky-skinned waitresses served Kokanee beer and pancakes for breakfast. I ate a lot of pancakes, sizing myself up against brawny men and women with two-stroke oil stained into their pants. I also drank a lot of Kokanee, but usually not until after lunch.

At Tok we turned south. At Glenallen, east. The road became dirt, and we followed it, grinding low gears for another three hours until we reached a dead end and a river surging with ice-melt and silt. A cluster of battered trucks and station wagons rusted on cinder blocks. A small sign pointed to a tram strung across the rapids on two-inch-thick pulley cable. In my memory, it says: WELCOME TO THE END OF THE ROAD. WEAR GLOVES. AND DON'T FALL IN.

Across the river, a narrow trail snaked through a dense alder thicket, abuzz with mosquitoes and birds. It was Sunday-afternoon quiet on a Tuesday—except for the shriek of a distant chainsaw and a little kid hooting in the woods. I broke out of the bushes and saw a cluster of log buildings with wildflowers blooming between the timbers: town square. Standing on the edge of the last civilization for ten million acres, I realized what most people realize when they enter the cultural hub of Wrangell–St. Elias National Park: McCarthy is a place separate from and in addition to the rest of the world.

I took to Alaska like I was born there. By June, I was living in a twelve-by-twelve-foot cabin at the edge of a massive glacier that flowed out of the mountains and into McCarthy. My friend Thea, who I'd met at St. John's, had arranged it so that I could live there in exchange for working for a family called the Millers. I would help Jeannie Miller in her garden, act as a de facto babysitter for the youngest Millers, Matthew (thirteen), and Aaron (seven), and wait tables at a pizza parlor the Millers were opening in town.

Jim and Jeannie had moved to McCarthy in the 1970s, after Jim was sprayed with Agent Orange in Vietnam. It turned out the Millers were famous in Alaska—in part because of their red Ford truck, which Sylvester Stallone commissioned for $500 and then drove off a bridge in the movie *Cliffhanger*, but more so because they had survived the day, in 1983, when a man named Lou Hastings set fire to the biggest, nicest lodge in McCarthy's sister town, Kennicott, and then gunned down six of McCarthy's twelve year-round residents. The shootout had started in a laid-back fashion, with Lou knocking on the Millers' neighbor Chris Richards's door and saying he had to kill him. A fight ensued, and Chris ended up with gunshot wounds to his eye and forearm. Chris survived, but Lou torched the lodge and proceeded to kill a half dozen of Chris's neighbors. Chris told me this story at a party on one of the first nights I was in McCarthy. The gory details were overshadowed by the message I heard in the story: that life beyond trauma continues, and where the blood pours into the ground, patches of fireweed later bloom.

When I arrived in McCarthy, Jim Miller was digging a leach field, and Jeannie was decorating the restaurant to appear as an old-fashioned tailor shop. The plan was that once the restaurant opened, I'd wait tables, serving dense, floury pies to gold miners and mountaineers while black bears picked through the garbage. Until the restaurant opened, however, I was free to roam.

Sometimes roaming meant walking the five-mile road between McCarthy and Kennicott three times a day, listening to the Root Glacier creak and moan off in the distance. Other times it meant running up Fourth of July Creek, past the old copper miners' houses on Silk Stocking Row and behind the dilapidated Kennicott Copper Corporation hospital and mine. When it was sunny, I hiked up the rock-covered moraine of the glacier, still afraid to venture onto the ice because of the bottomless crevasses and slick, blue wormholes called moulins. You can't rescue a person who falls into a moulin, though someday a hundred years from now you might find the sole of a boot, a rusty ski pole, or a chunk of leathery, ice-preserved flesh.

On days when I wasn't exploring, I weeded the Millers' garden with Jeannie. She was small but built of bricks. We crawled through the greasy black soil, pulling dandelion weeds from her rows of baby lettuce and bok choy. In the greenhouse, she showed me how to swab a squash flower with a paintbrush, manually pollinating the surrounding blooms. I followed her directions and watched baby squash balloon to life on the dense, mineral-rich earth.

Jim and Jeannie worked as fast as they could to open the pizza parlor before the summer rush ended, but there were permits to be signed, inspectors to placate, and loans to be applied for, granted, and deposited in downtown Anchorage banks. I followed Matthew and Aaron around, steering them clear of skinny-dippers and rescuing them from the silt pools we swam in when they stood up and became stuck in the mud.

When I wasn't swimming, I rode Matthew's bike up and down the five-mile dirt throughway, standing on the pedals to power up hills. I felt myself become stronger every day. I ate next to nothing—no breakfast, rarely lunch, sometimes dinner—which allowed me more time to roam. I'd been practicing this near non-eating for years, swearing off fat, which stores things like carcinogens and cancers as well as sorrow and shame. But in McCarthy, I saw a new body emerging, not anorexic but 99 percent lean. Sometimes I fantasized about the things my new body would do, once it was fully realized. It would climb to the top of Alaska's tallest mountain. It would build a warm, cozy cabin. It would cut the eyes out of any man who stared too long at little girls.

At night, after my various jobs ended, I sat at the McCarthy Lodge bar, enjoying the feeling of glacial silt and garden mud on my skin. Young guys bought me beers, and old guys asked me to dance, and I took full advantage of the attention, gyrating back and forth across a creaky wooden floor. A dozen men watched my and other girls' shirts inch up our bellies. We danced close to them and sometimes away so they could get a better look. I was careful to keep their attention and more careful still to seem unavailable when it was time to go home. The only person I wanted to go home with was Matt.

Matt was Thea's part-time lover, or occasional ex, or something like that. She told me to find him when I got to McCarthy, after her mother called her to say she had cancer and needed Thea to spend the summer in Anchorage, helping her try to survive. I didn't know it was Matt when I saw him, but I recognized something hungry in his eyes. He looked at me, I looked at him, he looked at me, and we looked down.

I knew Matt wanted to hike up the glacier, to feel the cold creep into his boots and to peer into the frightening ice chasms. And I knew he wanted to go there with me. The St. Elias Range looms beyond Kennicott, swathed in enormous sheets of ice and towering over the clouds and the birds and most bush planes at eighteen thousand feet high. It's big enough to create its own weather, and mountaineers have come back from three-week trips with stories of white-outs and avalanches when it's still summer in McCarthy.

One day, as Matt and I stood at the bar smashing blood-bloated mosquitoes onto our forearms, I asked him on a date.

"Would you want to go backpacking with me?" I said.

"With you?" He thought about it. "Hmmmm."

"What did you say?"

"I said, Hmmm."

"Oh, ha-ha, I thought you said 'yum.'"

We laughed at this, because it was absurd and silly and close to the truth, and then we searched our beers for something floating in the foam. The bartender played "Scarlet Begonias," and all the drinkers started swaying. Someone shouted Matt's name, and he went to investigate. When he returned, his eyes took up where they'd left off, looking at me like I was a caramel apple and he was a diabetic.

"Yeah," he finally answered. "I'll go backpacking with you."

"Okay . . . When?"

"I don't know, maybe this weekend?"

Three days later, we met at the edge of the glacier, far from the bar and in broad daylight, which made us feel different, more formal and stiff. While he fiddled with his pack straps, I waited, anxious to leave and worried I'd have nothing to say. But once we started walking, the words fell into place. We talked about books and music and girlfriends and boyfriends we'd loved but wanted throw off of cliffs. We discussed the virtues of Idaho and Virginia and argued for why ours was the better state.

"Virginia, totally," said Matt. "What's Idaho? The potato state?"

"*Yes,* potatoes. They're only, like, the staff of life."

"Uh, you might want to look that one up."

We kept walking until we reached the glacier proper, where we stopped to scan it for the crevasses and deadly moulins.

"What do you think?" said Matt. "Should we go for it?"

"Not sure. We don't have crampons or a rope."

"We'll be fine. You lead. Just pick your way carefully and we'll be *all* right."

Matt and I shared a healthy respect for glaciers, which crack and cleave, masticating the earth like Rototillers in garden mulch. We had heard how they heaved, surging and retreating several feet at a time, and we both knew stories of climbers who had fallen into crevasses headfirst, plunging forward as if diving until the walls closed around them. The lucky ones lost consciousness before they became stuck. Others were able to wiggle back out, assisted by ropes and pulleys. But the most horrifying accounts involved those who fell gently, slowed by the friction in those narrow shafts. I have often imagined their moment of reckoning, the terror welling up inside them when they realized that the glacier would become their coffin, and that they would wait there to die until their blood vessels ruptured, while their friends called down from the surface *It's okay. I love you. Close your eyes.*

I don't know how, but I saw a route through the crevasses and followed it on faith. Because it was summer, the death traps were obvious; we could walk up one side and look for a narrow spot to jump across. Guiding wasn't so hard when it came down to it; I just followed my instinct and looked a few steps ahead to make sure I didn't walk us into a trap.

We zigzagged down the ice, until sometime around late evening, when we made our way to a small lake hemmed in on one side by the glacier and on the other by land. Climbing across the moraine, we set up camp in a meadow of lupine blooms. A raven rode a thermal, circling up and swooping down. And the silence was a calling to pay attention to the moment at hand.

To the north we looked at Mount Blackburn with its stairways of ice. To the south, we saw nothing but glacier, and beyond it, raw wilderness with no end. Matt said he loved Thea; I told him I loved my dogs. It took us a long time to make dinner or to do anything but sit next to each other with the hair on our forearms touching.

At some point, gauzy blue turned to rose quartz, and a star burned itself into view. We watched it until the air grew cool, and then we went to bed, each longing for the other but each in our own sleeping bag. I lay there for a long time after Matt fell asleep, listening to the wind on the glacier and feeling grateful that two people could burn for each other without going up in flames.

The next morning, Matt slipped off his clothes, walked to the edge of the lake, and dove in. I watched him, trying to enjoy the sight of his body without thinking that I was a Peeping Tom. He splashed for a few short seconds and then came out, goosebumps beading the water on his slick, pale skin.

Then he wanted to watch me skinny dip too. I stood up, resisting the urge to laugh hysterically or jump around like a freak.

Being naked in front of men would never feel normal to me, and I was strict about who saw me nude and when. Mainly, I did not want it to happen—at least in daylight—under any circumstance. I changed clothes in bathroom stalls, even when it was just girls. I avoided hot springs and massages and always had sex in the dark. I had never skinny-dipped in broad daylight before. And yet, I wanted to take off my shorts, walk to the lake, and dive in. I wanted to feel beautiful in front of my new friend.

Matt tried to help relax me. "There's no one watching but me," he said. He grinned and raised his eyebrows, jutting his chin toward the lake. I stood there stupidly for several minutes and then made myself slip off my T-shirt and step out of my shorts.

When I was naked, I felt two things: a flicker of fear, reminiscent of every time I'd ever been naked with a man, and the electricity of the moment. I fought again to stay in one place, and when I couldn't stand it any longer, I jumped into the glacier-encased lake.

After our swim, we walked up the glacier, jumping across the tiny blue rivers etched into the ice. At an arbitrary point we turned around and started walking back, hot, sticky, and ready for something to eat. We talked about our families and how we felt separate from them. And when we got back to our campsite, we both knew that something had changed.

It was the lake. Or rather, the surface of the lake.

It was not where we had left it. It had dropped two feet.

Later, we would discover that scientists have an explanation for this disappearing act. Something about equilibrium and water pressure causing the glacier to lift. At a given point all the water rushes from its icy prison, flooding the river plain and tearing out bridges downstream.

We watched the lake recede for what felt like several hours, then made ourselves go to bed. In the morning, a giant bowl remained where the lake had been, and we slid into the basin, turning up dirt and inhaling the last thousand years. A wall of ice rose before us, fifty feet high and an entire valley wide. We crawled on our hands and knees, digging our fingers into the rich black ground and throwing the silt-heavy mud toward the sun. Matt found a shaft of bamboo, the remnants of an ageless ski pole. For the moment we were like children, called into the gleaming blue hallways of the glacier and its haunting, frozen vaults.

17

Father-Daughter Road Trip

Matt and I saw each just a few more times that summer. He was still in love with Thea, and I had gotten restless. A friend talked me into doing a wilderness EMT course in Crested Butte, Colorado. It sounded perfect; I felt like I could spend the rest of my life exploring Alaska, but the whole town of McCarthy shuts down at the end of summer. Since my friend's job ended later than mine, we'd get to Seattle each on our own and then drive the rest of the way to Colorado together.

Our arrangement meant that I would have to drive all 1,400 miles of the Alcan alone, something that sounded as enticing as eating nails. I made a flyer requesting a travel partner and pinned it to the McCarthy Lodge, the old warehouse, and the hangar where St. Elias Alpine Guides outfitted tourists to ice climb on the glacier. When, after two weeks, no one had responded, I once again found myself in need of my family. I called my mom, who promptly passed me to my dad. "Heck, yeah," he said. "I'd love to drive the Alcan. Give me a few weeks to find a cheap flight, and I'll meet you at the airport in Anchorage."

Dad and I departed Anchorage in late August 1993. I met him at the airport and loaded his gear into my Subaru Justy. I didn't say it, but Dad seemed tired beyond his years. It had been months since we'd seen each other and, for some reason, as I reconnected with nature, I projected that he was doing the same. Maybe it was irrational, but I expected some version of my old dad to roll into Anchorage, stirred to life by the freedom of the road, the cool air, and the bright white glaciers, visible from the window seat of the airplane, in the Chugach Mountains. The man in front of me looked like he was carrying twenty-pound rocks in both of his pockets. We climbed into my Justy and started driving.

A soft breeze blew through the windows, smelling of rocks and minerals. Dad kept his hands in the pockets of his windbreaker, even though it must have been seventy degrees. I took off my sandals, and drove in bare feet.

You have to go north to go south when you're leaving Alaska, so Dad and I drove the Glenn Highway, heading back toward the McCarthy cutoff. We passed moose in swamps, with algae hanging off their racks, and bald eagles sitting on nests perched atop telephone poles. In Glenallen, Dad was hungry, so we stopped at a gas station and stuffed ourselves on Slim Jims and Hostess Chocodiles before pressing on to Tok Junction. To the east, we could see the Wrangell Mountains, and to the west, 20,320 foot Mount McKinley. It looked so dense and massive, I thought it created an indentation on the horizon.

I could tell my dad was loving the adventure. He chatted up the waitresses at every roadhouse where we stopped. He loitered around guys with big, bushy beards and stared at the cuts—from fishing knives and motorcycle wrenches—on their blackened, gnarled hands. In another lifetime, or under different circumstances, my dad would have thrived in Alaska, where your outdoor skill set—from how accurately you can fire a pistol to how quickly you can change a carburetor—mattered more than things like reading and writing. A part of me wished we could go to McCarthy, so I could show him the glacier, the frothing Copper River, and, near Kennicott, the old angle station, where a friend once fired his rifle over my head to warn me that a black bear was following me. But I hadn't suggested turning when we came to the cutoff, because I didn't want to jeopardize the magic I'd felt living there. Yet even without my personal discoveries, my dad could barely contain his excitement. He *ooohed* and *aaahed* over every mountain that appeared in our windshield, and screamed "Stop the car!" when we saw a black bear or moose. In British Columbia, we followed two gangly caribou down the center of the road for what must have been fifteen minutes. Dad couldn't decide if he wanted to shoot them or take their picture. When I reminded him that he didn't have a gun, he settled on a photo. The road lurched up and down, aggravated by frostheaves, and the needles on the million-strong spruce trees smelled wholly different than the spruce-scented car freshener dangling from my rearview mirror.

On it went for hours. Wild animals materializing out of the brush as if put there purely for the sake of making our drive more entertaining. In one thirty-mile stretch we counted four black bears, three more caribou, a moose, and a golden eagle. Dad stared at the miles of wilderness surrounding us and said, "There's just no end to it, is there?"

"No end and no beginning," I answered.

Mostly what we did on that long drive, though, was sit together in silence. And during those times I'd start to get antsy, despite the arresting power of the landscape. I still wanted my dad to tell me the truth about what he'd done to me during my adolescence, but, at the same time, I didn't want to be the one to bring it up. When I got cranky from sitting in the car, I'd scooch against the window, glare out at a million acres of black spruce, and conjure up imaginary conversations.

I realize now just how much of my life I'd spent bringing enjoyment to my family. And how sick I was of shouldering the burden of making us whole and healthy. I constantly had to remind myself that *I* was the victim. *I* was the one who needed saving. After so many wrongs, it was up to my family to make things right for me.

Looking back, I know I felt too conflicted to tell my dad how I truly felt. At twenty-two, some deep, dependent need made me continue accommodating my dad. Why didn't I call someone else when it was time to drive the Alcan, or wait a few extra weeks until the summer officially ended? I *knew* college kids who needed rides back to schools in the Lower 48. But instead of waiting, or searching broader or wider, I defaulted to what was familiar, to what I wanted so desperately to be innocent.

We spent most nights on the drive down the Alcan sleeping in gravel by the side of the road. Clouds of mosquitoes drained us of blood, and the rain came down in heavy brown sheets. Anyone else—my mom, Chris, and every friend except maybe Ladan— would have wanted to rip my head off if I put them through such a "vacation." But every time I looked at my dad, he was smiling. I couldn't help but smile back.

In the end, Dad and I never found the words to say what we were feeling. Not on that whole drive from Alaska to Seattle. We sat in our separate worlds, staring out our separate windows. Knowing my dad had once—maybe still—craved me made me want to reach across the car seats and punch him. But the moment would pass, and I'd feel sorry for him again. I even thought that maybe I was just as sick as he was. But the soft part of my heart felt that he deserved another chance. I knew the day would come when I'd be strong—and hard-hearted—enough to finally force him to fess up to every last one of his abuses. That knowledge—and the fact that I still wanted easy, palatable answers—is what allowed me to sit next to him for twenty-five hundred miles and say next to nothing.

One hundred and seventeen hours after we left Alaska, Dad and I pulled into the parking lot of a cheap hotel in downtown Seattle. Dad went into the office, while I did some pushups on the sidewalk. A few minutes later, Dad came out of the office. "I got us a double," he said. "I hope that's okay."

It wasn't okay, not really. But I didn't say so at the time. I told myself it would be easier if I shut up and went along with Dad's plan. We sat at the opposite ends of the two queen beds and gorged our senses on television. When it was time to eat, we walked to Pike Place Market, where Dad found some greasy fish and chips and I chose a big bunch of grapes. We ate as we walked, looking at shops, coffee drinkers, and the ocean. I felt proud and happy, as well as sad and confused.

Because I knew, sooner or later, that I'd want to take a shower. I didn't know how other dads and daughters felt about showering in each other's presence, but I didn't want my dad to be anywhere near me when I took off my clothes and stepped under the steaming water. I waited as long as possible before digging my tiny bottle of Clairol shampoo out of my stuffsack and unfolding my purple pack towel. When I couldn't stand the stench of my own armpits any longer, I got up and stood against the door of the bathroom.

Dad, of course, didn't notice. He was too busy propping his eyelids open so he could watch TV.

When I'd hedged as long as possible and dad's eyes kept drooping, I went into the bathroom anyway. But as soon as I'd slipped out of my bra and Carhartts I put them back on. It creeped me out to think of myself naked in a hotel room with my father, even if there was a wall between us. Sliding into my Teva sandals, I stepped back into the main room and woke up Dad.

"Um, Dad?"

His eyes clicked open. He grabbed his glasses from a table and put them on. When he saw me standing next to the bathroom, pack towel in hand, he said, "Oh, sorry, Trace. You need to take a shower. Let me grab my wallet and I'll head out for a walk."

Because I was uncomfortable with the words "you" and "shower" coming out of my dad's mouth in the same sentence,

I looked down at the carpet. "Yeah," I muttered. "I guess I do. But . . . is that cool? I mean, I'm sorry, Dad. It's just that . . ."

"Don't say it," he said. "I'm going. Out the door. This minute."

When enough time had passed and I was sure he wouldn't be returning, I went into the bathroom, took off my clothes, and placed them on the counter. Before I stepped into the steaming water, I draped my towel over the door handle even though it didn't have a keyhole.

18

Rebound Man

Less than a year later, I was back living in Alaska. I knew my wounds weren't healed and that my destructive impulses still roiled under my surface. But I also knew that the vast, unpeopled wilderness of Alaska had the power to inspire and soothe me. So in January of 1994, I moved back and lived for a brief stint with a man named Mark, in McCarthy.

To Mark's chagrin, we lived more like roommates than lovers. I didn't love him, because he reminded me too much of a grandmother: he was stout in build, with long red hair and a beard that brushed against his collarbones. His pantry held pounds of Copper River salmon he'd dip-netted under a full moon and put up in jars. Acres of dried vegetables—exotic mushrooms, leafy kale, turnips, carrots, spinach—all harvested from his garden, lined his plywood cupboards. If I'd met him ten years later, I would have loved his subsistence lifestyle and the fact that, to support himself, he wove gorgeous, intricate murals made from the hair of his huskies, which he spun into thread. He also built giant moose sculptures out of willow wands, the mooses' main forage. But at the time, looks mattered more to me than a man's creativity or clarity of spirit. When I wanted male attention, I'd ski to town and hole up with one local or another for an hour . . . or a couple of days. I knew I was taking advantage of Mark. I wanted to have it both ways. Someday I'll beg him to forgive me, because those days in McCarthy remain some of the best days of my life.

Throughout the winter I met people who didn't care where I came from, how long I was staying, or when I planned to move on. My neighbors shared homemade bread, store-bought cheese, and other prized possessions. We sat in wood-fired saunas drinking green, nearly brewed beer, planning adventures, and watching the northern lights furling and unfurling in bright greens, reds, and blues from one edge of the sky to the other. I stared into the strangers' winter-rough faces and thought I saw something I could trust.

By the following autumn, however, I needed a new place to live. So in September of 1994 I moved to Fairbanks, coldest spot on earth. I got a job training forty Alaskan husky puppies for a competitive dog musher named Jeff Conn. Jeff worked for the Department of Agriculture and spent $30,000 a year on seventy skinny huskies that never won a single race.

For the first time ever, I was in charge of something besides myself: four litters of pups named after things like Greek gods (Hera, Zeus, Athena, and Achilles), the space program (Sputnik, Armstrong, Buzz), and knives (Butter, Jack, Ulu). In the morning, we left the dog yard and ran a five-mile loop through the birch trees. As autumn folded into winter the sun never rose above the horizon. I fed the pups, watered them, and hooked them to a sled. They ran hard and fast with their tongues flapping against their jowls. I yelled the commands I'd learned from professional mushers, who ran the Iditarod and the Yukon Quest. When I yelled "gee!" the dogs turned right, and when I yelled "haw!" they turned left. It always amazed me that a whole team of twelve-month-old puppies would respond to the sound of one voice.

As much as I loved the pups, though, I didn't like Jeff. He worked me to exhaustion in exchange for room and board and a small monthly stipend which I augmented briefly by working the night shift at a Fairbanks grocery store smearing frosting on doughnuts. Needless to say, sleep deprivation made my day job all the harder, but I kept at it because of the pups. I didn't realize it, but by training them I was also acting as their de facto executioner. Every week at Sunday dinner, Jeff would ask how they were performing on their daily runs out of the dog yard, and I'd report on their gait, their responsiveness, and their willingness to please. I had no idea of the sentencing I was giving them until the day, sometime around Christmas, when Jeff walked into the yard, rounded up all the "underachievers" and, after trying to sell them to other mushers, took them to the pound. Shortly thereafter, I started looking for another job.

One day after I left Jeff's place, I was drinking beer at a bar called the Captain Bartlett when a different dog musher walked in. He wore a giant down parka, tattered Carhartt coveralls, and a pair of fur-trimmed, knee-high mukluks.

Colin James said he was from Scotland and that he'd been to base camp on Mount Everest. His next "little adventure" was to compete in the thousand mile Yukon Quest dog sled race, dubbed the "toughest race on earth." To raise the money for such an undertaking, he guided British and Scottish tourists on dog-mushing trips north of Fairbanks. When I first met him, he seemed like a British version of Jack London. He was ruddy from the cold and missing his two front teeth, the result of a climbing accident. I liked his accent, his adventure résumé (which included sailing the North Sea in a boat he'd hand-crafted, kayaking Europe's biggest rivers, and traveling through Afghanistan with his brother as a teenager during the Russian invasion). I also welcomed the fact that he could keep me warm, outside, in a sleeping bag, even when the temperature dropped to 20 below zero.

But before long, he began showing his true colors. And they weren't as pretty as the alpenglow I'd imagined shimmering on the Himalayas. Just two months after our first date, he became bellicose and possessive at a Fairbanks dance club called the Crazy Loon Saloon. A friend from the University of Alaska invited me out, and I asked Colin to come with us. When we got to the club, he said he wasn't into dancing. "I'll nurse a beer at the bar. But you go on without me," he said. I kissed his cheek and walked onto the dance floor.

I guess I was having such a good time that I completely forgot about Colin. Because some time after we started dancing, my friend poked me and pointed. Colin was standing on the edge of the crowd, motioning me to him.

I smiled and waved him over. When he didn't come, I did my flirty move when I wiggled my butt and used my pointer finger to say, "Get over here, gorgeous." But he just looked at me and shook his head. When the lights circling the dance floor moved over him again, I saw that he was coming toward me but was frowning. He weaved between the dancers and grabbed my bicep. I thought he was going to lean in and give me a big smooch, but he yanked me off the floor and into a corner.

I should have known that was my cue to leave. Not just the dance, but Colin. But at twenty-four, I still inhabited a long, dark tunnel. I repeated my cycle of love and despair, my most familiar emotional rhythm.

"You hurt me." I said, reciting what was now beginning to feel like the theme song of my life.

"Good," said Colin. "If that's what it took to get your attention."

It took me a second to believe what I was hearing. I was three beers deep and feeling like a comedian, so I might have stuck my fingers in my ears as if to clean them. When Colin didn't laugh, I realized he was serious. I turned my back and stared walking toward the dance floor.

This time Colin grabbed me again, pulling me out the door and all the way to the parking lot. I looked around to see if anyone was watching. A few kids were, but they were drunk and they turned their heads, clearly embarrassed for me. Colin kept tugging until we were sitting in my car, staring out the front windshield. He blinked his eyes and rubbed them, as if he were about to start crying.

"Colin?" I said, now wondering if I'd actually done something to hurt him. I could do that sometimes: get so caught up in the fun right in front of me that I'd forget to worry about the people I'd dragged along with me. Had I been flirting? Flaunting my body? I didn't try to defend myself—I couldn't understand why a thirty-two-year-old bar fighter would be so upset he was about to start crying.

"What's the matter?" I asked.

"Didn't you *see* me? I was standing at the edge of the crowd, waving at you for hours. I needed to get out of there, but you didn't even notice. You have no idea what you just did to me, do you?"

I tried to realize, but I didn't.

"Ireland," he said. "You don't remember? The war? The bombs? I *told* you what they did to me."

"I'm sorry," I said. "I'm not remembering."

"I can't believe it. I can't *fucking* believe it. You tell someone you love the most important thing about yourself and they can't remember?" Colin yelled. "That's the most ridiculous thing I've ever heard."

I scooted closer to the passenger window, stammering, "I'm sorry, Colin. But you've told me so many things. And they're all so amazing. How can I remember everything?"

"I don't care about the rest of what I told you. I'm talking about the war I fought in Northern Ireland. That club is exactly like the one I went to right after a bombing. Bodies everywhere. Bloody, dismembered teenagers with their trainers still on their feet."

"Oh, Colin," I said. "I really am sorry."

It took a long time for Colin to calm himself enough to accept my apology. I stared past him, wishing that I could resume dancing. But when someone tells you how wounded he is—partially on account of your actions—a pair of shackles materializes out of the air and binds the two of you together. I knew I'd crossed a line. I also knew there was no retracting.

I took his hand, smiled, and pressed it against my cheek. I palmed the back of his neck, pulled him to me, and gave him a kiss.

"It's okay," he finally said. "But can you promise me one thing?"

"Sure, yes. Whatever you need."

"Just promise this is the last time we go dancing."

That night, I waited until Colin was snoring before I snuck into the living room and called my parents. It must have been four in the morning. My dad answered first, saying, "Chris? Tracy? Who is it? What's the matter?" and then a few seconds later my mom got on the other line.

She was out of breath, even though I knew she'd just been sleeping. "*Tracy?*" she said. "Oh my God. Are you alright? What is it, honey? What *happened*?"

"Calm down, Mom," I said. "Nothing happened." But then I started crying.

"What?" said my mom. "Are you hurt? Are you *injured*?"

I tried to talk but a sob caught ahold of my words. Trying to be brave, I made myself keep talking.

"It's Colin," I whispered. "He's freaking me out. I think he can be *violent*."

"*Violent!*" said my mom. "What do you mean *Violent?* Did he hurt you? Who's Colin anyway? Is that the dog musher you've been seeing? Are you okay? Are you in the *hospital?*"

"*No Mom!*" I whispered back. It was one of those whispers that was also a shout. "Just shut up and let me finish. All I'm saying . . . is that tonight he did this weird thing when we were out dancing. He *grabbed* me. And I don't like to be grabbed by anybody."

"Of course you don't, honey," my mom's voice quaked. "And nobody should be grabbing you. What do you mean by grabbing anyway?"

"Jesus, Mom," I said. "*Grabbing.* You know, *yanking.* He pulled me off the dance floor in front of everybody. It's like he wanted to show me that he *owned* me. I didn't like it, that's all."

"Oh, God," my mom said again, but I was waiting for my dad to chime in. Though I knew he was on the other line, he was being strangely silent. Before, when I'd had a spat with a boyfriend, he'd puffed his chest and made a point of telling me how easily he could "go down there and show that guy a thing or two." But for some reason, he wasn't weighing in on this conversation.

"What do you think she should do, Don?" said my mom. "How can we help Tracy?"

I could almost hear my dad going over his checkbook log in his head, calculating how much spare cash he had and if it was enough to fly me home. He cleared his throat, which I'd noticed him doing a lot more often lately. Then he said, "Trace? What do you want us to do? This Colin character sounds like trouble. Do you have somewhere you can go to if he gets truly violent? You know if you need us we're always here. If you think Colin is really going to hurt you, you know you can come home."

"Home?" I said. "Dad, you know Las Vegas isn't my home. And I can't come home anyway. Colin just bought me a plane ticket. I'm going with him to Scotland."

We flew to Edinburgh in June 1995, and I got a job at a water sports center called Loch Insh in a small town in the country's Highlands. Colin knew a couple who agreed to rent us an apartment. While I worked—waiting tables, helping Loch Insh's owner Sally Freshwater in her garden, and picking up the occasional early morning baking shift—Colin "sorted out his business." He traveled to his home on the north coast, where he told his common-law wife that he'd met someone and we were starting a life together. She retaliated by saying she was keeping everything they owned, including his six-year-old daughter, Freya. When he returned to Aviemore, he was too despondent to find work or be patient and loving. A few days later, when I said I wanted us to go to a party with a new friend, he answered, "Your friends don't like me."

"How do you know?" I asked. None of my new friends had ever expressed anything but curiosity and interest in Colin.

"They scrutinize me."

"They don't scrutinize you. They don't even know you. How can they scrutinize you if they don't know you?"

"They look at my teeth. They think I'm ugly."

"Colin. They don't think you're ugly. Besides, who cares what they think? I don't think you're ugly."

"Well, I don't want to go. I want to go climbing. Come with me."

"Come on," I whined, "I don't feel like climbing this week-end. I want to go to the party. Why don't you call your friend Allen? You stay here and I'll go to the party. That way, we can each have fun and come back ready to see each other again after the weekend."

If Colin had been a cartoon character, smoke would have started billowing out of his ears. He went to the closet and started packing a small, yellow duffel with rock-climbing gear and a sleeping bag. I thought for a second that maybe he was going to trust me enough to give me a little space and freedom. But I must have wanted it too badly, because he turned around and said, "Ahhh, now I see what you're up to. I know your *friend*. It's that kid from British Columbia. I know exactly what you're trying to do. You want me to leave so you can have him over and fuck his brains out. You'll wiggle your ass just like you did to me. I'm not stupid. Pack your gear. You're coming with me."

This time, I let my parents buy me a plane ticket back to them: was there another choice?

I'd sold my car, was living at "home," and had lost most, if not all, of the self-confidence I'd built up before meeting Colin. So when he called, saying he'd spent several weeks rethinking our relationship and that he had come to realize how truly special I was to him, I let him back in. I was nothing but a recidivist, and the pattern was now entrenched. I asked my parents if he could come live with us, and they said yes, for a little while.

Two weeks later, Colin was back in America. And two months after that, he was hounding me to get married. He said if we didn't, he'd never be able to make money. If he tried to work without a visa, he'd be deported. Believing his claims that I'd "seduced" him back to the States, I agreed to marriage. I also believed I had no other options. We went to the courthouse in downtown Las Vegas on February 23, 1996, and signed our names on the dotted line of the King County marriage certificate. A date was set for two weeks later.

It just so happened, though, that Mayz, the angel from Twin Falls, was coming through Las Vegas. For years, she had sent me cards, bought me presents, and prayed for my well-being. We'd kept in touch through letters while I went to Interlochen and Cornish; Mayz kept all of mine in an extra-wide Manila envelope, which she eventually sent me. Now she was coming to visit, and I had to tell her about my wedding.

Never was a marriage undertaken with less hope but more fatalism. Mayz knew something was wrong the second I answered my parents' phone. Her husband, Steve, was attending a conference, and she said she wanted to see me. We agreed to rendezvous at a Catholic church near the strip, with sculptures on the outside that looked like Power Rangers. Neither of us thought I should bring Colin.

Just seeing Mayz always made me want to crawl into her lap and start bawling like a little baby. She was the one person I believed wanted only good things for me. I knew when I told her about Colin she'd be shocked. She'd met him—and disliked him—before we went to Scotland. The second I sat down next to her, a water main burst behind my eyelids.

"I'm sorry," I said.

Mayz stared at me, surprised.

"Sorry for what, honey? You have nothing to apologize to me about."

"Yes, I do. Because I didn't tell you about the wedding."

"What wedding?"

"*My* wedding," I continued. "Colin and I are getting married."

Mayz stared at me for a good long while, slowly shaking her head. She looked at the cross of Jesus at the front of the church, suspended over a bright gold tabernacle. When she finally spoke, her voice sounded grave and serious. "I know you, Tracy," she said. "You don't seem happy. Are you sure you want to go through with this?"

"I have to," I said. "Colin's counting on me."

But Mayz didn't agree that I couldn't get out of my marriage. Holding my hand, she looked into my face with her beautiful nut-brown eyes. "Please tell me that you won't go through with this if you don't want to," she said. "Because you don't have to, Tracy. You don't."

"Why not?" I cried.

"Because no one can make you do something if you don't want it. Not if you don't give them power over you."

"But Colin *does* have power over me," I said. "He's counting on me. He'll kill me if I back out of the wedding now."

Mayz put one arm around my shoulder. She grabbed my hand in her free hand. I sobbed quietly, tried to keep my hiccuping to a minimum in case other people were praying. As she held me, she whispered, "Colin can't kill you, honey. No one can. If you do this it has to be because *you* want to. *You* count for something, Trace. I want you to believe that."

Because I didn't believe her, I had nothing to say.

Mayz continued. "I want you to tell me one thing, Tracy. Let it be the first thing that comes to your mind. What do *you* want? Try hard and tell me if you can see it."

I closed my eyes and waited for a picture to form in the oxbows of my grey matter. It wasn't hard, because I'd often dreamed this dream. What I wanted was so simple anyone could have had it.

"All I want . . . is to live in the mountains. With a dog, and a job that lets me do things. I could work at a health food store. And ride my bike, all the time. I'll ride through meadows full of wildflowers. And I'll write poetry. I doubt it'll ever happen, but it'd also be nice to find someone who actually loved me."

I wish Mayz would have called my mom right that minute and told her to come get me. The two of them could have packed me up and Mayz could have taken me back to Twin Falls. But I believed that I'd gotten myself into another mess that I couldn't possibly get out of. There were too many people counting on me. My mom had already bought me a $50 dress from the Gap.

Two months after the wedding, Colin and I moved back to Alaska. This time we went to the town of Talkeetna, which had four hundred year-round residents but swelled to five times that in the summer, when climbers from around the world congregated there to climb 20,320-foot Mount McKinley. I got a job in a small liquor shop-slash-grocery store, Nagley's, and Colin found work as a raft guide. We spent our first several weeks camping in a tiny, two-person mountaineering tent at the end of the town airstrip. While

Colin kept busy showing our new neighbors—climbing guides, commercial fishermen, and Denali National Park rangers—how to do things they'd been doing for decades, I got to know the local color.

One of them in particular stood out. He was a soft-spoken raft guide with scraggly brown hair and eyes the color of blue glass. He looked to be twenty-two or twenty-three to my twenty-six years on the planet. When he walked into Nagley's, he instantly gave me a spark. He introduced himself—Shawn Edmondson—and said he worked with Colin at Talkeetna River Guides. He and his giant black malamute, Tank, had driven up the Alcan from the University of Montana, but he had no intention of returning to school at the end of the summer. Once the snow flew, he and Tank would head to the ski slopes of Colorado.

The boy with the cobalt eyes lodged in my mind and wouldn't leave me. He continued dropping by Nagley's, where he'd reward himself after a long day of guiding with a freezer-cold bottle of beer. If we were alone in the store, we'd stand in front of the cooler with the doors swung wide and let the icy air cool our bodies. Shawn told me he'd grown up ski-racing in Connecticut and that he'd been raised solely by women, including his mom, grandmother, and two sisters, Courtney and Shannon. The way he spoke of them—half smiling, half complaining, but with obvious respect—made me instantly trust him. When he talked about the one thing in his life that was missing—a girl who loved the mountains and skiing as much as he did—I wanted to reach across the counter where the cash register sat and grab him. "I'm that girl," I wanted to shout. "Say the word and I'll run away with you!" But we never made it that far in our conversations. We'd talk until the glass on his beer bottle started to sweat and then, brushing finger-tips against palms in the exchange of money for a buzz, smile and say, "*Good-bye, take care, I'll see you again sometime.*"

During my days off, I rode my bike, picked blueberries, and stood on the banks of the Susitna River, staring at Mount McKinley and dreaming of the day I might climb it. But every night I had to go home to Colin. Even though we were newlyweds, he treated me like I was going to run off on him any second. I might have sent the subliminal signals; in a vague, uncertain way, I was already planning my escape.

In October, with money from my parents, we bought two acres of birch- and spruce-studded property outside of Talkeetna and built a tiny cabin on it. I helped with the construction and cared for our growing team of huskies. Though we could barely afford to feed ourselves, Colin was collecting dogs like another person might collect expensive shoes or foreign money. On my days off from Nagley's I pounded nails and swept the job site until one day, when I was having trouble hammering together a two-by-four, Colin screamed—driving all interest in helping out of me.

"Need a hand?" he said. He was standing behind me, watching my progress.

"I think I'm okay," I answered.

"Fucking hell, woman. I didn't ask if you were okay. I asked if you need a hand."

My ears burned. I slowly put down the hammer and took off on my bike.

But from that point on, Colin's temper started flaring up so often and unexpectedly that I began constantly guarding myself against it. A friend who knew me then says she thought of me as two different people inhabiting one body. She says when I was alone, I was gregarious, creative, and joyful, but when Colin came near me, I became visibly smaller and constricted. She was right on both counts: my new neighbors brought out the best in me, but when Colin's shadow came over me, I withdrew into myself. Once the cabin was built, I did everything I could to stay away from the tiny confinement, overpowered by Colin's emotionally demanding presence. I worked back-to-back shifts at Nagley's, built a small network of women friends, and started teaching yoga at the Talkeetna Community Center.

I only knew what I'd learned in my book *Yoga for Runners*, but in those days in Talkeetna, it didn't matter if you were an expert. My students came to me needing an antidote to the poundings their bodies took while chopping wood, wrenching on Cessnas, and hauling tons of live crab out of Cook Inlet's marathon commercial netting sessions. I led the hardened men and women through carefully planned asanas, teaching them simple poses like Mountain, Triangle, and Warrior. Afterward, I relaxed their minds and bodies with soft-spoken guided meditations. I was never paid for my time, but my students more than reimbursed me with gifts from their various trades. They brought me grocery bags stuffed with two-foot-long king crab legs, mittens knitted with home-spun husky fur, and, from the famous bush pilot and musician Doug Geeting, huge jars of cantaloupe juice that tasted better than any milkshake I'd ever sipped.

My yoga practice was also helping me. Moving in the heat of my wood stove, I'd bend and flow while the sweat of a million bad memories dripped from my pores and onto the floor. The slow, meditative movement calmed me; it allowed me to drop in to my feelings for the first time ever. Always before, I'd run, climbed, hiked, and skied away my fears. With yoga, I found a way to experience my emotions.

And what I felt was that old, profound sadness that lived in each of my cells. It was dense and heavy, like mercury or chocolate pudding. But what surprised me was how much I liked my sorrow, which seemed like the single most important thing about me. Few people I knew had been to places as dark as I had. I figured my journey to hell had made me better able to empathize with others' suffering.

It extended beyond me, to a neighbor named Krista Maciolek, who, in January of 1997, asked me to help her train her sled dogs for the 1,161-mile Iditarod race. Krista was brave and afraid; her boyfriend, Pecos, was dying of cancer. To deal with it, she was preparing herself for the second-toughest race on earth; I recognized that, like me, she was pushing herself to the physical extreme in order to process her anguish. I helped by feeding her dogs, stringing them on the gangline in front of her sled, and handling for her at races. Occasionally, during training runs, I mushed my own team of dogs behind her.

In order to qualify for the Iditarod, Krista had to prove herself competitive in two separate races. In mid-January, we agreed to meet at the start of the Kuskokwim 300, near the town of Big Lake. The second I saw her pull into the parking lot, I could tell she'd been crying. It was 30 below zero—without figuring in a wind-chill factor. She kept crying as we unloaded her huskies from their dog boxes and led them to the start line. She cried as we hooked them up and booted their paws. She was still crying when she thanked me for helping her, before unhooking her sled and yelling "Get up!" to her string of yapping, screaming huskies. She was beginning a three-hundred-mile round-trip journey to the Kuskokwim River, where the temperature would drop another 10 degrees to 40 below zero. I knew she was crying not only because of the terror that must come when you set off on a race that will last between twenty-four and forty-eight hours. She was also crying because a few days earlier, she'd been told that Pecos had only a few months to live.

So moved was I by the five-foot-two-inch Talkeetna librarian that I went home and wrote a story about her on the back of a grocery bag. Colin and I were so poor at the time that it was the only blank paper I had. Scribbling the scene that still held in my imagination, I burned the last of our white gas writing by the light of a Coleman lantern. When the lantern light died, I turned on my headlamp and wrote until I'd completed the story. In the morning, I took it to the local radio station, where I read it over the airwaves.

The tale of the dog-mushing librarian wasn't great, but it was honest. And in the weeks after it aired, dozens of people congratulated me on its humor and compassion. Not only did my neighbors in Talkeetna love it, Alaska Public Radio Network picked it up and aired it two weeks later, on the start of the Iditarod, which in Alaska is akin to Super Bowl Sunday.

That's when I realized, for the first time in my adult life, that I might have a gift for writing.

Krista and I went to Anchorage, where dozens of mushers were milling around 4th Avenue, loading their sled bags with all the required provisions for the long, strenuous trek. I tended to Krista's dogs' feet, while she fed them a final prerace snack. As I smeared each paw with an ointment of eucalyptus and wax, I heard the sound of mukluks padding across snow behind me. They belonged to a native Alaskan woman who said she lived in the village of Unalakleet, several hundred miles to the west. She told Krista about a story she'd heard on the radio that featured her and her dog team. It was so good, the lady said, she knew she'd remember it forever.

Bent over booting a dog paw, I closed my eyes and listened to the praise being bestowed upon me. I had reached someone. I'd made a difference.

19

The Great Escape

I f only that story could have been the true beginning of the
life I was about to encounter. The good life, with nice people,
heartfelt love, and grand, amazing adventures. But there was one
more obstacle I had to overcome. And it had to do with Colin.

The winter of 1997, Colin's violence escalated to the point
where I feared he'd physically hurt me. We'd argue, and he'd
scream until his face was flaming. One fight was so bad, I ran out
of the cabin in my stocking feet and spent the next several hours
shivering in our broken-down Subaru. I sulked back to my now-
calm husband only when I realized that if I didn't, I might have
died of hypothermia.

From then on, I started seriously looking for ways out. Big
escape plans, like saving my money and disappearing to a yoga
colony somewhere in Hawaii or Costa Rica. When I realized that
I wasn't going to save a penny while caring for Colin and feeding
our (now twenty-five) sled dogs, I began secretly exploring different options with my neighbors.

A woman named Bonnie-Ann told me about a ranger job in Denali. She said I'd be perfect for it and that I should apply. The job would require that I move to the park for the whole summer. Family housing didn't exist; there'd be no place for Colin. Not only that, but I would get to spend seven to ten days at a time "patrolling" Denali's six-million-acre park. Patrolling meant hiking over passes and into pristine river valleys, making sure people were storing their food in portable containers impenetrable by grizzlies. I swooned at the thought of living and working in a place where, for most of the year, lynx, wolves, and wolverines outnumbered humans. In early March, I told Colin I was going on an all-day yoga retreat with Bonnie-Ann and then drove two hundred miles with her to Denali.

By the time we were done visiting Bonnie-Ann's friends at Denali headquarters, I knew I had to be a backcountry ranger. I applied, right on the spot. People who live in Alaska year-round have priority for ranger jobs with the park service, so I figured I had a good chance of getting one and of banking the big bucks ($11/hour!) that came with it.

The only trouble was, Colin would never let me go. I decided I'd wait until I had a job offer to tell him. Bonnie-Ann and I agreed to put her PO box as the return address on my application. When the letter came, either offering me a job or denying me one, she'd signal to me by sending a message on the local radio station's *Denali Echoes* program, which sent messages to bush dwellers who didn't have phones.

On the day the letter came, Bonnie-Ann sent me an Echo. Just like we'd planned, she kept it short and coded. "To Tracy in Freedom Hills from Bonnie-Ann. The rabbit has left the water." Colin heard it too, but when he asked what it meant, I told him it was Bonnie-Ann's way of informing me that a date she'd gone on went well. I knew he didn't believe me, but I didn't care. I was going to work in Denali.

The question, though, was how. I knew when Colin found out about the offer, he'd threaten to call the park service and tell them I'd lied on my application. He'd say I was too stupid to be a ranger, that my sense of direction was always off (which would have been honest), and that I couldn't start a fire even if someone handed me a Duraflame log and a can of jet fuel. I knew he'd grind down my confidence until I gave up completely. So Bonnie-Ann, another friend named Cheri, and I planned my great escape. They would come to my house on the day I told Colin I was going to Denali. Cheri would drive her car, because she was rich and had a good one. She and Bonnie-Ann would stand at the end of my path and make sure Colin didn't come after me. All of us were so scared of what might happen, Cheri offered to bring a gun.

On the big day, Cheri and Bonnie-Ann sent another Echo that said they'd be over at eleven. I walked the snow-covered road in front of my house until I saw Cheri's bright red truck. She and Bonnie-Ann hopped out, gave me quick hugs, and told me to be brave. I breathed in their smells of woodsmoke and rose water before going into the dog yard, where I found Colin shoveling poop.

I picked up a shovel and started digging with him.

"I need to talk to you," I said.

"Oh, yeah? About what?"

"Oh, you know. Things."

"What kind of things? Things I'll like or things I won't like?"

I paused, because I knew that I was about to say it. Flexing my muscles under my raincoat, I reminded myself that it was now or never. "I want to tell you something important," I said. "Let's go make some tea."

I probably shouldn't have said the tea thing, because we usually made each other tea *after* a huge argument. I waited for Colin to signal that he was on to me, but he didn't act the least bit suspicious.

"Tea, huh? Okay, I'll be in in a minute."

I went inside and made some tea. Orange pekoe for him, Earl Grey for me. As our bags steeped, I peeked through the door and saw that my day pack was where I'd hidden it, sitting behind a tree and loaded with essentials. I'd filled it with everything I'd need if Colin went crazy and tried to kill me.

He came in, took off his work boots, and sat down in a rocking chair by the window. "Okay, I'm here. Now what is it?" he said.

For a second, I almost felt bad. Colin's eyes were glinting with anticipation. I thought that maybe he was hoping I would tell him I was pregnant, but I knew before I'd married him that I'd never give birth to his kids. If anything would bond me to him forever, our progeny would be it. He rocked back and forth, smiling.

Still, I didn't speak. Only stood against the ladder to the loft with my heart lurching toward my teeth. I knew if I didn't tell him now, it'd never happen. I didn't want to lose my nerve or, with it, my ranger job. I waited as long as I could and then said, "I—"

A dog barked outside. Another howled. Soon they were all

howling. I hoped they hadn't seen Bonnie-Ann and Cheri. It would have sucked to have dogs blow my cover.

"You what?" asked Colin. The glint had left his eyes. Now he was just staring. The hair on my arms stood up, along with more hair on the back of my neck. *Just say it.* I pleaded with myself. *Please, just say it.*

Okay. Here we go.

"I'm going to work in Denali."

Colin stopped rocking.

"You're what?" he asked again.

Don't stop. Keep going. Bonnie-Ann is right outside.

"I said . . . I'm going to Denali. I applied for a backcountry ranger job. And I got it. Aren't you happy?"

At first Colin was calm. He held on to the arms of the rocker and started cranking it again. He put his elbow on the arm of the chair and rested his chin in his hand. I thought for a millionth of a millisecond that he might be okay with my leaving. But in the next millionth of a millisecond he said, "Well, how're you gonna get there, then? You don't have a car, do ya?"

My insides were quaking, but I kept going.

"I was thinking Bonnie-Ann could take me. She works up there every summer."

Colin's face darkened. "So that's who's behind this, huh? *Boney Arm?* She's the one who's encouraging you to leave your husband. Why am I not fucking surprised?"

"It wasn't Bonnie-Ann," I pleaded. "It was my idea. I want to be a ranger. I just want to. It sounds fun."

"Fun?" said Colin. "And why should you get to have fun? Fun is staying here and helping me care for these dogs. The last time I checked, fun wasn't running off and leaving your husband for an entire summer."

"But we need the money," I went on. "And it could be good for me. I'd get to spend ten days in the backcountry at a time. I'd get to help. Imagine . . ."

I knew as soon as I said it that I should have left that last part out. I should have made it seem like the job was actually for Colin; that while I'd gotten the summer gig, he would get to know the dog mushers at the park kennel. "*Imagine it*," I should have said to him, "*we could move to Denali and you could run the park dogs all winter.*"

But I didn't say it. And that's when Colin stood up, climbed into the loft, and started pinging me with my belongings. Shoes, books, and clothes rained down on me like giant hailstones. I dodged a small, wooden jewelry box that my mom had given me. It flew past me and smashed onto the floor, spewing turquoise necklaces and hoop earrings around my feet. When I looked up again, my 20-below sleeping bag was flying toward me. Then my journals, all five of them held together with a giant rubber band.

Without a word, I bent down and started gathering my things. Colin stormed down the ladder and grabbed them out of my hands. He went to the kitchen and found a giant, black garbage bag. Saying things like "bloody hell" and "I should have known," he jammed in everything he could fit.

I waited until he finished, then took the bag from him, very carefully. If this was his worst reaction, I would take it. Because I was afraid to look him in the eye, I bowed my head. As I did, I saw his hand raise, as if he were going to hit me.

"It's not even worth the trouble I'd get in," he said, turning around and walking away. "You're not worth it. I've known it since the second I met you. You're just a stupid, worthless little cunt."

I have that word bound up in a piece of cloth and stored in the back of my memory. Because as much I hated hearing it, it sounded like the sweetest send-off in the world. Colin stormed after me as I ran down the path to Cheri's getaway truck, screaming that I was a little bitch who should never have been born. But when he saw my friends—prepped and ready to support and defend me—he stopped chasing me.

I sprinted the last forty yards to the truck, ripped open the door, and jumped into the front seat. Bonnie-Ann squished against Cheri, making room for my garbage bag and me. Cheri threw her truck in gear, and we spun out in the snow. The back end fishtailed a couple of times as if waving good-bye to Colin.

I waited until we were all the way down the steep face of Freedom Hills Drive and onto the plowed pavement of Comsat Road before I gathered the courage to look behind me.

Three weeks later, I was living in Denali. I'd moved into a small, rustic cabin in employee housing, completed a week of ranger training, and now split my time between ten-hour shifts at the backcountry desk in the visitors' center and ten-day backcountry "hitches." Traveling with one or two other rangers, I would hike up one enormous river drainage and down another, crossing paths with grizzly bears, caribou, and moose. With no established trails to guide us, we made our own paths, always keeping the Alaska Range in our vision. Singing, so that the park's resident bears could hear us coming, we bushwhacked through walls of sticky, thick alder and side hilled across scree- and snow-covered mountains.

All of the park's major rivers flow directly from glaciers that pour out of the Alaska Range, and we waded through their icy, waist-deep currents. Once, I fell in the McKinley River with my backpack on and nearly drowned; the silt-choked water sucked me under before I could unlatch my waist belt. At first I flowed backward and could see my hiking partners disappearing behind me. Eventually the current turned me around, until I was facing forward. My foot became lodged in the rocks at the bottom of the river, and I got stuck, with the muddy waves piling up behind me. My chest constricted and my fingers turned wooden. Knowing I would die if I didn't free myself from my backpack, I beat at my waist strap until the buckle came open, but my chest strap remained latched. The water filled my sleeping bag and pulled against my shoulders. For a few terrifying seconds I thought I would drown, right there, in the shadow of Mount McKinley, but at the last possible moment, when my face was inches from going under, I unlatched the top buckle, wormed out of the straps, and exploded out of the river.

Even though I knew that the wilderness could really, actually kill me, it didn't stop me from crossing rivers. The following day, I started another patrol in a different part of the park and spent four days hiking in a downpour. My group and I watched the Chulitna River rise and fall with each change in the rain's intensity. We hiked along the bank the entire time and made several waist- to chest-deep crossings without incident.

Through May and June, I became even more adept at backcountry travel. It never got dark, but I took a flashlight when I went hiking. Sometimes I patrolled the park solo, leaving the visitors' center in my scratchy grey uniform and riding the backpacker's bus to my favorite drop-offs. Tourists would point at my gold badge, and I could see admiration—and confusion—in their faces. I could tell they were trying to piece together how a girl like me ended up with a job as scary and important as a Denali backcountry ranger. As we bumped down the ninety-mile road to Wonder Lake, I'd mind my own business, but inevitably someone would wobble to my perch near the back of the bus, slide into the nearest empty seat, and ask, "Are you a ranger?"

Folding my arms across my chest, I'd say, "Yep."

"What are you doing?"

"Going out on patrol."

By now, several people would be listening.

"You're going alone?" one would ask.

"Seems that way," I'd say.

"But what about all the bears? And aren't you afraid you'll get lost?"

I took my time answering, aware that by now the whole bus was rapt. But I knew I had the time to string them along. The one-way ride to Wonder Lake took six hours, longer if that particular bus driver stopped every time he or she saw a ptarmigan on the side of the road. Forty people would cram against the windows trying to snap pictures of the fluffy brown bird. I'd hang back, making it obvious that I'd seen more than my share of ptarmigans—as well as golden eagles, wolves, and lynx. When the photo op ended, I'd wait for the tourists to resume our conversation, then answer their questions.

"I'm not afraid," I'd tell them. "Because Denali bears are used to people. No one's ever been killed by a grizzly in this park. Just let them know you're coming and they'll usually steer clear. Of course, store your food properly, and never run if one of them charges, but other than that, no problem. As for navigating, that's even easier. The park road runs east to west. The Alaska Range lies south of the road, and all the rivers run south to north. It's big and wide and goes on forever. Beyond that, I don't know anything."

20

Love, Actually

I t would take another year before I could finally extricate myself from Colin's clutches and serve him divorce papers enough times for him to realize I was serious. After the blowup in Talkeetna, he followed me to Denali, but I continued to assert that our relationship was over. He lived in our cabin, even though it technically belonged to me. I did everything I could to remove him, including calling the police and trying to get a restraining order, telling the Department of Immigration that he was working without a visa, and barging in on him at unexpected moments. In the end, I left Alaska altogether and embarked on a six-week trip to South America.

When I returned, a friend named Julia offered me a place to live with her and her sister in Winter Park, Colorado, a small, noncommercial ski town seventy miles from Denver. It was separated from Interstate 70 by 12,000-foot Berthoud Pass. The first time I drove the pass, on New Year's Day 1998, a huge storm was raging across the Rocky Mountains. Avalanches ripped down the snow-loaded faces, covering roads and closing them. Fortunately the road on I traveled stayed clear long enough for me to get to Winter Park.

On the night I arrived, a guy named Greg gave me a free lift ticket to go skiing. On the second day, I rode the lifts from nine to four and found my new calling. On the third day, I went to the season pass office and bought my first all-access season pass. I skied every day that winter, after finishing my job at the local bagel shop, pouring coffee for tourists and smearing cream cheese on round bread. Colin followed me to Winter Park, and for a brief period I lived with him again. But I quickly realized that there was nothing worth salvaging between us, so I moved in with Julia's younger sister, Melanie. Melanie gave me a couch to sleep on, friendship and love, and the encouragement I would need to leave the toothless dog musher once and for all.

By February of 1998, I felt like the world had given me the gift of freedom. The previous October, I'd left Alaska to spend six weeks bike touring through Ecuador. Traveling with an audio digital recorder, I reported stories from my journey and sent them back to Talkeetna. The stories focused on everything from the food we ate—boiled fish with bulging eyes—to a women's prison where mothers were raising their babies, and were so popular that the local radio station agreed to run the whole series twice.

I was finally beginning to take my writing more seriously. Over the next few years, between going to school at the University of Alaska and then, later, the University of Colorado, I'd get a degree in English with an emphasis on creative writing. While living in Winter Park, I'd start writing for the local paper. Stories in publications like *Climbing, Skiing, Outside,* and *Powder* followed—all of which solidified my belief that I possessed the skill, voice, and life experience to become a professional journalist. It would happen, and at a rate I couldn't believe.

But on that day in February, I wasn't writing or even thinking about writing. I was standing in the Berthoud Pass parking lot getting ready to go skiing. Ten inches of new snow had fallen, and my friends were itching to get going. I was attaching my avalanche transceiver, which lets people know your location if you get buried in a snow slide, when out of nowhere, a fluffy black malamute head-butted me in the side. He was running around the parking lot, chasing his own tail. It took me a while to place him, but I knew I had seen him before. Alaska. Cold beer. A boy with scraggly hair and eyes the color of blue glass. Wait! The malamute was Tank Edmondson, and Tank Edmondson was Shawn Edmondson's dog!

"Tank!" I shouted. "What are you doing on the top of Berthoud Pass?"

Snow was falling in big, fat flakes, piling up on steep slopes lined by dark green trees. All around me, giant mountains towered above a sleepy postcard valley, where I had now acquired a handful of ski buddies and friends. Almost daily, we loaded up in someone's car, drove to Berthoud, and skied laps through untracked powder, which billowed up like clouds of smoke around our chests.

Tank waddled back, his huge black tail wagging his massive black body. I kneeled down and scratched his forehead but immediately began scanning the parking lot. Heat crawled up through my belly, settling in my neck and cheeks. Somewhere in this lot was the sweet, handsome boy I'd dreamed about since leaving Talkeetna.

"Tracy Ross?" shouted a voice from across the parking lot. "What are you doing in Colorado petting my dog?" I followed the voice until I spotted Shawn. He was dressed in navy blue ski pants, a bright yellow raincoat, and big, black ski goggles, but even in all his layers I could see the outline of the body that made my insides quiver in Talkeetna. The closer he got, the more I had to fight the urge to run up and hug him.

"What are you doing here?" he asked again. "And where's Colin?"

I didn't tell him that Colin had followed me because I knew right then and there that within a matter of days I'd be ending things for good. I would follow the advice of Julia and Melanie, who would tell me to confront him in public. I would take him to a restaurant so we could discuss things "out in the open," and tell him, adamantly and decisively, that I wanted a divorce. When his voice started to rise, I would look around and say, "Do you really want to scream at me in front of all these people?" Then I'd pack my things and move in with Melanie, a photographer who once ran the photo desk for the Midwest bureau of *Time* magazine.

Shawn and I circled around each other, smiling.

"So what's up? How are you doing? Are you here alone?" he said.

My heart pounded and my head buzzed. "Colin's here, but it's over between us. Do you want to go skiing?"

On our first date, Shawn and I skied from the opening of the lifts at nine a.m. until the closing, at four. We ducked in and out of trees and hit wind-lips until our legs could barely support us. Shawn flashed through the spruce stands so fast I could barely see him. But every few minutes he'd stop, call out my name, and make sure I was still with him.

We spent the entire winter skiing, riding the lifts or hiking up the steep, windblown slopes surrounding Berthoud Pass. Shawn knew where the wind deposited snow in deep, buttery pockets that were also relatively safe from avalanches. We skied together every second we could, learning about each other in the place we both felt most alive and comfortable.

I don't know when, but at some point early in our relationship, I told Shawn about the abuse. We were probably skiing, because I wouldn't have wanted to make it into a big deal. I thought he needed to know, in case we were planning on taking our relationship further. When I told him, he responded with the same low-key, not-a-deal-breaker attitude with which I'd presented the information.

I'm glad that when he heard, he didn't fly off the handle and pretend like he wanted to kill my dad. I never wanted him to bare his chest and beat it on my behalf. Maybe I'd gotten used to no one truly caring about my wounds; maybe I only wanted to tell him so that when I fell into my inevitable sadness, which still hit me unexpectedly even though I'd surrounded myself with so much love and beauty, he would know that I and my history were the cause of it—not him.

That spring, I was going back to Denali. My ranger job awaited, and nothing could keep me from it. Shawn hadn't applied for jobs in Alaska and had a good job working for an excavation company in Winter Park. We'd loved spending the winter together, but both of us were adamant about not "diving in" to a relationship. Still, when the ski season ended, neither of us was in any rush to extinguish what we'd only begun.

At some point that winter, my parents had bought me a round-trip ticket from Las Vegas to Alaska, I think to ensure that I'd come visit them before I left the Lower 48 again for who knows how long. So Shawn offered to drive me down from Winter Park. We left in early April and stopped when we got to Crested Butte, Colorado.

The resort offered free skiing at the end of each season, so we hit the slopes, skiing terrain I never would have imagined possible before that year. We rode the Poma lift and picked our way through no-fall cliff bands and 40-degree faces. Shawn said I was the coolest girl he'd ever met and took a picture of me doing a spread eagle off a jump. I watched him launch off rocks and straightline his skis down cliff-peppered slopes, wondering how I had gotten so lucky.

We spent our nights sleeping in the back of his pickup. It was freezing, so we zipped our bags together. We'd roll around, creating sparks big enough to start a wildfire, then lie side by side, staring up at the constellations. I should have frozen in my 15-degree bag when the temperature dropped to near zero, but with Shawn beside me, the heat trapped in our sleeping bags never left us.

We kept telling each other love was for losers. I said it was stupid, and Shawn said that if you had to tell someone you love her, you really didn't. We kept it up all the way through Colorado and into Utah and then Nevada. The land transitioned from sky-scraping peaks to red-mud hoodoos to bleached ocean-bottom-like desert.

It was there, in the desert, on the eve of Shawn's departure to Colorado and mine to Denali, that we finally said the three words we pretended to scorn. We said them almost at the same exact moment. Salty tears streamed down our faces as we tried to come to terms with separating from one another. Mine stopped when Shawn told me that in a couple of weeks he was following me to Alaska.

Shawn and I were always in a live-or-die situation. At least that's how it seemed, our first summer in Alaska.

At my cabin alone, we counted ten grizzly bears wandering through the devil's club past the front porch. Thanks to Colin, the cabin door was a piece of reinforced plywood, and the windows were Plexiglas insulated with Styrofoam cutouts. The door's lock was a piece of bungee that attached to a driftwood handle. One day, Shawn and I heard whimpering under the house—my sled dog Merlin's litter of puppies. When we looked outside, we saw a giant grizzly sow with twin two-hundred-pound adolescents. We opened the door and stood on the porch, because, without a gun or even supposedly bear-repelling pepper spray, if the bears wanted, they could have pushed down a wall and eaten us. Each time the puppies whined, the bears came closer. Each time they came closer, Shawn and I shouted them off. Eventually Merlin returned from eating a neighbor's garbage, at which point the bears lost interest in the puppies.

If we'd had an animal totem that summer it would have been the grizzly. They found us everywhere we went. On a river trip down the remote East Fork of the Chulitna River, in our tiny, inflatable raft, we drifted past three, all walking on the silty banks. This time we carried a loaner rifle, but neither of us ever thought to grab it. Vulnerable as babies, grizzly finger sandwiches, we floated silently, back paddling away from the shores they walked on, each hoping the bears wouldn't notice us.

When we'd finally had enough close-call encounters with grizzlies, we went on one final adventure: this time to the no-bear zone of the snow- and ice-covered Alaska Range, which one of my bosses at the park agreed to let me use as a "patrol." With three other climbers, we took a bush flight into the Ruth Amphitheater, near a tiny stone hut constructed on a pile of rocks in the middle of the glacier called the Mountain House. Shawn and I had little climbing experience, so we put our trust in two dudes from Telluride, Colorado, who knew how to travel as a rope team across the Ruth Glacier's gaping crevasses.

The trip was plagued with problems from the beginning. It turned out our "guides" didn't have all that much experience. We made it through the crevasse fields safely, but when we tried to climb Pittock Peak across from the famous Moose's Tooth, we encountered hip-deep sugar snow melting on top of featureless black granite. If the snow had slid, we would have fallen to our deaths.

We retreated just as our pilot was flying overhead trying to make contact. But our radio was shoved in the bottom of someone's pack. Later, we'd learn that he was trying to signal us, to tell us that bad weather was coming, which would shut down flights into the amphitheater. Instead, we retreated to a place called 747 Pass, where, within hours of setting up camp, the temperature rose, the clouds socked in, and the mountains started "shedding their skin" in avalanches like you can't believe. Through the haze of clouds we could hear them ripping in every direction around us. We thought ourselves safe because we knew we were on an island. But we didn't know when or if they'd stop, when or if we'd be able to retreat to safety.

For three days we sat in our tents, worrying. I felt bad for our tentmate Julia, who suffered the sound of Shawn and my smooching to pass the time. As the days before our eventual pickup passed and the tension in our group rose because we truly didn't know if we'd make it out or get buried by an avalanche, Shawn and I never argued once. Since then, we've been in more than our share of killer fights that have taken us to the brink of divorce and scared our kids so badly we've made them cry. But we always manage to get back to the foundation we built in Alaska.

Shawn and I married in Winter Park on July 10, 1999, in a meadow overlooking the Continental Divide. Patches of snow still clung to the mountains, which shimmered in the thin, high-altitude air. For as far as the eye could see in every direction, giant, bald peaks fanned into the distance. A red-tailed hawk skimmed the meadow, searching for dinner. Lily pads floated on the surface of a pond that someone had dug to attract small birds and animals.

Though the forecast had called for afternoon thunderstorms, the weather held, bright pink and sunny, until after the ceremony, when we turned up the music and started to dance. I wore a long, cream-colored gown with a modest bustle in the back. Shawn wore a smart green suit. We both had grass stains on our bare feet.

Mayz officiated, standing between Shawn and me, the three of us contained in a circle of family and friends. In one of the photos, her hand has just fluttered up to her heart in response to the vows we wrote each other, which were tender and aching and true. But what doesn't show up in pictures is the impact she had on me just hours before the ceremony, the message she shared that dampened the happiness I forced myself to exude outwardly. It was so awkward and disturbing, it almost made me call the wedding off.

In the years since Dad and I had driven down the Alcan, his apologies had become more flagrant and heartfelt. But he still talked euphemistically about "hurting me" and "making my life difficult." On the surface, I'd played like we'd made amends, but underneath my gracious exterior I still burned. The flames of my anger often licked at both of my parents; the previous March, however, they had flared up at my mother.

"You're going to let your dad give you away, aren't you?" Mom had asked. She'd come to Winter Park to help me pick out napkins and a real wedding dress. Unlike my wedding with Colin, this one would be a big, serious ceremony. But even though my dad and I were on decent terms, I refused to let him hand me off.

"Let him give me away?" I exploded. "If he were going to *give me away*, don't you think he would need to *have had* me in the first place? I hardly think either of you have done *anything* to deserve the *honor* of giving me away."

Mayz had watched me level my parents, who'd driven six hundred miles and spent hundreds of dollars to make my wedding a special event, for two days. I could tell my behavior was making her sick, but I couldn't help myself. In the midst of all this holiness, I wanted my parents eighty-sixed.

Now, two hours before the wedding, Mayz wanted to have a heart-to-heart. We sat in the parking lot of the salon, where several girlfriends waited to watch me get my hair and makeup done.

"Tracy, there's something I need to say."

A pang of guilt stabbed my gut. *My behavior.* Mayz had seen the worst of it and I was fully expecting her to call me out.

"I know. I've been a monster. And I feel bad about it, okay? Don't worry, after the wedding I'm going to apologize for everything. I promise. But can we just not talk about it now?"

Mayz reached over and grabbed my hand.

"Tracy, honey, I need you to listen. This is not about your mother. It's about you. And Shawn. And Don."

I turned to face her, expecting another blessing, a final invocation of grace. But Mayz was finished with blessings.

"Tracy . . ." she said. "You are going to be given a moment. I don't know when, but a door is going to open. You're going to be given a chance to give your heart completely to Shawn. The door is going to open, and you're going to walk through it. You're going to be given a chance to forgive Don."

Up the road, a dozen friends were setting tables and arranging bright flowers in a circle on the lawn. Two sets of relatives had driven hundreds of miles before winding up and over Berthoud Pass, bearing gifts. Mom, Dad, and Chris stood in the crowd, smiling awkwardly, anxious to see the daughter-sister-bride. I was feeling guiltier by the second because I hadn't relented and agreed to let my dad hand me off to my new husband. And now Mayz had stuck me with the heavy burden of God.

When she was finished, Mayz got out of the car and went into the salon. I sat there for twenty minutes, maybe more. At first I thought, *Screw you, Mayz—and your "mystery."* And then I thought of a way to get around the hard part. I would be brave, and walk into the circle where Shawn and I were to be married even though I felt like the lowest life form on the planet. I would smile and pretend that I was having the time of my life. I'd never let on that Mayz had almost ruined it for me, with her ill-timed prophecy or whatever it was. If and when I encountered Dad, I would say *I forgive.* That way, I could forgive the *situation,* which may, or may not, include him.

That's how I decided, at the last possible moment, to walk into the center of the circle, where Shawn was waiting to promise me love, support, and protection for the rest of my life.

21

Shooting Stars
(or Birth Stories)

S hawn and I spent the first year of our marriage skiing, thinking about skiing, or dreaming up ways to ski more often.
Five days a week from December through April we arrived at
the lifts in time to hear the first avalanche bombs detonate, then
ripped through stands of timber until the sun set. We fed our hab-
its by working low-wage jobs at Winter Park Resort. Come summer, we returned to Alaska, where Shawn continued to raft guide
and I worked at Denali. But when autumn came, we circled home
to Winter Park. It was there that our first son, Scout, was conceived, in a big lonely basin just below the Continental Divide.

It was late August, a year and month after our wedding. We'd
thrown our sleeping bags in a meadow full of columbine husks.
Though we knew it could snow at any moment, we carried no
tent; just our bags, zipped together and reeking of woodsmoke,

wilderness, and sleep. Because we were in a basin, the sky created a giant dome around us, framed in by the bald mountains of the divide, the dark, craggy cliffs jutting here and there, and the trees fifty feet high and crowded together like people at a silent wake. Sometimes we thought we could hear a train whistling down in the valley, but it could just as easily have been the wind, kicking up somewhere near Tabernash and wrapping over the Divide.

I remember the feel of Shawn's body, tight and lean, with broad freckled shoulders and a skier's ripped torso. This was when we hardly ate and kept ourselves mildly dehydrated at all times because we believed it could curb our hunger for food. This was when we wanted to be hungry only for each other and despised the thought of excess flesh coming between us. In the dark we pressed our bodies together, chest to chest, hipbones knocking, attempting to dissolve into one person.

We had been talking about babies, even as we'd wound down the Alcan Highway on our way home from Alaska. Shawn wanted to be a father because his own dad had failed so miserably. A violent alcoholic and product of Vietnam, he had run out on Shawn's mother when she was still pregnant with his little sister. Shawn was looking for karmic comeuppance: he wanted to spirit a family across the West, read Ed Abbey to his children while they camped in the Escalante Desert, stargaze and fly-fish, build snow caves they'd actually sleep in. More than anything, he hoped to spend a few more summers in Alaska, where he could teach his kids the value of hard labor, independence, and good friends.

There was a huge barrier to his plans for fatherhood, however. I knew that if I had kids, I would just screw them up. Not only did I have plenty of parent disqualifiers—I drank beer while driving, dabbled in hallucinogens, and could live for weeks out of a truck—I was also the product of abuse. According to the National Criminal Justice Reference Service, this made me five times more likely than the average person to inflict the same horrors on my own kids. Thanks to Dad, I was statistically doomed not only to hug my babies when they were crying, but to console them by putting my hands down their underpants.

Having babies and caring for them was for someone loving and stable, with a stomach for carnal intimacy that included breast feeding, diaper changing, and, in some cases, placenta eating. That someone was not me.

Apparently, though, none of this mattered to Scout.

That night, high above the Continental Divide, he was already winging through the autumn sky, crossing the Pleiades and the other constellations, his star form dead or currently dying. When he saw me lying in a field of columbine husks, he thought I looked like the perfect place to stop his trajectory and settle in. Burning hot and full of energy, he dropped into my belly, ready to become a boy.

Nine and a half months later, the day after Mother's Day 2001, Shawn and I drove to Steamboat Springs, Colorado. At thirty-eight weeks pregnant, I felt bigger than a helium balloon. Brimming with water, blood, and adrenaline, I knew that I was carrying a baby boy.

We cruised past the cattle ranches in Kremmling and the bald eagles perched on tree branches along the Colorado River. Tank and my sled dog Merlin rode in the back of the truck. Today's plan was to hike, for hours maybe, after we met with our baby doctor, whom we already knew would be flippant and terse. A small-town obstetrician with time to kill, Dr. Schaller didn't seem to care that I'd gained thirty-five pounds despite obsessive overexercising and undereating.

At the clinic, a nurse came into the exam room, all smiles and questioning.

"How are you feeling?"

"Good, good."

"How are the contractions?"

"Good, I think. I'm not sure I'm having them yet."

"Are you nervous?"

This one I had to think about. Nervous wasn't the right word. Mortified, yes. Uncomfortable, certainly. A tankard moving through a sea of molasses, farting and burping and suffering fat ankles, esophagus burns, and hemorrhoids, hell yeah. Oh, and did I happen to mention that pregnancy had brought with it the added benefit of making me profoundly emotional? "I guess we're nervous." I said. "Who wouldn't be, right?"

Shawn slipped his fingers through mine and smiled weakly. We were both scared out of our minds, because of the unknown, because we were small and young and unsure of ourselves, and because we'd decided—weeks earlier, after the first Lamaze class— that we'd rather wing the birthing process than hang out with a bunch of fat, boring pregnant people who would give up everything they love to become parents.

We are not like them, we told ourselves. *We are strong, free, and independent! We are so connected to the rhythms of the earth that we don't need Lamaze! Let's go skiing instead!* (What we really meant—

what I meant, and Shawn went along with it—was that I was so sickened by the thought of focusing on my "area" in front of other people that I would rather have blundered my way through childbirth than sit in the living room of the local sheriff and listen to his wife say things like, "cervix," "perineum," and "vagina.")

It states in my personal rule book that I never, ever discuss anything having to do with my period, ovulation, or contraception, and I remember wishing that everyone associated with my pregnancy had been given a copy so that they could do the same.

I had made a decision years ago to put a clamp over my sexual organs and seal the edges with a blowtorch. While my dad ground his hipbones into me, I built plutonium-enriched shields over my breasts, vagina, and uterus. Psychologically, this had the effect of making me feel as fortified as an army bunker and toxic to the touch. Physically, it made me alternately numb and torturously sensitive.

But on that day in May, none of that mattered. What mattered was that I was thirty-eight weeks into one of the least-prepared-for pregnancies in history. And sooner than I could imagine, I was going to have to coax a baby through an area so foreign to me it might as well have been the moon. Back in the doctor's office, the nurse wrapped a blood-pressure cuff around my fat upper arm, pumped the rubber ball, and counted my pulse with two fingers while my forearm turned purple. I practiced slowing my heart rate by holding my breath, smiling, and thinking of cherry Popsicles. When the red needle on the monitor stopped, the nurse frowned and made a note. She removed the cuff, rewrapped it, and pumped the ball again.

This time her fingers rested on the exam table, tapping the

crinkly white paper, tat-tat-tat. Her eyebrows strained toward each other as she waited for the result. When the needle paused, once on the systolic number and once on the diastolic, she wrote on her clipboard again. The third time she frowned, unwrapped, rewrapped, and pumped, I asked, "Am I dead?"

"Nooo, but did you bring your overnight bag?"

Oh, no. "What?"

"I'm just wondering if you came prepared to stay. It's a long drive back to Granby, and you might be here awhile."

Shawn and I looked at each other with hard, dilated eyes. We had no idea what this cryptic nurse meant, but we felt instantly like we needed to laugh, throw up, and cry, as it dawned on us that in a matter of hours, we would no longer be just Shawn and Tracy. We would be Shawn and Tracy and the baby we jokingly called Number Three until we saw him on the sonogram pictures and felt our hearts momentarily short-circuit, at which point we named him Scout. The nurse put the cuff next to me on the exam table and said, "Have a seat, both of you. You're not going anywhere."

Two hours later we checked into Yampa Valley Medical Center. Tank and Merlin were still sitting in the back of the truck. At some point, Merlin would manage to jump out the window and run wild through the streets of Steamboat. An excellent tracker taking advantage of our distraction, she would find a fresh pile of steaming horse manure and roll in it before being picked up by the Steamboat dog catcher and landing in doggie jail. Meanwhile, Dr. Schaller would have come to the hospital to recheck my blood pressure, which now read 140 over 88. This is a great blood pressure if you are a 250-pound sixty-year-old who dines regularly on cheese, butter, and beef. On an extremely active thirty-year-old it meant hypertension, which, left unchecked, could have been bad for Scout. We were staying in Steamboat until I pushed him out.

By the time Shawn called the dog catcher and realized Merlin had been locked up, I'd had my blood pressure taken for the fifth of possibly 120 times. I'd changed into a hospital gown that wouldn't close in the back because my stomach was too enormous. I'd called my parents, who were not invited to the birth, and Shawn's mother, Linda, who immediately began packing for a two-day stay. And Dr. Schaller had decided that induction was a good idea.

He asked me to lie back and spread my legs, good and wide, so he could see all the way up to my throat. He poked my cervix, which made me want to vomit, and then told me that I was days, if not weeks, from dilation. "You're not even softening," he said, and I thought, *No shit, I'm not softening. I will never soften. I am a lead shell of fear.*

Fortunately, there are drugs to take care of that. Dr. Schaller spread some magical softening cream on my cervix, placed a gel tab of labor-inducing Pitocin inside, and left the room. I was relieved he left but then worried about the contractions he promised would come. I switched on the television and waited for a python to squeeze my belly. I continued waiting but nothing happened. The nurse watched my blood pressure rise and fall, creeping into the danger zone and back out again without explanation.

Several hours later, Linda arrived from Denver. She planted herself on a wooden chair directly across from my bed; I could see her smiling over the tips of my feet. The next time Dr. Schaller came in (twelve hours later, with more Pitocin), Linda had a pervert's-eye view of my labia. Respectfully, she turned away, while the nurse checked me for softening. Hours of bad sitcoms passed. Linda smiled encouragingly, asked if I needed anything. I did: a temporary lobotomy. I began to retain water, taking it on like a capsizing boat. In photos I look like my brother, who weighed 220 pounds at the time. Sometime after midnight, I fell asleep to the muffled rhythm of Scout hiccupping in my belly.

The following morning arrived, and with it more devices, encouragement, and hope. Linda said, "This is the day, I know it!" And Dr. Schaller returned, carrying a long, plastic poker with a hook on the end. He explained that he would use the hook to break my water, which would kick labor into high gear. It took significant poking, but he persisted. With a sharp sting, my water bag broke, sending a burst of warm fluid down my inner thighs. Now the contractions would come, and with them, Dr. Schaller promised, a new boy.

He didn't lie. Within minutes of the manipulated water-breaking, the contractions arrived, violently and without warning, making me buckle in pain. Because of the induction, I was confined to bed, hooked up to a series of monitors that tracked my vital signs along with Scout's. All along, Scout had been a trooper, sleeping and gently swimming, moving a shoulder across my belly, jamming a knee into my spleen. I couldn't believe I would meet him in a couple of hours. I hoped he would like me as much as I already liked him.

Then—all of a sudden—there was trouble, as Scout's heart rate began to skip and flutter, weakening with each contraction. Summoned to my room, Dr. Schaller shoved an electrode into my uterus, fished around for Scout's head, and stuck a white pad sprouting red wires to his temple. The snake-squeeze contractions continued, but furtively. When the nurse checked my cervix for the umpteenth time, she frowned and said, "You have to relax." I wanted to relax, but I started to cry. Twelve hours after my water had been broken, I was dilated one centimeter. The nurse said, "Don't worry, one way or another, we'll get this baby out of you."

But I did worry.

I worried that I had made the shield too strong. I worried that even now, because of something my dad did twenty years ago, I was too damaged to experience this joy. How could I tell the nurse and Linda and Shawn that there was no way a baby could get past the clamp? How could I tell them that it is a medical impossibility for something so bright and beautiful to move through a place that is so black and blue?

In the end, I couldn't—tell them, or deliver Scout vaginally, even though for a few electrifying minutes, it seemed like I might. At 2:30 a.m., on the morning of May 18, 2001, I was overcome with the urge to push. At first I whispered it: "I need to push." And Shawn, unknowing, said, "Yes!" But something told me I needed Dr. Schaller's permission. I held off until I was overcome again and then shouted, "When can I push?! When is it okay to push?"

All at once, it was as if an alarm went off in my room. The nurse rushed out and ushered Dr. Schaller in. "Your cervix is hard as a rock," he said, stating the obvious. "If you push, you could rupture it, which could kill you and your son. What you have to do is wait and resist the urge to push, and maybe something will start happening.

"Then again, maybe it won't. There's no guarantee that you won't have contractions for several more hours and still never fully dilate. The baby is fine, we're monitoring him, but you've been going at this for days. You're exhausted. Your uterus is worn out. If you want to, we can take him by Cesarean. If you're rea—"

"I'm ready," I said, cutting him off and looking around for Shawn. He was standing right next to me, holding my forearm. "Is it okay if I'm ready?"

Shawn's eyes filled with tears. He squeezed my hand and nodded.

At three a.m., the sun has not yet poured over the horizon, and it's still dark enough to count a million stars. This was when I told Dr. Schaller to cut Scout out of my body. Shawn put scrubs on over his rumpled clothes and walked alongside the stretcher as they wheeled me to surgery. A curtain dropped in front of my face, so I couldn't see them making the incision, which is in the shape of a half-smile a few inches below my belly button.

On the operating table I felt the doctors digging into my uterus, rooting around for Scout. He was lodged deep in my pelvis, his shoulders in a tight, determined hunch. It took serious tugging, but they lifted him out of the blood and entrails and put him up to the light. He was the most perfect baby you've ever seen, except for one thing: when they held him in front of me, I noticed that the top of his head was pointed in the shape of missile.

He had only been trying to move out of my body and into the world.

He had been interrupted by damage already done.

248

Seventeen months later, on October 18, 2002, Scout's brother, Hatcher, was born with the same complications. Shawn and I tried for a VBAC, a vaginal birth after Cesarean section, at a hospital in Denver. Hatcher was two weeks late, and the weather forecast predicted heavy snowfall in Winter Park. When women go into labor in our former ski town, their offspring are often born in an ambulance screaming over Berthoud Pass. I called my midwife and told her it felt like my water might have broken. When she summoned us to the hospital, Shawn and I knew that the next time we came home, we'd be bringing a fourth member of our family with us.

A doctor induced me on the afternoon of October 16. Once again it didn't work. After two more tries, I finally went into labor while Shawn slept on a stiff, plastic-covered recliner in our birthing room. I thought I was going to be brave and open enough to let Hatcher slide into the world without incident. Even my obstetrician was optimistic. After I'd labored for several hours, he examined my cervix and said, "Looks great. Keep going. You should be having this baby within hours." Shawn called our parents with the good news. But then my cervix clamped shut, forcing Hatcher to be surgically removed from my body.

Not that any of this matters to Scout and Hatcher. Both of them believe that before they were babies gestating in my body they were shooting stars. The stars could see. They had eyes and they could think. They knew they wanted me for their mother; they knew Shawn was going to be their dad. Whether the boys were stars or not before they were babies, I believe they chose us for parents because we seemed just right. Not too much of anything. Wild but not gamey. Wounded just enough to sympathize. Younger than we should have been for all we'd been through.

"I'm going to tell you how this happened," said Scout.

We were sitting at the kitchen table a few days before Christmas 2005. The boys were coloring their birth stories on big pieces of white paper. Scout, who was four, had sandy red hair, lapis-blue eyes, and a smattering of freckles sprinkled across wind-burned cheeks. At three Hatcher was shorter and slighter, with auburn hair and skin that felt like warm milk.

The boys pulled dried-out markers and colored pencils from a shoe box, spreading glitter glue over planets penned in ink. Hatcher drew Harry Potter, who symbolized himself, in the middle of a starburst. When he was younger, Hatcher always drew Harry Potter. When we played Harry Potter, I was always Hermione.

It was just after lunch, and bright sunlight filled the kitchen. Scout and Hatcher were feeling light and special because I was coloring with them, a rare afternoon when I was not too distracted by *my plans, my dreams* to fall completely into theirs. We'd already been out skiing, cutting tracks across hard-crusted snow as we zigzagged through the woods that surround our house. Years ago, when I was pregnant with Scout, Mayz told me that my little boys would become my best friends, the playmates I'd always wished for but never had the good fortune to meet. I'm glad I didn't believe her, because they are so much more than that.

One day, when they are old enough to finally read this, I'll want my sons to know they rescued me. That even though I was terrified by their raw, needy bodies, I loved them the second I touched the silky hairs covering their rice-paper skin. Ever since they were born, they have forced me out the darkness and into a bigger, happier world. Before them, there was me. And I was lonely, even with Shawn. With them, there are puppies, and friendly postmen, and maybe God—plus strangers I realize it's okay not to talk to. With my sons come mystery and wonder, a universe of smells and sounds, and, mostly, their trusting faces whispering hilarious, zany secrets into my ear. When they do this, their cheeks are so close to mine that I can push out my lips and kiss them. Sometimes I do. And it's always okay.

In case I don't say it enough when they are little, I want Scout and Hatcher to know that despite the cloud that sometimes engulfs me, because of them, I am more *here* than I have ever been.

"Okay, tell me," I said to Scout, handing him a marker that smelled like a watermelon.

"So you were sleeping," he said. "And you had your mouth open."

"Yup, that's right."

"And Hatch and me, we were floating around in the sky. Were we the same star?"

"Nope. You were two separate stars."

"Were we stars at the same time?"

"I think you were. But you had probably never seen each other, the cosmos being so big and all. Plus, I'd say you were on a different rotation, because Hatcher was born in October and you were born in May."

"Were there other babies up there floating around?"

"I'm not sure. I bet there were, though, since if we go by your theory all babies choose their parents, and they could have been stars for millions of years before coming to Earth."

Hatch looked up from his picture, screwed his mouth to one side. His eyes are not green or brown but the color of humus in the spring when the ground is in thaw.

"So, we flew down into your mouth and then we went into your tummy?" he asked.

"That's what Scout says. I'm pretty sure that's how it went."

"Did you know when it happened? Like, did it burn you?"

"No, I didn't get burnt. But I'd say I knew when it happened."

I mean it when I tell them I remember. On the night Scout was conceived, though we knew it wasn't safe, Shawn and I didn't use protection. The ground was too cold. The air too clean. Shooting stars were zinging through the inky sky with amazing regularity. We made love like we meant it. And when the moment before the moment came, I told Shawn to stay where he was, inside of me. I'd even say my mouth was open, so that a star could actually have fallen in.

Hatcher, influenced by Scout, has been contemplating his own accidental arrival on the planet since he was three. At first I told the boys they had been angels before becoming our kids. But angels scare them in the same ways skeletons do: they signify death and the vast emptiness that will eventually envelop the great time we're having on Earth. Skeletons are less scary than angels, because angels, being formless, can't swim, or ski, or jump on the bed in their underwear. A shooting star, on the other hand, seems like a perfectly reasonable prehuman incarnation to Hatcher.

"I remember you," Hatcher said, hoisting himself onto his

elbow and leaning in close to my face. "I saw you waiting for me."

"You did?"

"Yes. You were just standing there. And then I surprised you! Flying into your mouth and down into your tummy." He was gaining momentum, building on the images flooding his brain.

"Then what?"

"Then you got fat and threw me up."

I couldn't tell Hatcher this because it would have disturbed him too much, but I would have preferred giving birth out of my mouth, even if it required extricating every tooth to make room for his skull, his shoulders, his feet. Cut out my tongue, fine, as long as you can put it back in. Snip the sides of my mouth—let that be my episiotomy. Dislocate the joints in my jaw. I would have done it to avoid the prodding and pulling, the hands-on examinations, the scrutiny and extreme focus of nurses and doctors, midwives and medical students, all seemingly injected into my life (not once, but twice!) to remind me of the six years my dad held me down and treated me like a motion-activated version of a Raggedy Ann blow-up doll.

You see now why the boys aren't the only ones who prefer the birth-by-star-vomiting story.

22

PTSD

At the wedding my dad told Mayz he'd received a miracle, and it's true. I'd said all three words: I forgive *you*. He and my mom immediately started patching things up. They held hands and went camping, later buying a brand-new bright silver Airstream they paid for with cash. My dad, who'd done well for himself selling natural gas to developers in Nevada, surprised my mom with diamonds buried in long-stem roses and fancy candlelit dinners on Lake Las Vegas. One time she even called to tell me they were rediscovering feelings for each other they hadn't had in years.

Dad and I talked on the phone like old friends too. We met at campgrounds and on barstools whenever work or play brought us in close proximity to each other across the West. Twice my parents returned to Alaska, to see more of what the fuss was about. And when Scout and Hatcher were born, my dad fell for them like a meteor shower.

He hadn't expected to love them so much, I don't think. And at first he was afraid. But soon they had replaced me as the brightest light in his diminished life. By the time Scout was walking, Dad was asking when he and my mom could come babysit for a week.

In the beginning I let them, believing that my dad would never touch a baby, especially my baby, after what he had done to me. I convinced myself that he had suffered enough and that it wasn't up to me to prolong his punishment. It was obvious that his life had been a long string of sadnesses and disappointments, and I felt obligated as his daughter to cheer him up. More to the point, opening old wounds was inconvenient. Everyone finally seemed so happy. I didn't want to ruin the high.

You'd understand my willingness if you could have seen how he held my boys, treating them as if they were precious and never letting them linger too long on his lap. They'd climb all over him, like little kids do, entirely unaware of where they were jamming their hands and feet. He let them smash his nose and smear their chocolate-pudding-covered hands all over his favorite Ralph Lauren polo shirts. But he was always searching my face for a sign of approval to assure him that, *yes, it's okay if you hold my children and whisper sweet nothings in their ears.*

This need for constant permission was a kind of currency for me, something I could hold against Dad when he did something I didn't approve of, like snap at me for leaving dishes in the sink, or lust after women in the casinos in Las Vegas. He knew, in some deep, primeval place, that he was on borrowed time and that one misplacement of a hand or finger on my sons could mean the end of our relationship.

Then one day, something changed. Scout was two years old and Hatcher was seven months. We'd taken them back to Redfish Lake because I thought it would be romantic to introduce them to my favorite place. Shawn was working a construction job, so he couldn't make the seven-hundred-mile drive from Boulder. In the soft light of summer's evening, I removed my sons' diapers and let them wade among tiny flickering minnows that flashed like silver paperclips between their chubby legs.

We spent the first few days of our vacation digging sand castles, hiking, and watching ranger programs at the outdoor amphitheater near Fishhook Creek. While my parents napped in our rented cabin, I loaded Hatcher in my kid carrier and held Scout's hand across a boardwalk that stretched over the wetlands of my youth. I knew the boys were too young to see the magic lingering beneath the mossy green logs at the bottom of the creek, but I hoped this trip would create an early childhood imprint that would make them want to go camping forever.

At first, all of us felt lazy and idyllic. But then Mom started to get restless. She said she wanted to drive to Sun Valley to go shopping, just her and me. Dad would stay in our cabin with the boys, pushing them around the gravel parking lot in their double jogging stroller until they fell asleep. It would be simple, Mom said, and a good test of my dad's grandparenting ability. I was uneasy but agreed. With two babies under the age of three, I took all the help I could get back then, especially when it came from family.

Mom and I made it fifteen miles down the road to Sun Valley before a vision in my mind made the air around me turn to ice. Without explanation, I skidded my dad's truck off the side of the road, spun an out-of-control U-turn, and sped back in the opposite direction.

Mom's eyes bugged out behind her glasses. "What are we doing?" she asked. I was so frantic I couldn't answer. Just jammed the gas pedal into the floor mat and screamed back down the highway.

"Tracy," my mom said again. "Where are we going?"

"Back to the cabin," I practically shouted.

"Why? Did you forget something? What's the matter?"

Fighting hot tears that were surging against my eyelids, I snapped, "Stop asking so many questions! I just have to go back. I'm worried about the boys."

"The boys?" she said. "Why would you be worried about them? I'm sure they're fine. They're with . . ."

She stopped speaking as soon as the realization hit her. I looked over and saw anger flash across her face. Her mouth dropped open, and I knew she was going to defend my dad. But for once she didn't try to talk me out of the sickening way I was feeling. She gripped her purse, nodded her head, and said, "I understand. Let's go back."

The image stayed with me all the way to the cabin, of my sons, lying on one of the beds with their diapers pulled down around their legs. They were crying and squirming, trying desperately to crawl away. Standing before them, I saw a man, also with his pants dangling off his hips. It was my dad, leaning over Scout and Hatcher.

Swerving into the gravel lot, I jammed the truck into park, not even bothering to lock it. I ran to the door and started pounding.

"Open up!" I yelled. "It's Tracy. Let me in!" Dad opened the door, looking surprised to see us.

"Hey Trace," he said nonchalantly. "What are you doing back here so soon? What'd ya do? Forget your wallet or something?"

Instead of answering, I tore past him, looking for Scout and Hatcher. The room was tiny, so I found them instantly. Scout was sitting in his portable high chair, sucking on a handful of Cheerios. When he saw me, he smiled and raised a grubby fist. Scanning the room, I found Hatcher lying on the bed in his diaper, drinking a bottle of milk. He smiled when he saw me, too, which caused the milk to dribble out of the side of his mouth.

Without looking at my dad, I unbuckled Scout and lifted him out of his high chair. With my other arm, I bent over and scooped up Hatcher. Pushing past both of my parents, I carried my boys out of the darkened cabin and into the bright Idaho sunlight. Kneeling because I could no longer stand, I smothered my sons in kisses. When I finally assured myself that they were happy and unharmed, I turned around and faced my father.

He stood in the doorway, slowly shaking his head. He started to speak, but I held out my hand to silence him. I knew that he was going to tell me nothing happened, but I didn't care about what he had to say. The last thing I wanted to hear was his voice, trying to overrule my instincts.

Dad didn't touch the boys, I'm certain of it. And the look of dread when he realized why I rushed back to the cabin still fills me with wrenching guilt. But on that day, the Earth shifted. I saw for the first time the risks I was willing to take to be my parents' perfect daughter. I saw the compromises I'd made to keep Mom and Dad happy, by being the well-adjusted, forgiving girl they needed to maintain the illusion that they had been redeemed.

If I am to be completely honest, I must admit that I was also still ruled by my own weakness. It takes time to sand away a wish that's carved into the stones of our psyche. All my life, I had longed for a happy, normal family. I'd convinced myself that my own memories were overblown; the truth couldn't possibly have been as terrible as I remembered it. At some point I assigned a number to the times my dad molested me: twelve. And I told myself that twelve times wasn't such a big deal. Millions of kids had suffered far worse. It was probably better if I stopped thinking about it. It took work, but I had managed to bury the past deep inside of me, especially when I was around my family. What else could excuse that feigned "forgiveness" I had shown my dad at the wedding? How else could I have spent more than ten minutes with my mom without trying to kill her? What emotional amnesia could allow me to let my parents babysit my precious little boys?

As I stood in the parking lot outside the cabin, I felt like a girl who had just been trampled by a herd of cattle.

The vision told me I was fast approaching my break point. I knew if my dad was going to stay in my life, everything had to change. I needed vindication. He had to explain what he had done to me as an eight-year-old, a fourteen-year-old, the child who trusted him and loved him beyond belief. He had to confess—not only to me but to my whole family.

It took some time, but after my outburst, I regained my composure. But for the rest of the trip, I kept Scout and Hatcher close beside me. Mom never asked me to go to Sun Valley again, and I never offered. When my sons were around my father, I didn't want to take my eyes off of them for a second.

23

Crash and Burn

A few years after Hatcher was born, I nearly died. It wasn't an almost-death of the body but an almost-death of the soul. Shawn and I were riding our mountain bikes on a trail near my cabin above Boulder when I missed a turn and skidded into the dirt. The sun was shining on tight blue buds that would soon flower across the hillsides. The boys were at home with a babysitter. And I was falling apart.

"I can't do this," I told Shawn. "I can't hold up the weight."

Shawn began untwisting my legs from my bike. "What do you mean?" he asked. "You were flying back there. You looked good."

Most things in my life were looking good. After Scout and Hatcher were born, I kept writing, first for the Winter Park newspaper and then later for *Skiing* magazine. When Scout was still breast-feeding, I traveled back to Jackson Hole, where I got to do a steep-skiing camp with a pro skier named A. J. Cargill. The following winter, with Hatcher nursing, I scored an assignment for

Outside Traveler, in which Shawn and I got to climb and ski a big couloir on Mount Heyburn, in the Sawtooths. All the while I was penning a weekly adventure column for the *Winter Park Manifest*. I barely made any money, but slowly and steadily, I was gaining respect as a journalist. In 2003, an editor at *Skiing* called to ask if I'd consider working on staff. I went to Boulder, applied for the job of associate editor, and got it. Shawn and I packed up the boys, bought a house, and moved to the mountains above town. For the next three years, I skied, hiked, and backpacked all over the country (as well as Canada and Iran) while honing my skills as a feature writer. Through it all I made enough money for Shawn to stay home with the boys.

We made our life on two wooded acres at eight thousand feet surrounded by the Roosevelt National Forest. Nearby, the Continental Divide snaked toward Wyoming and Montana. Black bears, mountain lions, and bobcats wandered through the aspens and ponderosa pine trees that provide shade—and hawk and songbird habitat—on our land. Scout and Hatcher spent their youngest years playing in a seasonal creek that swelled past its banks when the snow in the high country melted. During the summer, we sat on our deck watching stars shooting across the sky. In the winter, with snow blanketing the ground, we listened to a quiet so vast it created its own sound. And yet, despite all the joys of my home, work, and family, I still wasn't happy.

Despair and loneliness had chased me ever since my awakening in Idaho, and it got worse as I fell into normal familial patterns with my parents. I'd invite them—or they'd invite themselves—to Colorado, and I'd clear my schedule for their weeklong stay. The boys would barely sleep on the night before their arrival, knowing that they were bringing toys, goodies, and new pajamas for them to sleep in. For the first few minutes after they showed up, I'd feel an overwhelming relief that they'd made the drive from Las Vegas safely. But as soon as Scout or Hatcher climbed into my dad's lap, I'd feel like I wanted to vomit. Never once did I pull my sons off of him or ask my parents to leave early, but every time they visited, I would start counting the seconds until they left. I knew lots of grown kids had the same reaction to their parents or in-laws coming to visit, but I doubted many of them felt that way because of the abuse they'd suffered. The second my stomach started contracting, I would know that I shouldn't have invited my father anywhere near Scout and Hatcher. But I kept doing it—even asking him and my mom to babysit while Shawn and I went on short vacations—because I was afraid and selfish.

More and more, I also began to feel the deep, abiding betrayal of my entire family. Dad had created the lie, but Mom and Chris had let me carry it all. Never once did either of them ask me what had happened during all the years I'd been molested. In some ways, their refusal to ask was more painful to me than the actual abuse.

It came out at home, when I was playing with the boys or having sex with Shawn. With depression sapping my energy, I never felt that I could give any of them my full attention. Shawn's normal hunger for sex made me feel dirty and disgusting. Even though I was five foot five with a lean 125-pound body, I thought I was too ugly for even my husband to desire. As the years had passed, we'd been intimate less and less often. I tried to explain why I couldn't close my eyes and relax enough to enjoy the feel of his body, but as soon as I opened my mouth, I knew I couldn't say what I was thinking. I could barely admit to myself that twenty years after my abuse had ended, when I closed my eyes at the wrong moment, I still had flashbacks of my father.

In March of 2006, I stayed in bed for a week. Shawn put heavy wool blankets over the windows and kept the boys quiet, so I could sleep. For days, I lay under a mountain of covers, listening to my children playing in the woods. The music in their voices soothed me, but they also made me think of my dad. I let my mind stay on him, and the abuse, and the million chances I'd given him to fess up. And then, one afternoon, another vision changed my life.

In my mind I saw the shores of Redfish Lake, and on them, a trunk battered and half-buried in the loam. Autumn light slanted through the lodgepoles, and small birds flickered through the leaves. Though the trunk was locked, I could see inside it, the walls invisible to me. What I saw were several pairs of little girl's underwear, a pair of men's pants, and two pale yellow, soiled bed sheets.

As I stared at the trunk, I knew that there was only way I could unlock the secrets that still haunted me. If my dad wouldn't tell me the truth, I'd go seek it out myself. That day, I started plotting my return to the place my abuse began on a cool autumn evening in 1979. Going alone, I would return to Redfish Lake.

October 2006: I stood at the counter of River One Outfitters in Stanley, Idaho, waiting to pay for a map. Outside, the thermometer read 41 degrees. A man in a red flannel shirt stepped behind the cash register, sizing me up. "What's a pretty girl like you doing hiking alone?" he said.

"I'm prepared and conservative," I told him. But it was only a brave front. Though I'd done it—come back to the Sawtooths—I hadn't wanted to be on that trip. It was coming on three decades since my dad put his hands down my pants at Redfish Lake. During those years, I'd been to therapists, astrology workers, and priests. I'd even visited a psychic, who told me that going into the mountains with my abuser would be the most dangerous thing I would ever do. That's part of the reason I went back the first time on my own. I wanted to see if I could find the answers that I needed without the trouble of involving my dad.

My plan was to backpack—because I loved it—while opening myself to the memories I hoped would flood me if I returned to the scene of the crime. People had done that recently, after the World Trade Center bombings: put flowers at the location their loved ones were believed to have landed after leaping from the burning towers. In a sense, I was trying to mimic them. I wanted to find the child who had been traumatized near the streams filled with decaying salmon, and offer her a proper burial.

It was late afternoon when I finally started hiking, leaving the trailhead for Sawtooth Lake. I climbed through yellow aspen leaves and up switchbacks littered with scree. At a dead ponderosa, I took a picture of myself and my pack, a memento to prove to myself that I had actually done this. But as the sun began to fade, thoughts of wolves crowded my brain. I knew they'd been reintroduced to Idaho during the mid-1990s but that wolves in general don't attack hikers. But something about the trip, and my own heavy heart, made me see myself as the perfect prey for any predator. I found a campsite next to a small lake ringed by razor-edged mountains. I ducked into my tent, and burrowed into my sleeping bag without eating supper.

Through the night, I lay as still as possible, waiting for an epiphany to shock me. The memories came—of me in the camper bunkbed, of me running toward a bridge in my Tweety Bird night-gown. But no resolution. I tried hard to make myself remember the events that led up to the abuse, and to see if I had been a willing accomplice to them. My body had the same reflex it always had when I thought back to the tickle sessions or the mid-afternoon fondling. The hairs on the back of my neck stood up, my eyes clamped shut, and my mouth contorted around the words *No. No. Not me. Not you.* But answers to why it had happened? Only one person could provide them.

Condensation, caused by my breath clouding my small non-breathable tent, kept sheeting off the ceiling and falling onto my face. Tiny daggers of ice pelted me, forcing me to think.

Deriding myself, I said that my quest was in vain; that *I* was vain for leaving Shawn, Scout, and Hatcher and hiking alone into the Sawtooths. Going into the backcountry solo was stupid, of this I had proof: just two months earlier a congressman's kid had gone missing on a solo hike. A search was mounted with helicopters, volunteer ground crews, and rangers all picking and flossing the granite teeth. There'd been no sight of him until a search dog got onto—and then lost—his scent. I was acting as selfishly as he had, and the stark reality was that if something happened—a bad fall, for instance, or an aneurysm—I could never see my family again. Worse yet, I would leave them, as my own father had left me, in a state of shock and anguished bewilderment. I shuddered at footsteps I thought I heard outside my tent. I tried to console myself, but all I wanted was to go home to my husband and sons.

Just before dawn, I couldn't wait any longer. I slid out of my bag and shoved my still-frozen tent into my pack. Jamming my feet into ice-cold boots, I began running, revolting against my own need for answers. The people I passed on the trail looked at me like I was a madwoman, maybe because I was. I knew then that the next time I returned to the Sawtooths, it would be with my dad.

24

Return to Redfish Lake

For the first time in years, I am truly afraid. It's July 2007, and my dad and I sit at a picnic table on the far side of Redfish Lake. The boat we took to get here has left, along with the worried Texans who looked at my dad and me, shaking their heads. When we reached the edge of the lake, none of them bothered to help us. Even as they motored away, I thought I could hear their voices carrying across the water. "Where are those people headed?"

Today, my dad and I will hike through the yarrow-dotted hill-sides, stopping every minute for Dad to catch his breath. We'll walk along a river full of slippery green rocks. When we come to a place where the water rushes over a natural slide made of granite, we'll stop, so I can take off my hiking boots and slide fifty feet into an emerald green pool. Dad will stop, shoot pictures, and take a deep slug of Gatorade. After I swim, climbing from the water dripping wet and freezing, I'll sit on a rock a few feet from my father. An awkward silence will rise up between us when my dad offers—and then retracts his offer—to let me use his T-shirt as a towel to dry my skin.

Now we are heading into a mountain range that looks imposing and mean. When I talked to my dad months ago, separated by five hundred miles and a satellite signal, this trip seemed noble, necessary, and, in a twisted way, fun. This will be the first and last time we go on a multiday backpacking trip, just the two of us, in the place we love most on Earth.

I'm scared, because when I am with my dad, I am eight years old. We will walk for days up valleys covered in trees. We will camp in places so lovely we'll want to weep. Fish will rise to the surface of a dozen glassy lakes. And he might try to lie on top of me when I fall asleep.

"I've made some rules for myself," he announces, then rattles them off. "I won't ask questions. I won't speak out of turn. I won't be vulgar or too descriptive. I won't get pissed off at you."

I stare at him. *You won't get pissed at me?* I think. *What the hell is wrong with you?*

Instead of denigrating him, I remind myself that my father is sixty-four going on sixteen. A week ago, at a party in Utah, he tried playing on a rope swing that hung out of a tree. When he caught the edge of his shoe on a root, he held on and scraped himself over some rocks, rubbing the flesh off of his knees. Now the scabs are deep, dark red, and crack open when he walks.

We continue hiking until we reach the sign for Alpine Lake. We've covered five miles and gained 2,500 feet, but our next campsite is still a mile away and another thousand feet higher. Dad looks weary, like he could lie down with his pack on and sleep until morning. The trail is becoming steeper with every step.

At the fifth switchback, he's fallen fifteen minutes behind me and I consider waiting, then clip along at my own pace. I know Dad is getting older and is out of shape and that in his condition he could be back there somewhere having a heart attack. I keep walking until I reach Alpine Lake.

That night, we set up camp, eat dinner, and drink a gallon of water. I slip away, hiding behind a tree to change into a clean pair of clothes. My dad heads down to the lake and casts for rainbow trout. I scoot my sleeping pad as far from his as possible, until I'm lying in the corner of the one tent we brought to share.

Even on this hike, I am still willing to capitulate against my best interests, my own damaged instincts. My instincts were damaged, along with my boundaries and my sense of personal protection and self worth, when I was abused. Scientists now say that children sustain lasting nerve damage when they are physically or sexually mistreated. It's taken unimaginable strength for me to come this far in my relationship with my father. I'm not going to berate myself for conceding to sleep in the same tent.

Nor will I forget, as I put my dad through the interrogation that's coming, that he has always been my father. When my mom was in danger of falling apart completely, he swooped in and brought joy to our lives. I spent too much time as a child worshipping this man who stole my innocence and almost ruined me. But I can't help myself. The weak places in my heart tell me that he, too, has suffered.

I'll never know the urges that existed inside him, driving him to prey on a cherub-faced near-baby. But I have seen him pay for it every day of my adult life. I also know things about him now that make his actions toward me somehow more understandable;

before our trip, he told me that he had been molested as a child. An older cousin sodomized him at a family gathering when my dad was five. It went on for years, said my dad, but he didn't think he was scarred by it. "It taught me that sex wasn't something you should be ashamed of," he said. "It was how you showed your love."

Twisted or not, he now sees the damage that he has created in me. The fact that he and my mom stayed together means that he gets to watch his damage play out, daily, on the one person he claimed to love more than anyone else in the world.

I know that I should hate him. But however flawed, weak, unforgivable, revolting, or treacherous it makes me, I can't. For better or worse, I believed him the one time he cried over his crimes against me. It was in the car after a bluegrass concert when I was twenty. And before that—before everything—there were the years at Redfish Lake. I hold those early memories with care, knowing they are like pressed wildflowers: if shaken too violently, they'll turn to dust.

Still, the tent is a terribly uncomfortable place. And so, this too becomes a crime, because one of backpacking's greatest virtues is that it makes instant bedfellows out of strangers and friends. When else do we lie side-by-side under a star-filled sky separated by a thin piece of nylon and a few cubic inches of down? In the tents of my past, I have fallen in love and whispered my greatest longings and dreams. I've huddled with friends while lightning flashed just inches from our heads. We have wept and laughed until we peed our pants, knowing that in the morning, we will have created a shared history at 10,000 feet. This is one of backpacking's true beauties, beyond the stunning vistas and close encounters with wildlife: it creates an intimacy that transcends normal friendships and eludes even some of the best marriages.

This is the first time my dad and I will lie shoulder-to-shoulder since I was a teenager in Twin Falls. I will wear all my clothes and never really fall asleep.

The next morning, we pack up, eat breakfast, and head back down the switchbacks, which murder our knees. As we walk, my dad fills the silence I create. He reminisces about bird hunting with his friend Gary Mitchell and fishing for the eight-pound trout that used to feed on freshwater shrimp in Richfield Canal.

He sifts through his better memories, until we come to a big log on the side of the trail, where we break out our lunch. Then this: "I was sixteen the first time I killed a deer," he says. Bob Murphy and Gary were there, when a four-point buck "that would have been an eight-point by eastern standards" walked into the crosshairs of his gun. When Dad pulled the trigger, he got so excited he started shaking uncontrollably. It was buck fever, and he had it bad.

"You can hardly grab your breath," he says, grinning mischievously. "Just knowing that you can actually kill something—it's the height of excitement. It makes you weak in the knees.

"I got away from shooting does," he says, "after I killed one with a fawn." The fawn's cries echoed through the South Hills, and my dad couldn't stand the sound. So he put a bullet in its head.

We chat, nibble on sausage, and dry our sweaty shirts in the breeze. While they sway in the wind, we take off our boots and wade into a bottom-clear lake. The silence comes back, bigger than it has been all week. A giant rock leads into the water, then drops off like a cliff. The fish are rising now, and my dad is following the ripples out to the weeds that line the lake. Watching him, I rehearse different ways to interrogate him when the time comes.

So, Dad. When was the first time you . . .

. . . abused me? (Too clinical. This isn't an after-school special.)

. . . touched me? (Too tactile. Might make him fantasize about me.)

. . . completely fucked up my bearings? Yes, that's it. That's how I'll start the conversation when we get to The Temple and he's so tired he can't retaliate. I join him down by the water. "Feels warm enough to swim," he says.

Two days later, my dad and I finally reach The Temple. We're in the middle of the boulderfield that threatened to break us in half. Dad collapses the second we reach the altar. Sweat drenches his torso and his face looks punched and weak. Before we left the trail, he stopped to peer up at the stone minarets surrounding us. "Beautimus," he whispered. I heard the bones cracking as he craned his neck.

Crouching behind him on the altar, I dig into my pack. This is the moment I've been waiting for: when the truth will shine down upon us and the heavens will break open beneath the weight of a million white doves. I take out my Dictaphone, test the battery, and push record, beginning the interrogation I've waited twenty-five years to enact. I have only four questions. The entire conversation will take less than twenty minutes.

The Truth in One Act

[The lights come up on a rock in the middle of a boulderfield. Don, a once athletic man in his mid-sixties, sits slightly in front of his step-daughter, Tracy. She holds a reporter's tape recorder in front of his face.]

Tracy: So . . . this is going to be hard.

Don: It's okay.

Tracy: [Hands spread on the rock, absorbing its heat.] All I have are four questions. And I don't want to know details. Because I know. I was there. And so what is important to me is to know your version of the truth.

Don: [Nodding, looking down.]

Tracy: Okay. When did it start?

Don: [Clearing his throat] On a camping trip up here at Redfish. I had been drinking. I lied. I was tucking you in. My hands went to a spot, which surprised me, and I kept them there. But the severity—it wasn't that often at that age. Just periodically.

Tracy: But I was eight. Couldn't you see what that did to me and say, "Oh my God, oh my God, I did that. That was a mistake"?

Don: [Choosing his words.] A person who does what I did . . . you make things up. You don't think of the other person. You just need that closeness. If I had ever known how it would have affected you, I probably would have done something completely different.

Tracy: So . . . that day on the log. I wasn't upset?

Don: I don't think so. I don't remember. I was trying to cover things up. I had feelings for you. I thought of you as my fishing buddy. The only thing I could do was lie. I wasn't thinking of you.

Tracy: Just so you know . . . in case you were wondering . . . I was thinking about what would happen if I jumped in the river and died. [Starting to cry.] I was eight. That's so fucked up.

277

Don: [Tenderly.] No, it isn't.

Tracy: Yes, it is. When you're eight years old, you're a little kid. It wasn't a physical thing?

Don: Not then, but later I was put in a position where you were going through puberty. These were your teen years; you were probably twelve or thirteen. Your mother stopped being intimate. I leaned to you for closeness.

Tracy: Okay, okay. So mom wasn't interested in being intimate? Why didn't you go have an affair?

Don: That's what I shoulda done. By all means.

[A break. Tracy takes a drink of water, shakes her head. Stands up, sits down. Don looks across the valley. A hawk skims the trees.]

Tracy: Okay. Now, how many times did it happen? In various degrees of whatever it was. Coming into my room . . . whatever that was. Till it ended.

Don: Between twenty-five and fifty times maybe. You know, I never kept track.

[A long silence.]

Tracy: [Fighting tears.] Well, you must have felt like shit about that, right? I mean, I didn't want that, right? I wasn't a willing accomplice . . . right?

Don: You weren't a willing accomplice. I didn't expect you to be willing. I really felt screwed up. Why would I jeopardize my family like that? And I'm not using this as an excuse, but I was abused when I was real young.

Tracy: I know, Dad. You told me. Did you do it to Chris?

Don: [Quickly.] No, no. It's never boys.

Tracy: Okay, Dad. Okay. [Another long silence. The wind picks up, wrapping around the rock towers and pouring into the basin, blowing Tracy's hair in her face. A hawk finds a thermal and rises toward the clouds. It seems as if the conversation is winding down.]

Tracy: There's one more question, Dad . . . I have to know. Scout and Hatcher . . . What about them? Because people ask me. They say, "How can you let him stay with your kids?" And truthfully, I . . . I . . . I don't know what to say. If anything ever happened to them, I would have to kill you. I could never forgive myself. So why would I even risk it? Why put them in that position when I know what you're capable of doing to little kids?

[Don's eyes begin to water. He shakes his head.]

Tracy: I'm asking you again, Dad. If you ever had those thoughts toward my kids. I'd have to know that so you could never be with them again. Because they know. They feel. They're intuitive. They know when something doesn't feel right.

Don: [Still shaking his head. Looking Tracy directly in the eye for the first time throughout the whole conversation.] Trace . . . I haven't had those feelings for anybody, ever since.

Tracy: Since when?

Don: Since you. It ended when you left, when you ran away.

[They're both crying now. The wind has picked up.]

Tracy: So one day it was just . . . over?

Don: No, it's never over. You have those feelings, but they're just like this tape. It replays but you learn how to stop it. You learn how.

Eighteen minutes after I pushed record on my Dictaphone in July 2007, I ended my dad's and my conversation. I knew that I had heard all I could take. My dad sipped water from a clear, blue bottle, and I bent down and started loading my backpack.

We sat, listening to the wind scream along the ridge directly behind us, and before long, we both knew it was time to go. I struggled to stand up, because it felt like someone had cut open my chest and crammed it with boulders. Dad creaked into a standing position and for a second acted like he was going to hug me. I shook my head, and backed so close to the edge of the altar that I almost tumbled off it. From that moment on until we were back in Twin Falls, I made sure to keep myself out of my dad's arms' reach.

We recrossed the boulders beneath The Temple and then continued down the trail to our last campsite. When Dad asked how much longer I wanted to stay, I said, "Let's get the hell out of here." We packed our things and started hiking back in the direction we'd come from. I knew I'd walk all night if that's what it took to cover the fifteen or so miles back to the boat ramp. I also knew that if my dad and I missed the last shuttle boat of the evening, I would keep walking, circumnavigating the lake, until I was finally back among other people.

Dad and I drifted down the trail, barely speaking to each other. I didn't know whether to scream at him or thank him. Twenty-eight years had passed since he first abused me, and now, finally, I had the truth. I liked knowing that I'd caught his confession on my tape recorder and could now share it with anyone I wanted. But no matter how hard I tried to rouse myself into a feeling of lightness, my heart felt a thousand times heavier than when we'd started.

I knew my dad had done me a magnificent favor by being honest, but nothing could have prepared me for the things he'd told me. All my life I'd convinced myself that I was overblowing my abuse—that I was the selfish, melodramatic girl my parents, brother, and grandparents had always called me. But twenty-five to fifty nights of molestation? When I looked through family albums from the years I was abused, I saw a girl who, though awkward looking, was often smiling. Not once did I see the strained smiles or tear stains I'd imagined I would. Two years later, when I asked my dad to decode my apparent happiness, he said, "You didn't suffer as much as you could have. I drugged you with your mother's sleeping pills."

I reeled from him in horror.

"What?" I choked.

"I knew from what happened after the trailer that you wouldn't be able to handle what I needed to do. I gave them to you at night, when you were already groggy from sleeping. I'm sorry, Tracy. I was sick."

So much for the oft-touted "closure." That revelation is the thousand pound weight I now carry around my neck. It turns out the truth doesn't quite set one free. But would I rather know the full story? Yes, absolutely. This disclosure turns my dad into a premeditated predator, not "just" the admittedly sick individual he had to be to molest a child. But now I understand my sleepwalking through so many years, the phantoms that formed in the shadows around me.

All along I'd thought that my dad's confession would be my ultimate vindication—the moment in the movie when the colors fade and the beautiful music starts playing. Dad's revelation at The Temple wasn't anything like I'd expected. It only raised more questions. Some of them I knew would never be answered, because

I wasn't brave enough to ask them. Like how he'd been able to watch me suffer and still put his own needs first. Now that I was a mother, it horrified me that he could take a child's trust and twist it into a form of bondage.

Around dusk on the last evening of our trip, Dad and I descended the final switchbacks to Redfish Lake. Waves lapped against the boat dock, and crows argued in the trees. My dad removed his boots and stuck his toes in the water. I looked at his bare ankles and felt the urge to vomit. He smiled up at me and said, "Talk about a little piece of heaven," and I wanted to tackle him and throw him into the lake. My hands strained against my wrists, wanting to punch, scratch, rip his ears off. But I was too pathetic. I sat on the hillside above him and drew circles with my fingers in the dirt.

After a while the boat arrived, and we boarded it, shoving our gear into the stern. Dad clambered to the back and said, "Man, a beer is gonna taste good." I silently agreed with him, imagining the cold, yeasty liquid sliding across my tonsils. But my heart was plagued by a feeling that a much larger mystery remained.

Could I still forgive him? I moved past forgiveness into an acid understanding etched in pain. I had explored the perimeters of love, however warped, and saw that love could retain some value while wreaking destruction at the same time. There can be no resolution of my childhood suffering, but I have the best life I can dream of. My main goal is to protect my own children from such injuries to body and soul. I refuse to let past pain intrude on the present possibility of joy. Shawn, Scout, Hatcher, and I all share the beauty of wilderness, the adventures that helped save me. My sons are spirited, outspoken, and instructed on the dangers of pedophiles. Shawn is a kind, compassionate companion, and my job is the envy of everyone I know.

But where to go, how to be, with this new information? Before the hike, I had started to accommodate my parents into my children's lives, allowing them to babysit, have unchaperoned access to my sons. That ended with the word "drugged." For months after hearing it, I severed all ties.

Love cuts with a serrated blade, and there are shreds of my feelings that form an unbreakable bond to my parents. They're getting older and weaker. I now see them, but rarely, on special occasions. At those "holidays," the damage between us floats like static electricity. I never let my parents watch my kids alone and try, diplomatically, to keep space between the boys' bodies and my father's. When my parents depart, I turn to Shawn, Scout, and Hatcher and know that though I've just compromised I've been a better, more protective mother. So maybe there is peace, however hard won.

I often think back on the last morning of Dad's and my father-daughter journey—how we packed up, stopped at a bakery for coffee, and left for Twin Falls. I listened to my favorite Neko Case album, *Fox Confessor Brings the Flood*, three times in a row. As we drove south, I could see the Sawtooths receding behind me. I thought it was nice that for the first time in a long time, my dad didn't ask me to change the music.

Two hours later, Dad dropped me in Twin Falls. As he drove away, the more lasting impact of my journey began to percolate up into my consciousness. Over four days in July, I had retraveled the fateful path of my eight-year-old self's last innocent trek into the Sawtooths. I'd passed the signposts of my past—Russian John hot spring and the ranger station on Highway 75.

This time, I noted the small wooden sign, barely visible from the overlook on Galena Pass. Through a camera lens you might not even notice it, dwarfed as it is by the mountains. But if you know where to look, you'll find that sign, and below it, a tiny spring buried in overgrown grass. The narrow silver streak of water trickles upward—the headwaters of the River of No Return. It seeps out of the earth, gathers volume and speed, and becomes so fierce one hundred miles from here that it cuts a trench in the earth a thousand feet deep.

People say the river was named this because the current is so strong it's impossible to travel upstream. But when I was a little girl, I stood on the banks watching sockeye salmon struggling toward their ancient spawning grounds at Redfish Lake. Nine hundred miles from their starting point in the Pacific, they arrived redder than overripe tomatoes, their flesh already breaking apart.

In the early 1970s, thousands of fish returned here to lay their eggs and die. Then we put in dams along the Columbia and Snake rivers. By 1975, eight concrete dams stood like barriers between the Pacific Ocean and Redfish Lake; by 1995, the sockeye population had dwindled to zero. Many people took this as a sign that the world had become too corrupt for something as pure as native salmon to exist. I might have believed that, too, until the summer of 2007, when four Snake River sockeye made it home.

The ultimate irony began to buoy me—in that same year, I, too, had reversed the trip. I had managed what the river declared was impossible. Just like those salmon, I had fought my way upstream on my own impassable river. Now, it was time to return to my real life and see if I could carry out my own, new equilibrium.

Not long after my trip, I was schooning down the Snake River in a boat with Mayz Leonard and her family. It was evening, the air was warm, and blue-and-purple dragonflies darted in the pale, tall grasses. Giant whitefish rose to the surface of the water and swallowed clouds of gnats and mosquitoes. The mud on the river's edge smelled like life—and a million years of granite and volcanoes. To our sides, the blocky walls of the Snake River Canyon rose skyward. And stretching between them, like a silver thread nearly five-hundred feet feet above the water, was the Perrine Bridge.

BASE jumpers now flock to the bridge to climb onto its steel railing and leap off over the water. Twenty-three years ago, I would have died jumping off the bridge. If I had been lucky, my body would have floated up against the lava-rock-cluttered embankment, so that everyone would know I was not some runaway but a girl with too much pain to continue living. But when BASE jumpers leap, they free-fall for several seconds and then pull a cord attached to a small parachute. Using risers to control their direction, they hover over the water and then land in the scraggly bushes at the river's edge. We drove the boat until we were bobbing directly below the bridge and the jumpers. I found it beautiful to sit with Mayz's family and watch the bodies floating toward us.

It looked effortless, the way they drifted on the wind currents rising off the river, but I knew that they'd taken measures to protect themselves from danger. With their parachutes, they could have the experience of flying and still know that they were in for a safe landing. As I watched them, I began to realize something about my own experience.

I put myself in the shoes of the BASE jumpers, who—unknown to them—were flying off the first great turning point of my life. I realized that although I had just done something life threatening in the Sawtooths, I'd been my own protector. And I thought that maybe, after all these years of looking for someone else to save me, I had finally become my own salvation.

Author's Note

I've recounted the events in this book as I remember them; they are my memories, told from my point of view. Others may remember events differently, but I have tried to be honest, fair, and accurate on all counts.

Acknowledgments

This book never would have happened without the early support and encouragement of two outstanding editors: Jon Dorn, editor-in-chief of *Backpacker* magazine, and Peter Flax, editor-in-chief of *Bicycling*. Together, they took an incredible risk sending me to Idaho three times to report the magazine version of *The Source of All Things*. Their deep care and exquisite editing led to that story winning the National Magazine Award, and to my eventual meeting of both my agents, Todd Shuster and Lane Zachary, and my book editors, Dominick Anfuso and Leah Miller. I don't have words to express the bottomless gratitude I feel for Lane and Todd, who did more work on my behalf than any person should ever have to, and bolstered my confidence over and over when I believed I couldn't do this. Dominick and Leah provided encouragement during my darkest moments and helped to elevate my book from mere life story to work of art.

Melanie Stephens, Mayz Leonard, Meredith Mahoney, Amy Burtaine, Julia Stephens, and Linda Edmondson (sisters all, plus one mother-in-law), were inexhaustible champions, full of love and support, and constantly cajoled me to write more. I'm lucky to have such dynamic, generous friends. Max Regan helped me organize my thoughts and kept me interested in my own work by pointing out metaphors, connections, and meaning I didn't know I was creating. Michelle Theall, Angela Hart, Rachel Odell, and Hannah Nordhaus all read the manuscript in its various stages and gave insightful (though sometimes hard-to-hear) feedback.

Special thanks to the magnificent Claire Dederer and Mike Kessler, who came in at the end of the process and helped immensely. Claire loved my book unabashedly (giving me a final jolt of confidence), even when it was still covered in blemishes. Mike, master storyteller and soldier of truth, pressed me to tell all, especially when it came to the final revelation that I had been drugged, lest I shortchange my readers.

I don't have words to express my love and gratitude for my husband, Shawn, and my sons, Scout and Hatcher, who keep me grounded, focused on the good things, and laughing. I love you to the moon and back, and through the Earth, to China.

And finally, after all is said and done, I thank my father, who, from the second I started this search, promised complete and total honesty. His choice to do so has severely impacted his life and will mostly likely only continue to do so. I'm grateful to him, my mom, and my brother, for having the grace to let me tell this story.

About the Author

Tracy Ross is an award-winning journalist and contributing editor at *Backpacker* magazine, an ASME award-winning outdoor publication with 1.2 million readers. Her work has been published in the United States, England, South Africa, and Australia. Her essay "The Source of All Things" won the National Magazine Award in 2009 and was selected for *Best American Sports Writing* and *Best American Magazine Writing*. Her assignments have taken her to the wilds of Alaska, the ski slopes of Iran, and into remote reaches of Ecuador. She writes about exotic places and intriguing people, but mostly about the wilderness and how it intersects with the most important issues of our time.